HELLFIRE AWAITS

HELLFIRE AWAITS

150 Years of Redruth RFC

Nick Serpell

Foreword by John Inverdale

pitch

First published by Pitch Publishing, 2025

(pitch)

Pitch Publishing
9 Donnington Park,
85 Birdham Road,
Chichester,
West Sussex,
PO20 7AJ
www.pitchpublishing.co.uk
info@pitchpublishing.co.uk

A CIP catalogue record is available for this book
from the British Library.

ISBN 978 1 80150 934 3

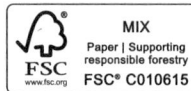

FSC	MIX
www.fsc.org	Paper | Supporting responsible forestry FSC® C010615

Printed and bound in the UK on FSC® certified paper in line
with our continuing commitment to ethical business practices,
sustainability and the environment.

Typesetting and origination by Pitch Publishing
Printed and bound in India by Thomson Press India Ltd.

Contents

'Many are the famous matches that have taken place at Redruth, and over the years the legend of Hellfire Corner has emerged. It has become almost as well known to rugby footballers as is the Kop at Liverpool in soccer; both are renowned for their partisanship, their good humour and their noise.'

M.R. Steele-Bodger
RFU president 1973–74

This book is dedicated to the players, officials and supporters of Redruth Rugby Club, past, present and future. You have all played your part.

Foreword by John Inverdale

Award-winning television and radio presenter

THE ALARM went off at 4.30 in the morning, but kick-off wasn't until 3pm. Matchday. The first game of the season. There's no day like it, whatever the sport. All that hope bubbling up uncontrollably within. Nobody's lost yet, even though by five o'clock half of us will.

It was dark in Newcastle, the sun just peeping over the Tyne Bridge as I ran for the earliest train probably anywhere in Britain that morning. Heading south, and then further south, and then west, and then further south-west. Destination, Cornwall. Crackers really. It wouldn't have taken much longer to get to Caracas.

But that's the point. First game of the season or not, you can't miss the chance of going to Redruth. Of heading for a club where it genuinely matters. Of rushing out of the station at ten to three (yes it was late) and shouting at a random person walking the other way 'Where's the rugby club?' and them instantly shouting back directions. Of getting to a club which for 80 minutes screams history and heritage in a robust accent, before wrapping its arms around you afterwards with rich Cornish hospitality.

I'd gone to bed early the night before, much to the disdain of my workmates. 'Early start,' I'd said. 'Rugby.'

'Where are you going?' they asked.

'Redruth.'

'Don't be daft,' they said. 'What the hell are you going all the way there for?'

'Because there really is nowhere else quite like it.'

John Inverdale recalling
Redruth v Esher in September 2019

Introduction

I WAS queuing for a pie and a bottle of Steinlager at the Wellington rugby ground in New Zealand when I fell into conversation with two local supporters. 'Where are you from?' they asked. 'Redruth,' I replied, assuming they would ask me where it was. 'Ah,' said one of them. 'Hellfire Corner.'

Not only had these two Wellington fans, 12,000 miles from Cornwall, heard of Redruth, they knew the name of the most famous feature of the ground. It was the memory of that conversation that would spur me on, a decade or so later, to attempt to write a history of the club as it celebrates its 150th anniversary.

I suppose I should not have been surprised. The Cornish have colonised large parts of the English-speaking world and taken both their hard rock mining skills and their love of rugby to Australia, South Africa, South America, the USA, Canada and New Zealand. Over the years, players with Cornish ancestry have turned out for their new countries, ranging from Wilf Trenery for the Springboks in 1891 to Brodie Retallick for the All Blacks in more recent times.

In his book celebrating the 100th anniversary of the Cornwall rugby union, Tom Salmon writes that, in some indefinable way, Redruth has become the undisputed home of Cornish rugby. This was underlined in 1908 when the members of the Cornwall team all voted to play at Redruth for their match against Durham, one which saw Cornwall lift the County Championship for the very first time.

Redruth is a club sunk deep in its local community, in a town which has not seen the best of times since the collapse of the mining industry. Despite its geographical location, and the economic situation in the local area, it punches well above its weight in the rugby hierarchy. The professional approach of its officials, the quality of its players and the enthusiasm of its supporters have carried this club through a century and a half, with all its ups and downs. I am sure that someone in 2075 will be updating this book to mark 200 years of rugby at Redruth.

Nick Serpell
Autumn 2024

Chapter One

Beginnings 1875–1880

IT IS 1875 and 19 young men have gathered in a field on the edge of a mining town in West Cornwall to pose for a photographer. They are not wearing the formal clothes of the typical late Victorian studio shot, but instead the rough jerseys and leggings of the sports field, for this is the earliest known photograph of a Redruth rugby team. In the back row, holding a rugby ball, is the captain of the team, William Willimott. Sitting at the front wearing his house cap from Clifton College is Henry Grylls.

These two men had a great deal in common. Both had been to public school before returning to their homes in Cornwall and they moved in the same social circle. It was, therefore, inevitable that they had come together to discuss forming a football team. We do not know exactly when and where they met, but we do know why they were so keen. Grylls had excelled at the game when at Clifton College, while Willimott had fond memories of his playing days at Marlborough. Both wanted to find a way to continue now they were back home in Cornwall.

They could not have foreseen how rugby in general, and the Redruth club in particular, would develop over the following decades. They were probably just looking for comradeship and an opportunity for some strenuous exercise in the fresh air, an outlet for their excess energy after long hours at their desks. But someone must have felt this fledgling venture was worth recording for the future. So a photographer was invited to capture for posterity this first Redruth side, posed near to the tall granite rubbing post that was an unusual feature of this, their earliest playing field.

The photograph is an invaluable record of this original team, the first of many generations of players who would, over the following century and a half, turn out for a club which would indelibly stamp its name on the game of rugby union in Cornwall and beyond, in a place that is still seen by many as the undisputed home of Cornish rugby.

Henry Grylls, who had been born in Redruth, was the 18-year-old son of a copper agent and banker. On leaving school in December 1874, he became an articled clerk at the office of Samuel Downing, a local solicitor. In later years, he would form his own law practice, the successor to which still bears his name. Willimott, who was three years older, was the son of the vicar of St Michael Caerhays, near St Austell, and worked for Henry's father as a bank clerk.

In 1925, Grylls sat down and wrote an account of the founding of the club for a booklet celebrating its 50th anniversary:

> 'Redruth Football Club was started in 1875. It was the first to be formed in West Cornwall I think, with the single exception of Bodmin, in Cornwall. Mr W.M. Willimott and myself were, I believe, mainly responsible for Redruth's start.'[1]

Few clubs are lucky enough to have a first-hand account of their founding and Redruth is especially fortunate to have a photograph annotated with the names of the players. The only sources for the earliest dates of most Cornish sides are reports in local papers, but the press was slow to catch on to this new sport; football coverage was subject to both the whim of the editor and the dedication of the teams in sending in a letter describing the encounter.

The name 'football' is used to describe the games of this era because this was then the accepted name for the sport. The term 'rugby' was adopted in 1871 by the newly formed Rugby Football Union for no other reason than that the three men who drew up the new laws of the game had all attended Rugby School, which had first come up with a set of rules some 40 years earlier. The generic term 'football' remained in common use in Cornish newspapers well into the 20th century. In Cornwall, 'football' was rugby; the other game was 'association'.

The style of football played in the early 1870s by Grylls at Clifton and Willimott at Marlborough would seem alien to those familiar with the modern game of rugby union. Rugby football was a game of the fee-paying public schools and was played according to the laws drawn up at Rugby School, but with local variations and interpretations. The newly emerging clubs followed whichever traditions the players were familiar with and that frequently meant differences between two neighbouring sides or even within the same game.

The development of rugby as a separate sport from association football owes much to the book *Tom Brown's Schooldays*, published in 1857. It contains a detailed account of a game of the 1830s, which is when its author, Thomas Hughes, attended Rugby School. It owes very little to a certain William Webb Ellis, the fabled schoolboy instigator of the carrying game. The story of him picking up a ball and running with it at Rugby in 1823, 'contrary to the normal laws of the game', has long been discredited by most rugby historians as a myth.

Before Grylls arrived at Clifton or Willimott at Marlborough, their two schools had met on the field of play in 1864. Clifton's rules allowed hacking, the term used for deliberately kicking the shins of opposing players. The Marlborough players were unfamiliar with this tactic and reacted strongly to having been invited to what they regarded as a brawl. Unsurprisingly, a mass fight broke out and there were to be no further fixtures between the two schools for the next 27 years. It is clear from the account written later by Henry Grylls that it was this robust style of football that he and Willimott brought home to Redruth.

It found fertile ground. The roots of rugby in Cornwall can be traced back to physical contests between teams of men as early as the 16th century, with historians such as Francis Marshall and O.L. Owen suggesting that hurling, a popular Cornish pastime for hundreds of years, was one of the forerunners of the game. The cartographer, John Norden, who surveyed Cornwall in 1584, witnessed games of hurling on his travels:

> 'The Cornish-men they are stronge, hardye and nymble, so are their exercises violent, two especially, Wrastling and Hurling, sharpe and severe activities; and in neither of theis doth any Countrye exceede or equall them. The firste is violent, but the seconde is daungerous: The firste is acted in two sortes, by Holdster (as they called it) and by the Coller; the seconde likewise two ways, as Hurling to goales, and Hurling to the countrye.'[2]

Norden recorded the folklore surrounding three Bronze Age stone circles near Minions on Bodmin Moor, known for generations as The Hurlers. Legend claims they are local people turned to stone for hurling on a Sunday.

The historian Richard Carew also wrote an account of Cornish hurling in his Survey of Cornwall published in 1602:

> 'Two bushes are pitched in the ground eight or 12ft asunder directly against which, at a distance of ten or 12 yards apart, two more bushes in like manner which are called goals. The hurlers to goals are bound to observe these orders or laws. In contending for the ball, if a man's body touches the ground, and he cries "Hold" and delivers the ball he is not to be further pressed. That the hurler must deal no foreball, or throw it to

any partner standing nearer the goal than himself. In dealing the ball, if any of the adverse party can catch it flying ... the property of it is thereby transferred to the catching party; and so the assailants become defendants, and defendants, assailants.'[3]

Carew's description is of what Norden had described as 'hurling to goals', where the game took place on a fixed piece of ground, the equivalent of a modern pitch. The similarity of his account and some of the rules of modern rugby are striking. They allude to a handling game, rather than one restricted to kicking, and describe the forerunners of the goalposts, the need to release the ball after a tackle, a prohibition on the ball being thrown forward and an interception.

Some versions of hurling had fewer, if any, rules and could take place over a wide area of the countryside. The object was to get the ball from one designated spot to another, usually the end of the parish. This game was once widespread in Cornwall, but only the hurling of the silver ball that is still played at St Columb Major and St Ives remains. This was a form of what historians describe as 'mob football', versions of which were common across the country. It was often fuelled by large quantities of drink and was usually violent, leading to bruises, broken bones and worse.

The Camborne parish registers of 1705 record the burial of William Trevarthen: 'Being disstroid to a hurling with Redruth men at the high dounes the 10 day of August.' It did not help that much of the action took place on the slopes of Carn Brea, where the soil was thin and granite boulders could cause serious injury.

Cornish wrestling, described by John Norden in his survey of the duchy, can also be argued to have had an influence on the game. The two contestants face each other with the aim of taking hold of their opponent's canvas jacket and throwing him flat on his back, a skill with obvious value in rugby. Cornish wrestling's long history includes accounts of matches between

Bretons and Cornishmen dating back to the 15th century and it is claimed that Cornish archers at the Battle of Agincourt in October 1415 carried a banner depicting a wrestler's hitch. In 1602, Richard Carew wrote:

> 'Wrastling is as full of manliness, more delightful and less dangerous [than hurling] ... for you shall hardly find an assembly of boys from Cornwall and Devon where the most untowardly among them will not as readily give you a muster of this exercise as you are prone to require it.'[4]

During the great revival of Cornish wrestling in the 1920s and 1930s, a number of the club's players would take part in tournaments, including one of Cornwall's greatest exponents of the sport, Francis Gregory, who played rugby for Redruth before moving north to join Wigan in the 1930s.

A variety of sports, both team and individual, were being played in Cornwall long before the first organised games of football. A game described as 'football' often featured as part of the many feast days held around West Cornwall and there are references to these as far back as the 1840s, with scratch teams being raised for one-off matches.

In January 1864, there was a game of football at Penzance between a side representing the town and a Rifle Corps team. Over the years, these ad hoc games became more common. Henry Grylls played in at least two such games, at Truro in January 1873 and Penzance in January 1874, when he was home for the Christmas holidays. He later recalled of the Penzance game that there were few spectators but 'the game was not the less enjoyed by all who took part'.

This was typical of football games in early 1870s Cornwall. Clubs, as we understand them today, with a fixed ground, committees and management structure, did not exist. Players and spectators heard about games through word of mouth, letters of invitation or bills posted to advertise a feast day event. It was not until the setting up of the Cornwall Rugby Football Union (CRFU) in late 1884 that a framework for the game began to emerge and teams began to play with a more fixed allegiance. Even then, rugby remained largely confined to its West Cornwall heartlands and sides would come and go as enthusiasm waxed and waned among the players.

There is much argument among partisan supporters about which club can claim to be the oldest in Cornwall. There were two or three Cornish clubs already in existence before Redruth was formed in 1875, but these later fell by the wayside and were re-formed at a later date, often more than once. In the absence of any firm evidence to the contrary, and discounting breaks for the two world wars, Redruth has a well-founded claim to have the longest, continuously documented history of any Cornish club.[5]

The first hurdle facing the founders of the new club was to find some players. At the time, the game in England was dominated by professional men, overwhelmingly former public school pupils. Of the 21 clubs that met in 1871 to form the Rugby Football Union, no fewer than 14 were made up of public school old boys, many from Rugby School itself. The rest drew players from the ranks of professional occupations such as barristers, doctors and civil servants. All the founding clubs were based in London or the Home Counties.

The population demographic in West Cornwall at this time was completely different, as Henry Grylls was all too well aware. 'Professors from Marlborough', as he wryly put it in his account, 'were rare on the ground in Redruth'. This meant that early Cornish clubs, like many in Wales and northern England, contained men from a much wider variety of social backgrounds than the RFU's founding members. This fact would be responsible for many tensions in the game over the ensuing decades.

Clerks and tradesmen played alongside men who toiled underground in local mines, laboured on the land or worked in the foundries or factories of Holman, Climax or Bickford Smith. It is likely that many of the latter saw the game as a welcome release from the drudgery of their hard day jobs and those same jobs gave them a strength and stamina which equipped them well for the rugby field.

There was also another aspect of the game they enjoyed, as the Cornish author and mining historian Allen Buckley points out:

> 'The Cornish took to rugby like ducks to water. To the miners and factory workers of Camborne and Redruth, rugby seemed the only game to play; it was hard, physical and frequently violent, and suited their temperament admirably.'[6]

Writing 50 years on from Redruth's first season, and fortunately with a lawyer's propensity for recording detail, Henry Grylls lists some of the founding members of the team. Peter Preston was the managing clerk for solicitors Downing and Paige, where Grylls was articled. A fellow clerk, Alfred Meadows, was also persuaded to sign up. Thurstan Peter worked in his family's law practice, as well as being the registrar for births, marriages and deaths. He joined with his brother, Lewis, who later became a priest.

Edwin Bonds practised as an accountant and doubled as the town rate collector, while Martin Peters was a metal broker. John Penberthy, one of several of that name who would give sterling service to Redruth over the years, was a student who would later become a professor at the Royal College of Veterinary Surgeons.

The wealth generated by mining had given Redruth a bustling town centre and its many family businesses provided more new players. These included Cornelius Beringer, the son of a German immigrant who had co-founded a jewellery business. Alfred Thomas was another jeweller's son, whose father, John, had a shop in West End. Frank Woolf, whose playing career at

Redruth would span an amazing 29 years, ran a drapery business in Fore Street. He joined the son of a printer, Richard Tregaskis, and a music teacher, Robert Heath, who also played the organ in the local church.

Miners who took part in those early years included James Smith from Churchtown and Kit Williams, who lived at Mount Ambrose, while William Wilton and Henry Michell were sons of local farmers.

It was this disparate collection of men, some of whom had experience of football and others none at all, that Grylls and Willimott had to forge into a side capable of holding their own in a tough and largely unforgiving game. Grylls was very much aware of the challenge:

> 'It was not an easy matter to drill a lot of beginners, who had had no opportunity of seeing other people play, into a respectable team, but everybody was very keen and, knowing nothing about it themselves, they took as gospel what was told them by those of us who were "professors" and it was not very long before the hang of the thing was grasped and the rules and practice mastered.
>
> 'Some of us went in for serious training, mainly runs in the country after working hours. I remember on one occasion, a squad of us started for such a run and in Church Lane met Mr Freeman, the postman, I think at the time our only postman. He came back into the town and reported that he had met young Grylls and the football party running like mad in the dark with next to nothing on.'[7]

Redruth's first ground was a field below Brewery Leats, then owned by the Redruth Brewery Company; the ground is now sadly buried under a Tesco supermarket. Previously it had been a venue for bouts of Cornish wrestling. Let to the club on a rent-free basis, it had a natural grandstand by way of a raised path which allowed spectators to have a clear view of the pitch. The leat itself was a water-filled ditch that ran alongside the path and into which spectators would sometimes slip or be pushed. Given that this channel carried debris of all kinds, including dead animals, waste from the brewery and the sewage from numerous houses, immersion would not have been a pleasant experience.

Teams at the time officially comprised 20 players on each side, with 16 forwards and four backs, although many games kicked off with fewer than this if insufficient team members turned up. Grylls wrote an account of those early matches which gives a flavour of the game as it was played in the mid 1870s, almost entirely dominated by the forwards, who stood upright in the scrums, then known as scrimmages:

'Those in the front rows stood their own height and their business was to overpower their opponents by sheer muscle and weight, keeping the ball in front of them and hacking their way through. It was not then good practice to heel the ball out to those behind the scrimmage. The forward play was forward, not backward. The scrimmage broke up of course. I have known them to last ten minutes or a quarter of an hour and steam rising on a frosty day as from a huge cauldron of hot water.

'But you tried to break them on the opposing side and take the ball through. When a half-back got the ball, he ran with it, dodging and shoving off his opponents and sticking with the ball. Whoever, forward or half-back, got going with the ball, he stuck with it until he "died". No tossing it about on the chance of a better man than yourself got hold of it.'[8]

It was rare for the backs, especially on a winning side, to see the ball at all. If they were lucky enough to get it, they were supposed to kick it into touch, as far into their opponents' half as possible. Alternatively, they could, if they were close enough, attempt to drop a goal, no easy task with a heavy leather ball that was more plum-shaped than today's version. Anyone unfortunate enough to ground the ball for a try could find himself jumped on, or even throttled, to make him surrender it, in what was then termed a 'maul in goal'. Grylls wrote that this mayhem was taken in good part:

> 'It was marvellous that there was so little display of temper or bad feeling in those days, and I think it says a good deal for the sporting spirit that animated us all, that we very rarely had any serious evidence of anger.'[9]

The Rugby Football Union (RFU) agreed to reduce team numbers from 20 to 15 for the 1876/77 season, with most clubs playing with ten forwards, two attacking and three defensive backs. Further law changes were made over the following years to speed up the game, as interminable battles between the two scrums became increasingly tedious for the spectators.

In the early days, a try counted for nothing. If the ball was grounded over the line by an attacking player, it just provided an opportunity to kick for a goal.

From 1877, the RFU decided the number of tries could determine a game's result, but only if no goals were scored. Laws and scoring values were continually amended as the game developed.

By no means all clubs rushed to adopt the new ways of playing and the further they were from London, the more slowly they tended to make the changes. Cornish sides of the day largely played each other and, with the era of touring teams from elsewhere yet to come, it mattered little that football in Redruth was in the old style. Cornish clubs also took a long while to adapt to a faster, more mobile style of play. The sight of a strong pack inching its way forward is still much appreciated among

Cornish spectators, particularly when Redruth are driving into Hellfire Corner.

Inevitably, the new laws did, in time, produce a change in the roles of players on the field. Where there had been three or four full-backs, law changes meant that two of them needed to be closer to the scrum. At first they were called halfway backs, but this soon changed to half-backs, the modern scrum and fly-halves. With the growing tendency to pass from one player to another, something that had originally been discouraged, it was found that the space between the half-backs and the full-backs needed bridging. And so was born the role of the three-quarters. It would take the arrival of a mercurial Welsh player at Redruth, in 1892, to make the club fully embrace and take advantage of this new style of play. Until then, it was eyes down and push.

With so few teams in operation in Cornwall in 1875, it is likely that early games would have been ad hoc affairs between members of the club as the players learned their craft. The earliest mention of a Redruth game against another club is an account reporting a contest between Redruth and Truro on 22 January 1876. Truro ran out winners by one goal to nothing. The venue is not stated, but it was most likely at Truro, as the following month Redruth played the same opponents at the Brewery Field, the club's first documented home fixture. Ten days later, on 1 March, Redruth played Bodmin at Truro.

It was common for accounts of the game to be written by one of the captains or the secretary and sent to the newspaper. The tone of the report suggests this was one of those occasions:

'FOOTBALL BODMIN v REDRUTH: A well-contested match between these clubs took place at Truro on Wednesday first inst. in the presence of a large number of spectators. A most pleasant game was won by Bodmin by a goal and two touchdowns to one touch in goal. Both teams played well. Mr G.H.

Chilcott acted as umpire and discharged his duties in a most efficient manner.'[10]

The report indicates that Bodmin fielded 13 men to Redruth's 12, but such a disparity would not have been unusual in those early days. Games often kicked off with a shortage of players on one side or the other. It was common for teams to borrow players from their opponents to level up the numbers.

Two weeks later, Redruth had arranged to play another game against Truro:

> 'FOOTBALL: A return football match will be played in a field opposite the Maria Camilia School on Tuesday next the 14th March at 3.30pm against the Redruth team with rugby union rules.'[11]

The club members met for a supper at the Bullers Arms in April 1876 to celebrate the end of their first season. Each member was allowed to take a friend along, possibly in the hope they might sign up. Several speeches were made advocating the advantages of the manly game of football and complimenting the club on its success.

Redruth played their first game against a newly formed Falmouth club on 4 November 1876. There are no details of the location in the short report, but the game ended in a draw. Redruth met Truro on 23 November, in an away game, which Truro won by two goals to nil. The contest was described as having been a hard fight and a splendid game in front of many spectators from both towns.

The next mention of a Redruth game was on 19 December 1876 when the *Royal Cornish Gazette* found room for two lines stating: 'The Redruth football club have been successful in winning the recent match against their Truro competitors.' Presumably this was the return game from the away fixture the month before. Fixtures with Truro appear to have been a regular arrangement, with a train service making travel between the two relatively easy.

Given the small number of sides active at the time, games could be few and far between. Redruth only played an average of six games a season in their first five years. Not all games were recorded, either by the local press or the club. Eventually, as matches began to attract more spectators, newspapers began to improve their coverage and notices appeared pleading for match details.

Newspaper reports of the time often omitted the score and frequently left out the names of the players involved. If players were mentioned, it was almost always by surname only, making positive identification difficult. Football was seen as an opportunity for comradeship, exercise and fresh air, and, while teams set out to win, it was the playing of the game that was important, rather than the result. It made for rather anodyne match reports, but that would change as the rugged style of play became more contentious, local rivalries became more intense and decisions on the field were disputed.

In the early days, it was down to the team captains of the day to resolve disagreements. Mention is made at some games of an umpire, or even one for each team, but they would have been on the touchline, rather than in the role of a modern referee. It was the captains who took charge on the field, as Henry Grylls explained:

'The captains took command and, with rare exceptions, could be depended on to keep order and discipline. The only case I remember of disagreement between captains was in a match here with Bodmin captained by Bernard Edyvean. He and I could not agree a touchdown in goal and the game was blocked for a time, but we ultimately decided it by a reference to those somewhat nearer the spot in question than ourselves. Our matches with Bodmin were always the fiercest we played, but we won more than we lost with them.'[12]

The idea that disputes over touchdowns could be resolved by asking spectators for their opinion, or that the players could be expected to own up to a forward pass, seems strangely at odds with the undoubted passion Grylls shows for the game. In these days of television match officials, one can only imagine the referee at a modern Redruth game turning to the faithful standing in Hellfire Corner to enquire whether the Reds had grounded the ball. But it was the ethos of the game in Cornwall in the 19th century that rugby was played hard, but played fair, and the captain's word was law.

And played hard it certainly was. Severe injuries were not uncommon and reports of broken bones appeared regularly, as did accounts of players being knocked unconscious. Those who worked in the mines and factories invariably played in their heavy iron-shod working boots. There were few laws defining what might today be considered foul play and players saw no need to hold back when attempting to halt the progress of the opposing side. A rather tongue-in-cheek account of a game in February 1877 sums up some of the perils faced by players:

'THE PLEASURES OF FOOTBALL. A football match between nine each of Truro and Falmouth clubs against nine each of Redruth and Penzance clubs played at Redruth on Tuesday resulted in the victory of Redruth and Penzance although, unfortunately, not without accident, one young man of Penzance being severely injured in the neck and head and Mr G. Peters of Redruth, son of Mr Peters, hairdresser, having his collarbone broken.

'One of the Truro club is said to have had a severe blow just under the ear, but still went on with the play and one of the Falmouth club had to lament over a severe kick in the leg which, for a time, nearly lamed him. Notwithstanding these slight drawbacks the game is highly extolled as an exhilarating, delightful and healthful recreation.'[13]

Later the same year, in a game between Redruth and Penzance, Redruth's John Everett, a local schoolmaster, suffered a fractured jaw after receiving a severe blow in the face. There is no evidence that his assailant suffered any sanction for the assault.

Matches with Bodmin were some of the most intense that Redruth played during this period. The rivalry eventually spilled over into the local press after William Willimott, the Redruth captain, made a speech at the club's annual dinner in which he suggested that Redruth was now seen as the 'County Club'. This produced a swift response from an individual, whose letter was published under the pseudonym 'Old Rugby':

> 'Now then Redruth wake up! For you cannot be said to have the belt until you have won a victory over Bodmin Rovers [sic] who conquered you at Truro in their first and last match. When are you going to play the promised return match on Bodmin Beacon?'[14]

There appears to have been no official response to this challenge.

In May 1877, Redruth lost the services of its co-founder and first captain William Willimott, who moved to Penryn to take up a position as a bank manager. As well as his involvement with the football club, Willimott had played cricket for Redruth and the two clubs organised a presentation evening at the Church Society rooms on Station Hill.

Willimott was presented with what was described as a 'handsome timepiece'. One of the Redruth players, Robert Heath, joked that he wished the gift had been more costly but that 'tin was down', a remark received with laughter by those present. It would not have seemed so funny a decade later. It was not the end of Willimott's involvement in football; he continued to play for several years and went on to turn out for other sides.

By this time, the game was attracting spectators in increasing numbers. A match at Redruth against Falmouth on 20 January 1877 saw 1,500 people watch the visitors go down to a defeat and it was reported that the Redruth team seemed to carry everything before them. A game between Bodmin and Redruth on 29 November 1877 was reportedly played in front of fifteen or sixteen hundred people. The rise in the numbers watching football seemed to have persuaded the local press to increase the amount of coverage and the same edition of the paper carried a list of upcoming fixtures for December: Liskeard v Launceston, Camborne v Falmouth and two Redruth games, home to Penzance on 8 December and away to Bodmin on Boxing Day.

One of the newer clubs to appear on that list was to become Redruth's greatest local rival. In September 1877, a newspaper notice reporting a meeting of the Camborne Cricket Club ended with: 'Cannot a football club be formed instead of cricket?' In his book marking 100 years of Cornish rugby, Tom Salmon claims that one newspaper added the sentence: 'After all, Redruth have got one'.[15]

Whether or not this was true, it is just the sort of provocative remark to fire up enthusiasts in Camborne. It was not long before a report appeared announcing the founding of a football team in Camborne. However, the writer clearly had reservations about the code that Camborne had chosen:

'The club has adopted the rugby rules and, as a consequence, some of its members have already taken upon them the rugby game "trademark" in the shape of bruises, scratches, kicks, etc, of various designs, and one has even gone so far as to bisect his collarbone. However, the club numbers nearly 50 members, so there still remain plenty of collarbones unfractured. I doubt the wisdom of playing rugby rules in preference

31

to the association game. There are many who like football well enough, but who cannot afford a new "jersey" and "pair of pants" every two or three weeks, to say nothing of collarbones and sticking plaster.'[16]

Just two months later, on Boxing Day 1877, the first reported game between Redruth and Camborne took place at Rosewarne, on the edge of Camborne, with what was described as an unusually large crowd present, on account of it being a holiday. Redruth won the game by two touchdowns to nil, hardly surprising given that Camborne had only been in existence for two months.

For many years, it was believed that this match marked the first of what was later claimed to be the longest continuous fixture in rugby. Sadly, that is not the case. After that first game in 1877, only two further Boxing Day matches between the two clubs took place before 1900. A series of rows, which often suspended fixtures in the first two decades of the 20th century, means the unbroken run only goes back to 1928.[17]

Camborne joined a growing list of clubs established in Cornwall in the late 1870s. Over the first five years of its existence, Redruth played games against Bodmin, Falmouth, Penzance, Truro and Camborne. Matches were usually arranged by an exchange of letters or telegrams between the two captains, who would also have picked the respective teams. Redruth did have a secretary and a small committee, but these were roles filled by members of the team. Players provided their own kit, which varied in style and colour, as can be seen from the 1875 photograph. The boots were often their everyday footwear. Redruth's now traditional red shirts were something for the future.

There was no need for anyone to manage the club's finances, as these were almost non-existent. The club's accounts for 1877 showed subscriptions totalling £4 12s (£4.60), expenditure of £4 3s 9d (£4.18) and a total of 28 members. The only costs were paying for goalposts, marking the lines and buying the match balls. Nearly 50 years later, Henry Grylls still had strong views on money coming into the game:

'Everybody paid his own expenses, except in some cases, where a player could not manage perhaps a railway fare, when it was provided privately by some other member of the team better able to stand the outlay. So that our balance sheet, if one was ever prepared, would show an expenditure for the year of something well within £5 and this was met by a small subscription or, if this proved insufficient, by extra contributions from the two or three who could afford it. There was no gate money. I know that a gate is essential nowadays, worse luck. I am old fashioned enough to believe that the less the money element has to do with the sport, the better. The game is the game.'[18]

It is not difficult to guess what Henry would have made of the era of professionalism, but his views on the evils of money and the need to preserve rugby's amateur status were shared throughout the game in the 1870s. This stance would continue to be strongly defended by the Rugby Football Union for the following 110 years – to the detriment of the development of the sport, many now feel.

Despite Henry's remarks, part of Redruth's longevity can be attributed to an early adoption of a hard-nosed pragmatism when it came to administration. Club minutes dating back to the 1890s show that officials quickly demonstrated their belief that, while amateurism ruled on the field, there was a desire to run the club in a professional manner and ensure the finances were in as good a shape as the team. This attitude has certainly been a major factor in the club's success.

The first newspaper report of a Redruth club AGM appeared on 3 October 1878. John Everett, who had taken over the captaincy following the departure of William Willimott the previous year, was re-elected. Frank Woolf was elected as secretary, with Charles Lanyon taking on the role of treasurer. A committee of five was elected to look after the administration; Henry Grylls, Thurstan Peter, William Holloway, Frank Williams and Charles Williams, all of them players.

Redruth rounded off 1878 with a home game on Boxing Day against Penzance. Played in what was described as unfavourable weather, but in front of a large crowd, the match was completely dominated by the forwards. According to the report, not one Penzance back touched the ball throughout the whole game. Neither side managed to kick a goal so, under new rules which allowed the number of touchdowns to count where no goals had been kicked, the match ended in a draw in favour of Redruth.

Two weeks later, another game at Redruth had the local press buzzing, but not about the action on the field. On the evening of Monday, 13 January 1879, the first match in Cornwall to be played under electric lights took place. The encounter came just two months after a game played in Salford between Broughton and Swinton had entered the record books as the first floodlit game played anywhere in the world under rugby rules.

The game attracted more than 3,500 spectators, keen to experience this miracle of modern technology, many of them travelling on special trains laid on for the occasion by the Great Western Railway. It was not the first use of electric light in Cornwall – the Lizard lighthouse had been powered by a generator since 1872, but this was dismissed somewhat sniffily: 'It is true that the light has been for some time in use at the Lizard, but this is in far too remote a part of Cornwall to admit of a general inspection of it.'[19]

The floodlights were being toured around the country by a Manchester firm, C.W. Provis and Son. The company's founder, Charles William Provis, had been born in Redruth in 1835, the son of John Provis, a copper agent. The game took place, not on the Brewery Field, but on what the newspaper described as 'a large field at the end of Green Lane'.

It is possible that this may have been Hocking's Meadow which, four years later, would become Redruth's Recreation Ground, and remains the current home of the club. The match was played between two representative sides made up of players drawn from a number of other towns including Falmouth, Penzance, Camborne, Helston, Truro and Penryn. Half of the 32 players – 16 each side – came from Redruth, with one team wearing yellow badges and the other red.

Redruth took something of a risk in staging the match. Gales and heavy rain had battered the town for several days before the event and there were fears that many people would be put off attending. Just in time, the weather eased and the Redruth committee worked hard to lay down sawdust and cinders on the approach to the field and boards around the pitch on which the spectators could stand.

Those who came paid one shilling to stand in a reserved part of the ground and sixpence to stand elsewhere. The *Cornish Telegraph* article waxed lyrical:

> 'Redruth is to be congratulated on the public spirit which has enabled it to be the first town in the county to give to some thousands of people so excellent an opportunity, they had last evening, of witnessing public demonstration of the merits of a light about which so much is now being said.'[20]

The reporter was fascinated by the technicalities of the lights and devoted more than half his article to explaining how everything worked. Mains electricity was unknown at the time and each of the four lights needed a separate generator, powered by a 12 horsepower stationary steam engine. The pressure of the crowd around the supports holding up one of the lights caused it to go out, but the report states that it made little difference to the overall illumination on the ground, which was probably not that bright in the first place.

The red team, captained by Redruth's Frank Woolf, beat the yellow team, led by John Everett, also of Redruth. One of the players on the yellow side was William Willimott, Redruth's co-founder and former captain. By all accounts, it was a forward-dominated tussle, typical of the football of the day, and, in any case, the wet state of the ground would have hampered any attempt at a running game.

In his excitement, the reporter seems to have overlooked the fact that the lights echoed another significant event in the town's history. Redruth was once again pioneering a new form of power, some 80 years after William Murdoch's house in Cross Street had become the first in the world to be lit by gas.

Redruth's next scheduled game was to have been at home to Hayle at the end of January 1879. It would have been the first time they had hosted their visitors, but no one from Hayle turned up. It was not unusual for players to arrive after the start of a game, but it was less common, although not unknown, for no one to turn up at all. That month also saw the first reported appearance of a Redruth second team, a game taking place between the junior teams of Camborne and Redruth at Camborne on 29 January, with the home side winning by five tries to two. It was a sign of the growing popularity of the sport that the clubs had enough players to field two sides.

At the club's annual supper at Tabbs Hotel on 26 March 1879, the Redruth captain, John Everett, stood to respond to a toast, hailing the great progress which the club had made from the time of its formation, not only in numbers, but in thorough knowledge of the game of football. His speech was reported in the local press:

> 'This [progress] was shown on the previous day in
> their match with Truro, when they had to enlist the
> services of several of their juniors in consequence of

the absence of their forwards. From time to time, even with this disadvantage, they had successfully competed with some of the best clubs in the district, and seeing the large number of victories which they had scored, with scarcely an exception, he thought they were fairly entitled to be considered the county football club of Cornwall.'

Unlike the last time this claim had been made at a Redruth gathering two years previously, there was no recorded objection from Bodmin or, indeed, anywhere else.

In September 1879, the club organised what would be the first of an annual series of athletics events, held at a venue called the Golden Field. Local businesses were persuaded to donate money and prizes, and members of the football and cricket clubs took on stewarding duties. Competitors took part in a variety of events, including running and walking races over various distances, as well as long jump and high jump. The day was rounded off with what was intended to be a one-mile donkey race, but the animals refused to move more than a few yards and, following a letter they had received prior to the event from the RSPCA, the local police refused to allow riders to use any form of coercion to make their mounts go further.

The first match of the 1879/80 season to get any newspaper coverage was a game against Camborne at Roskear in which several players were reportedly injured, one sustaining a broken collarbone. Camborne won by one touchdown to nil. The club rounded off the year with December fixtures at Falmouth, in which a draw was declared after two Redruth tries were disputed, and a home match against Penzance, won by two tries to nil. A Boxing Day fixture against Bodmin had been arranged but no subsequent report appeared, so it is not clear whether this went ahead.

Redruth started 1880 with a home game against Falmouth on 16 January. The encounter was not at the Brewery Field but a field owned by Alfred Lanyon; he lived at Tolvean House, so it was likely the field was close to the present-day Penventon Park Hotel. Alfred Lanyon's 14-year-old son, Sydney, would later play for the club and act as secretary, going on to serve as president between 1903 and 1920.

It is not explained why the club had left their original ground by the brewery, though it could have been due to flooding, and the move was to be only temporary. An account of the game comments on the slippery state of the ground and that the play was almost entirely confined to scrimmage work in which the united effort of the Redruth forwards was especially notable. Redruth won by two tries to nil.

A home fixture against Hayle on 24 January had been keenly awaited, as both sides were undefeated that season. Redruth managed the first touchdown but a later try claimed by Hayle was disputed by the Redruth captain, John Everett. The response of the Hayle captain, Hockin, was to take his team home before time was up. The paper recorded a win for Redruth. Despite the disagreement, Redruth travelled to Hayle the following week for a return contest played in front of a large and enthusiastic crowd. The game was declared a draw in favour of Hayle because Redruth were forced to touchdown twice in their own goal area.

At the end of that 1879/80 season, John Everett took stock of the Redruth club's progress, once again addressing the annual supper at Tabbs Hotel. In those five years, 29 games had been played, of which 19 were won, four lost and six tied. He went on to say that the club he had the honour of managing was composed chiefly of what would be called juniors in many towns, but they managed, somehow or other, with scarcely an exception, to give their opponents a 'downright good licking'.

The Redruth club had come a long way since 1875, establishing itself as a major force in a game that was growing in popularity throughout West Cornwall. More clubs were being formed, football was getting greater coverage in the local press and spectators were turning out in increasing numbers. As they contemplated the start of a new decade, those involved with Redruth would have been keenly aware that the club was at the forefront of the development of the game in Cornwall.

Chapter Two

A New Home 1880–1894

THE 1880s was a pivotal period for Cornish rugby. The decade saw the establishment of the Cornwall Rugby Football Union (CRFU) and the move of the Redruth club from Brewery Field to the ground it still occupies more than 140 years later. Members of Redruth would give sterling service to the CRFU, and to the Cornwall county side, and the Recreation Ground would host important matches in the years ahead.

The town of Redruth was evolving to meet the challenges of a changing economic landscape. It was still dependent on mining, but the industry was in severe decline. The Cornish copper industry had virtually disappeared after the price crash of the 1860s and a decade later tin had begun to go the same way. Overseas producers in Malaya, Bolivia and Tasmania could produce tin far more cheaply than the mines around Redruth. Cornish mines had deep workings which needed the constant pumping out of water and, as world prices fell, the costs involved in coal and machinery made Cornish tin uneconomical.

John Everett, who ran a private school in Rose Row, had been re-elected as Redruth's captain for the new season, having previously succeeded Redruth's co-founder, Henry Grylls, following the latter's retirement from the game on medical grounds. Everett, the son of an Illogan tin miner, epitomised the concept of 'muscular Christianity', a philosophy advocating a commitment to health and manliness through discipline, self-sacrifice and athleticism, particularly as practised in team sports. It was an idea which had sprung from English public schools and was often associated with Dr Arnold, the famous headmaster of Rugby School.

Everett was a devout Methodist, teetotal and a prominent figure in the temperance movement. Along with many other Redruth players, he served in the local rifle volunteers. He was married to Sophie Heath, the sister of one of Redruth's original players, Robert. When she died of tuberculosis in 1884, aged 31, a match against Truro was postponed as a mark of respect. Everett was also an outstanding football player and often had to defend himself against criticism of his involvement with the Redruth club from those who held the view that organised sport was at odds with Christian teaching.

At a meeting of the Redruth Young Men's Debating Society, he told members that his physical nature required looking after as much as his mental and spiritual nature, and he believed all kinds of sport were beneficial. This philosophy allowed him to knock seven bells out of his opponents on the rugby field on a Saturday afternoon and pray with a clear conscience for their wellbeing in chapel on Sunday morning. One might see in Henry Grylls' description of Everett, characteristics that are recognisable in some modern-day scrum-halves:

> 'He was a very capable, if somewhat dramatic, half-back, and afforded a great deal of amusement to the crowd on the bank.'[21]

Redruth's opening game of the new season, on 16 October, marked a return to their original ground at Brewery Field after the spell at Tolvean. After a quiet November, the next reported game was an away fixture at Bodmin in early December, won by the home side by a goal against a try. The return match against Bodmin at Brewery Field was the first at which spectators were charged admission. It may well have been the first game in Cornwall at which people were charged solely to watch the action and even with a modest gate fee of 2d – less than 1p – the innovation did not find favour in the press:

> 'This arrangement is made ostensibly to prevent crowding; but the fact is that on that afternoon the Brewery Company, as a mode of advertising, intend washing out all their empty casks and allowing the refuse to flow into the leat. The spectators, during their whole stay in the field will have the privilege of living upon malt and hops, slightly flavoured with the essence of dead cats ... for the enjoyment of which the committee consider 2d a very reasonable charge.'[22]

In the second half of the 1880/81 season, a scoreless draw at Falmouth was followed by a home game against Camborne in February, which Redruth won convincingly by a goal and two tries to nil. The following week the club travelled to play a team representing HMS *Ganges*, a Royal Naval hulk anchored in Falmouth Roads and used between 1866 and 1899 as a training ship. The game was played at Devil's Roost, between Mylor and Flushing, and resulted in another Redruth win. The young trainees from the *Ganges* had scant opportunity for such sport and it would have been an all too brief respite from the harsh, sometimes brutal, conditions of life on the hulk. During the ship's time as a training vessel, 53 of the boys died, mainly due to disease from the unhygienic conditions on board. They are commemorated by a memorial in Mylor churchyard.

Redruth appear to have played relatively few senior games over this period, but the popularity of football was spreading fast and other new clubs were springing up in the area. During the latter half of the 1880/81 season, there were reports of games involving sides from Pool (between Redruth and Camborne) and North Country (an area north of Redruth, directly across what is now the A30), while Redruth Juniors were also in action. Occasionally, the names of established Redruth players appeared in teams representing other clubs. This was not unusual at the time. There was no contract between player and club and, if a particular side had no fixture, a keen footballer would look for a game elsewhere. The number of these smaller local clubs continued to grow throughout the 1880s, creating a feeder system that would play a major part in Redruth's later success.

On Boxing Day, there was a match against a team representing Pool. The visitors had beaten Camborne three weeks previously, but were no match for Redruth. In an era where scoring tended to be low, Redruth won by three goals and two tries to nil. Between 2,000 and 3,000 spectators attended the game and a young player named Luke Smith was singled out for mention in the match report. He would go on to become one of the club's early success stories.

A match with Falmouth was played at Redruth on 11 January 1882. It ended in a draw, with the report suggesting it had been chiefly a contest between the two packs of forwards. The game was one of many at the time to take place on a Wednesday afternoon, traditionally a time that English schools and universities devoted to sport, but as it still attracted a good crowd, it may also have been half-day closing in the town.

Soon after this game came a report that Falmouth, Hayle and Penzance had decided to end fixtures with the Reds due to the behaviour of their supporters. Any side which had the temerity to win at Redruth, it was claimed, would find its players being pelted with mud, turf and even stones. Crowd trouble was not unknown in the early years of Cornish rugby, with spectators eager to reflect the often violent scenes on the pitch. The *Cornubian and Redruth Times* was quick to respond, suggesting that, even if the accusation were true, this sort of thing could not happen very often as 'Redruth rarely lost at home'.

Any rift with Falmouth, if ever there was one, would appear to have been set aside when the two sides met again on 18 November 1882 at Brewery Field. The game resulted in a decisive win for Falmouth, by one goal and three tries to one, and it seems from the match reports that Falmouth players escaped being showered with bits of debris. Another defeat, this time away to Hayle, was followed by a win over Camborne just before Christmas and a draw at home against Hayle on Boxing Day in front of several thousand spectators.

February 1883 saw torrential rain fall in West Cornwall and a game away to Helston ended abruptly when the Redruth side walked off, having decided the pitch was too bad for them to continue. The account of this match in *The Cornishman* caused some confusion, as the paper's Helston correspondent thought the visitors were from Camborne, a mistake that would not have been well received by either town. The game predated team jerseys and it may be that any distinguishing features of the players had been obscured by mud, but a correction had to be published the following week.

Back at Redruth, the rain was also causing problems. A blockage in the brewery leat saw floodwater pouring down the hill, turning the playing area into a lake. The Redruth Brewery Company, then belonging to Strong and Neame, had allowed Redruth to use Brewery Field free of charge, but this was not the first time the low-lying pitch had been flooded and, with the granite post still presenting an obstacle in the middle of the playing area, it was clear that the club needed to find an alternative ground.

A meeting was held at Redruth's town hall on 13 March 1883 to discuss providing a playing field that could be used by sporting organisations in the area. After much discussion, it was agreed that a limited liability company should be set up and money should be raised from the sale of shares, with income from letting the ground for sporting events providing a return to investors. It had already been agreed that a piece of ground at the end of Green Lane, known as Hocking's Meadow, would be leased for an initial period of 40 years.

The shares were snapped up within a week and the first shareholders meeting took place just a week later. Of the 11 directors elected, no fewer than seven were members of the football club. By August, work was under way to remove hedges and build boundary walls. There was some concern that only three men had been employed for these tasks and that the ground might not be ready for the new football season, but there was to be no return to Brewery Field.

Redruth played their first game of the 1883/84 season between a captain's XV and a side raised by the secretary, so it was not until 28 November that Camborne became the first visitors to the new Recreation Ground, in front of what was described as a large attendance. Camborne led by a try at half-time, although Redruth came back strongly after the break. Redruth were inches from the Camborne goal line when the Camborne umpire called time. This was hotly disputed by the Redruth umpire, who insisted a further five minutes of play remained. With no agreement, the game ended with Camborne the winners by one try to nil.

The fact that Redruth was settled on its current ground within eight years of its formation is quite rare in rugby and few clubs have played continuously on the same ground for so long. In the early days of the game, it was normal for newly formed clubs to borrow fields as needed and generally lead a nomadic life. The Redruth committee decided early on that, whether for reasons of finance, security or increased affiliation from supporters, it wanted a ground it could call its own. As a result, it has one of the longest continuous tenures of its current ground in rugby union. Other than the short spell at Tolvean, Redruth has only had two grounds in its entire existence.

In the early days, however, it could not call the Recreation Ground truly its own and catering for a variety of different sports did cause some problems. One of the most contentious proposals was from the local cycling club, which asked that a cinder track be built around the outside of the ground. It was agreed to consider the possibility, as long as it did not interfere with the football or cricket. A subcommittee was set up, chaired by Redruth co-founder Henry Grylls and comprising mainly members of the football club. It seems they did not pursue the matter with any great urgency and eventually the cyclists pedalled elsewhere.

On the afternoon of 8 October 1884, representatives from Bodmin, Falmouth, Hayle, Redruth, Penzance, Tregony and Truro met at the Royal Hotel in Truro and resolved that a representative body be formed to be called the Cornwall Rugby Football Union. It followed a series of defeats of an ad hoc Cornish side by neighbouring Devon and it was hoped the new body could improve Cornish rugby. The Redruth captain, John Everett, was one of three members of the newly elected committee appointed to pick a side to face Devon for the upcoming fixture. Just over a year after Redruth had played their first game on the newly opened Recreation Ground, on 2 December 1884 they played host for the first time to a match between Devon and Cornwall.

These early games laid the foundation for Redruth to develop as the acknowledged home of Cornish rugby and, for decades, the Recreation Ground became a natural choice for County Championship matches. In the words of Tom Salmon in his history of Cornish rugby: 'In some quite indefinable way Cornish rugby and Redruth have become inseparable.'[23]

Redruth may have provided the ground, but they were far from dominant when it came to providing the players. No fewer than five of the Cornwall side that played that December day came from Hayle. The club, which had been founded in 1877, would prove to be Redruth's greatest rival throughout the 1880s. Redruth had hosted a Hayle side at the Recreation Ground just three days before the county game, losing by two goals to nil against a side that played a different style of rugby:

'The success of the winning team was solely owing to their superior and effective passing of the ball. This innovation has only become generally recognised since the match, last year, between Devon and Cornwall, when the former's brilliant passing secured the supremacy. Cornish clubs have now adopted this practice; and the team thus most efficient maintain the upper hand. It is hoped that our local players (in other respects a strong club) will practise this point.'[24]

On Boxing Day 1884, it was Penzance who visited the Recreation Ground, relations having apparently recovered since the earlier boycott. Penzance won by a goal and two tries to one try, but it would be stretching a point to say peace had broken out. Finding themselves trailing in the second half, Redruth players began slowing the game down by disputing every decision against them. The following year, Camborne came to Redruth on Boxing Day for only the second time. Redruth won by three tries to nil.

In the mid-1880s, Penzance, Hayle, Camborne, Truro and Falmouth formed the core of Redruth's sporadic fixtures, with occasional matches against sides from Devon. They were joined in January 1885 by a new club from Penryn, which would feature strongly in Redruth's future fixture lists. The first report of a match between these two sides was in January 1886 and it was not a happy affair. An early try by Redruth was hotly disputed by the Penryn players and fists began to fly. When Penryn crossed the line a few minutes later, another fracas broke out and the Redruth team walked off the pitch and went home. According to witnesses, the game lasted less than 15 minutes.

There was more unpleasantness later in the year when Redruth travelled to Hayle, losing by two tries to nil. The *Cornubian and Redruth Times* noted that the match was particularly rough and many of the Redruth side sustained injuries. Hayle, which was said to have a much heavier pack, played 'a most brutal game'. One Redruth player was reported to have been grabbed by the hair and pulled to the ground.

Redruth's performances on the field began to improve as the decade wore on. In the 1886/87 season, Redruth lost just one game and that was against the Albions at Plymouth. However, the club's continuing success had a downside. There were increasing reports of opponents calling off games at short notice, citing a shortage of players. In January 1887, both Falmouth and Hayle pulled out of visits to Redruth, claiming they could not raise a side.

Football columnists of the day usually wrote under a pen name, perhaps understandably given the rows that erupted between clubs. Reports seen as being favourable to one side or another often triggered irate letters to the editor. One row between Camborne and Pool over player eligibility went on in the correspondence columns for several weeks. Redruth were frequently derided by a man who dubbed himself 'Fullback' and wrote for *The Cornishman*, a Penzance paper, but they could rely on the support of the *Cornubian and Redruth Times*.

The *Cornubian* was predictably scathing about an announcement that Falmouth had challenged Hayle to a match to decide who was the best side in the county:

> 'Redruth is pre-eminently the home of football in this county. Not only does it furnish excellent players to the county team, and maintain a skilful local club, but its inhabitants attend each game in large numbers and with surprising regularity. The proficiency of the club is more remarkable as the personnel constantly undergoes changes. Many of the members emigrate, and they carry with them to foreign lands the pluck and push which made them successful players at home. But recruits are never lacking; and though this year the majority of the members are not out of their teens they have not yet lost a match. The game with Falmouth was won with surprising ease; and even the redoubtable Hayle team was set at nought.'[25]

These barbed exchanges in the pages of the newspapers only served to encourage the already rowdy behaviour of the spectators, who were sometimes more closely involved in the action on the pitch than was wise. At one game at Camborne, played on 5 February 1887, those in the home crowd repeatedly harassed opposition players. As Redruth's Tom Smith dashed down the wing, ball in hand, Camborne supporters pushed on to the pitch and tried to trip him up as he attempted to reach the goal line. He managed to get the ball to his brother, Walter, who evaded the clutching hands to put the ball down for a try. Redruth won by three points.

There was more crowd intervention when Redruth played Hayle on 12 February. Late in the game, Hayle claimed to have crossed the Redruth line, but this was challenged both by the Redruth players and some of the onlookers. The Hayle umpire, a man from Camborne, claimed it was a touchdown, while the Redruth umpire was emphatic that it was not. The referee, who happened to be the Rev. J. Stona, president of the Redruth club, disallowed the try. This triggered arguments from Hayle players and a number of the home side's supporters broke on to the pitch to remonstrate with both the Redruth players and the referee. The game was cut short.

October 1887 saw the introduction at Redruth of a new set of matched playing jerseys to replace the random selection previously provided by the players themselves. The shirts had a design of four squares in sky and navy blue, and were paired with blue stockings and white shorts. A pattern of squares was one of the easiest to stitch together and the early Cornwall county shirts were of a similar design, except in amber and black.

The season started late, with Redruth playing their first game on 29 October against what was described as a 'scratch' Hayle side. It ended in a draw. Fixture lists were fairly sparse, with several clubs struggling for both funds and players, the latter either through lack of interest or because players were moving abroad. This saw a number of reports of games featuring ad hoc teams, some of which contained Redruth players. The *Cornubian*'s robust claim that, at Redruth, 'recruits are never lacking' suggests that other clubs were not so fortunate as to have ambitious youngsters playing for feeder teams.

The Christmas period would usually bring a flurry of activity and, in 1887, two games were scheduled against a side from St Ives, the second one at home on Boxing Day. There were also matches at home to Penzance and away at the Plymouth side, Albion, on New Year's Eve. A total of five games were arranged in the second half of the season, with matches against Hayle, Penzance, Keyham – later the Royal Naval Engineering College in Devonport – and Albion, who also played at Devonport. The match against Albion on 3 March 1888 saw Redruth avenge their earlier defeat up in Devon, winning by a goal and three saves to one save.

One team is notably absent from this list and the task facing the Redruth fixture secretary became even more challenging with the news that the Camborne club had run into financial difficulties due to members not paying their subscriptions. A meeting of the club at the end of September 1888 formally wound it up. Fortunately, there was better news from Falmouth where the club was in the process of being re-formed after folding some months previously. Truro, too, was about to regain a football club following the demise of the previous incarnation.

The newly resurrected Falmouth club was one of only three sides to play Redruth in the first half of the 1888/89 season when it hosted them in November. Redruth won by a goal, a try and seven saves to nil. Boxing Day saw the visit of Liskeard, probably one of the most one-sided games the Reds had played to date. The home side fielded a second string and lent the visitors three players, but still won by one goal, eight tries and six saves to nil.

By the beginning of 1889, Redruth had established a two-year record of being undefeated on any Cornish ground. This continued with a win over Hayle in January in front of a crowd of nearly 1,500 spectators, more than had watched a recent Cornwall game against Devon. Redruth's continuing success was attributed in the match report to the club playing sides from outside Cornwall.

Redruth maintained their record against Cornish clubs until the end of the season. Of the nine games they played in 1888/89, they won eight and drew one, at Hayle. One of those was a match on 6 March against an invitation Cornwall XV, which became the second Redruth game to be played under electric lights. Technology had evidently improved since the previous such game a decade earlier, as the report claimed that every player could be as clearly distinguished as if it were bright daylight.

The resurrection of the Camborne club did little to lighten the load of the Redruth fixture secretary over the summer and, at the beginning of September, the club placed an advertisement in the press asking for matches with any clubs in Devon and Cornwall. Even after this appeal, their first game of the season did not take place until almost two months later, on 1 November, a home game against Devonport Albion, which was lost by five goals to nil. There were also a number of fixtures in the first half of the season for what was termed the Redruth B side, with the first XV described as Redruth A. It seems other Cornish sides were prepared to take on Redruth's more junior team, but baulked at the prospect of going head-to-head with the senior side.

One new name to appear in the Redruth fixture list was that of Western Albions, who played on a field at Trevingey, close to the original Redruth Churchtown. They had been founded by a player named Richard Garby, who had previously turned out for Redruth. He introduced the four three-quarter style of play he had seen in Wales. The first report of their existence was in February 1890 when they were classed as a junior club. It seems from the various match reports that other Redruth players occasionally turned out for this side. They came to the

Recreation Ground on 6 December 1890, losing to the Reds by a goal and three saves to nil.

Western Albions scored one success over Redruth in that they were able to reveal that the football correspondent of the *Cornubian and Redruth Times*, who wrote under the pseudonym 'Dropkick', was actually a Redruth player. Disappointingly, they failed to name the player, but this did help to explain the paper's clear bias in favour of the more established Redruth side. It was, of course, highly likely that players wrote the equally biased football columns in other newspapers at the time.

Redruth were at home to Camborne on 26 December 1890, the first Boxing Day encounter between the two clubs for three years. Kick-off was scheduled for 3pm but was delayed by the collapse of a grandstand which held between 300 and 400 spectators. The structure had been there for some time and was in poor condition, so much so that some spectators had been giving it a wide berth for a while.

There was only one serious injury, Mr Smith, a nurseryman, who had to be taken to the Miners' Hospital. Luckily, there were two medical men at the game to attend to the injured; a surgeon, William Hichens, later the Redruth president, and his brother, Frank, who was a GP. One paper related that: 'Of course, the untoward event caused excitement, but the play began and took off people's attention.' Given the lateness of the kick-off and the time of year, the game must have ended in near darkness.

Three months later, on 31 March 1891, there was much excitement at the Recreation Ground when a crowd of 2,000 turned out to watch a team from Newport take to the field, the first time a club from Wales had played at Redruth. It had been predicted that the visitors would be far too good for the Reds but, in the event, they were deemed fortunate to go home with a narrow win, by one try to nil.

After the match, Newport's players and officials were entertained to a dinner at Tabbs Hotel before boarding the late train back to Wales. It would be 30 years before Welsh clubs would become regular visitors to the Recreation Ground, but the foundation was laid for a mutual respect that would endure between the top clubs of these two rugby playing Celtic communities.

That evening at Tabbs Hotel, the speeches continued after the Welsh players had left. The chief subject of debate was the continued existence of their near neighbours, Western Albions. The Redruth captain, Alexander Suter Grylls, younger brother of founder Henry, told the gathering that it was a mistake to have two teams in the town and he expressed the hope, to loud applause, that they might merge the following season. In fact, Western Albions continued to feature in the local press for another decade, although their matches became few and far between and many of their players also took to the field in Redruth colours.

One imagines that there would also have been much discussion about Newport's style of play and about the lessons that might be learned from the big Welsh clubs if Redruth were to develop. The match had showcased elements of the game that were in their infancy in Cornwall and there was an appetite to learn more. And so it was that when the 1891/92 season approached and a new player joined Redruth, a Welshman with experience of rugby at the highest levels, he found fertile ground for his ideas. In just a few months he would transform the way they played the game and lay strong foundations for future success.

John Smith Longdon, known at the club as 'Jack', was 25 when he arrived in Redruth to take up an appointment as a teacher at the grandly named Redruth College in Clinton Road. Longdon was an Oxford Blue who had previously played for Neath and London Welsh, before moving to Swansea in 1889. His time at Swansea came shortly after the club had introduced the four three-quarter system which had originally been trialled in Cardiff. This involved moving one of the two full-backs into the three-quarter line to spread the game wider.

The result was what is fundamentally the modern formation of inside-centre, outside-centre, left-wing, right-wing and a single full-back.

Longdon's reputation had preceded him, following his stunning try for Swansea against Cornwall in a game played in Wales on 22 March 1890. He once said that the first thing he did when he arrived in Redruth was to ask friends if there was a local team and to join up immediately. With his easy, confident manner and aquiline good looks, he made friends quickly and was embraced by his new team and their supporters.

Redruth enthusiastically adopted his philosophy that kicking should be discouraged and that the job of the forwards was to win the ball and get it out to the backs. This was a major change from the traditional Cornish style of forward-driven play, when dribbling a ball forward with a player's feet was still an intrinsic part of the game. Longdon's debut for Redruth was keenly awaited by their supporters, but he did not have the opportunity to play a competitive game until their visit to Camborne in January 1892. Redruth won, with Longdon getting a special mention in the match report. However, it was felt that Redruth had not made the best of their new star.

> 'Everybody was eager to see Longdon play but he had not a chance. However, he showed that, given the opportunity he could do something towards winning a match. But a man cannot do anything without the ball.'[26]

Longdon shone again when Penzance visited the Recreation Ground in April 1892. The somewhat partisan *Cornish Telegraph*, printed in Penzance, reported, perhaps just a little tongue in cheek, that the visitors were expected to have such an easy win that many Redruth supporters failed to turn up on the assumption that their team would lose. In the event, Redruth won by three goals and a try to nothing. Much of the credit went to the pairing of Longdon and the fleet-footed Redruth winger, Harry Carvolth, whom it was said could do the 100 yards in even time (ten seconds) without turning a hair. The Reds finished the season having played 17 games and remained unbeaten by any other Cornish club.

Sadly, just a few months after arriving in Redruth, Longdon was gone. At the end of the 1891/92 season, he returned to Oxford to continue his studies, later taking up a post as a curate in Wales. At the club's annual dinner, in April 1892, he was presented with a silver cup by the club's treasurer, Sydney Lanyon, who said that Redruth's weak point had always been the performance of its three-quarters:

'I would say now that the three-quarters of the Redruth team are as strong as any others in the county. Mr Longdon had taught the three-quarters a great deal and they all appreciated what that gentleman had done.'[27]

Longdon played one final game for Redruth, against a touring Neath side which arrived on 19 April 1892. Having easily dealt with Exeter and Albions, both packed with Devon county players, the Welsh side were confident that Redruth would not pose much opposition. More than 2,000 spectators watched a hotly contested game in which Longdon made several attacking runs. Neath pushed hard towards the end, but Redruth held out for the draw. At some stage during the game, Longdon's jersey was ripped in two and the match report noted that:

'Lady spectators were much amused to witness the energetic way in which it was dragged off and another pulled on; but the new one proved too small and the ladies were again put to the blush, for the cup-holder had to take it off and swap with Hodge.'[28]

Redruth took their new style of play into the 1892/93 season and Frank Woolf was re-elected captain. According to a report in the *West Briton* newspaper, Woolf had played more games than any other player in Cornwall, Devon or Somerset. The paper also hoped for good things from Redruth's back division; Harry Carvolth, Harry Phillips, Jack Viant, Trevenan Peters, Williams, Paull and Howard Gray.

The provisional fixture list for the coming season showed that serious effort had been made to arrange games with convincing opposition. It listed Devon sides Torquay, Totnes and Newton Abbot among the opponents Redruth would face, as well as two Welsh touring sides, Penarth on Easter Saturday and Aberavon on Easter Monday. However, there was disappointment that it had been impossible to agree a fixture with the Albions, then Devon's premier side. It was a match that always attracted a large crowd.

Redruth's B team also had a busy programme ahead. The club had a thriving second XV and it was noted that, during pre-season practice, the A team had to work hard to overcome the second side.

Locally, the game continued to grow. In September 1892 there were more than 20 junior clubs active in the Redruth area, including the Midgets, North Country, Scarlet Runners, Carn Brea Grasshoppers, Greyhounds, Warriors and Hobnailers. Some of these clubs would later merge or, in some cases, disappear completely, but they were a valuable source of promising players whose ambition was to play for the Redruth first XV, by then becoming known as the 'chiefs', to distinguish them from the B team, later the reserves or second XV.

Off the field, the social side of the Redruth club, so important in modern times, was not neglected. The club enjoyed a Smoking Concert at Tabbs Hotel on the evening of Tuesday, 8 November 1892. These events, popular in the Victorian era, were an opportunity for men to gather for live music, songs, drinking and smoking. Women were not permitted. In this case, it was also an opportunity for a presentation to be made to Sydney Lanyon, who had just married a mine manager's daughter named Susan Tremayne.

The evening was chaired by the club president, Rev. John Stona, vicar of Mount Hawke. He admitted to being neither a drinker or a smoker, but he hoped such evenings would continue into the future. It is clear from the detailed report that once the teetotal president had left to go home, the evening became rather more lively, with impromptu songs and recitations – and many choruses of *For He's a Jolly Good Fellow* – before the striking of the town clock at 11pm brought the jollities to a close.

Redruth suffered their first defeat of the season on 19 November in an away game at Newton College, Newton Abbot, losing by the only try of the match. Redruth actually crossed their opponents' line three times, but each time the try was disallowed. The Redruth skipper, Frank Woolf, while described by Henry Grylls as 'the toughest forward I ever knew', also had a deserved reputation as a man of great courtesy. However, some felt he was being a little too polite:

> 'Capt. Woolf never permits his team to dispute with the referee and, instead of arguing, he puts his head into the scrum and the rest follow their leader. This is a good feature, but it may be sometimes carried too far.'[29]

The following month saw a convincing Redruth win at home to Camborne, by four goals, four tries and two saves to nil. The visitors arrived a couple of men short and had to borrow two Redruth B team players. On Boxing Day 1892, in front of a crowd estimated to have been between 2,000 and 3,000 people, Redruth avenged their only defeat of the season so far by beating visitors Newton by two goals and two tries to nil. The visitors had travelled down to Cornwall in a private carriage attached to the back of a GWR train and were met at Redruth Station by around 400 locals, who cheered them into the town.

There was more excitement a few days later when Redruth faced Penzance at the Recreation Ground. In terms of results, these were the two best sides in Cornwall at the time and the clash was much anticipated. On this occasion, Redruth's forward power was too much for the visitors and Redruth ran out winners by one goal, one try and two saves to nil. This was the first report of a Redruth game to record that the players were wearing red shirts and in which they were described as 'the Reds'.

Penzance had their revenge in the return match a week later when a weakened Redruth side were beaten by a try and two saves to nil. This was the first time Penzance had beaten the Reds in four seasons. *The Cornishman* got so excited it published a fake, if somewhat premature, death notice: 'In memory of the Redruth football team which was laid to rest at St Clare, Penzance on Saturday last at 4.30.'

By now, Redruth had become the uncontested premier side in Cornwall, the team everyone wanted to beat and, as with modern clubs with heaving trophy cabinets, the side everybody loved to hate. They certainly proved too good for their near neighbours, Camborne, who threw everything at them in vain, losing by a goal and a try to nil in January 1893:

'A deplorably rough-and-tumble, old-fashioned game it was the Camborne side who played their hackneyed, degenerated, chaotic miserable substitute for football which we were accustomed to see in years gone by. There is no doubt if the game had been played properly and without all the unnecessary roughness, Redruth would have had the satisfaction of a more decided victory.'[30]

The following month, on 10 February 1893, the police had to intervene at Redruth's home game against Totnes. The Redruth committee had appointed a Penzance referee by the name of Cornish, which did not go down well with the Redruth crowd, given the longstanding enmity between the two towns. The home crowd felt that Totnes were getting far too many free kicks and began hooting and catcalling the official.

When the referee called 'no side' to end the game, he found himself surrounded by a hostile group of Redruth supporters. A number of police officers, together with members of the Redruth team, had to escort Mr Cornish off the pitch for his own safety. This would not be the last time an official had to be protected from the Redruth crowd.

Redruth crowds were nothing if not keen to get involved. For many years it had been the custom of spectators to play an ad hoc game on the pitch before the teams came out. This was eventually stopped because it often turned the ground into a mud bath before the players ran out. Barracking of opposition players during the game was commonplace, as were attempts to interfere with the play if someone from the opposition looked like scoring.

The appointment of referees, and their subsequent decisions, increasingly gave rise to complaints from those both on and off the field. A game against Camborne in October 1893 ended in a predicted win for Redruth, the club being described in the match report as the 'champions of the west'. However, one anonymous Camborne supporter took issue with the referee's performance:

> 'Isn't it strange that the Redruth team cannot get an independent man to act as referee. Surely there must be something radically wrong when nearly every team that plays on their ground has to complain of the unfair decision of the referee? Isn't it time the Rugby Union looked into the matter?'[31]

The Redruth players focused their attention on the pitch and it secured them an unexpected draw against visiting Torquay

Athletic in the run-up to Christmas 1893. The Devon side was one of the best in the region and many, not least in Penzance and Camborne, had confidently hoped and predicted that Redruth would lose.

They also forced a 0-0 draw against Llanelli, one of the strongest sides in Wales, who were on a brief Christmas tour. More than 2,000 spectators watched the game at the Recreation Ground, where Redruth had to play in a change strip of yellow and white because the visitors had arrived with their habitual scarlet jerseys. There were complaints in some quarters about the rough play of some of the Welsh side and their continual swearing in both English and Welsh. One Llanelli player was quoted as saying it was the toughest match they had played all season.

The year ended with Redruth once again undefeated by any Cornish side, but this record was soured by the announcement that Penzance and Camborne were pulling out of any future fixtures at Redruth. It is not clear what the reason was; perhaps the alleged bias of Redruth match officials. It could be argued that decisions went in Redruth's favour because they were outplaying their local opposition, who infringed the rules out of frustration. The football correspondent for the *Cornish Telegraph* felt there were other reasons:

> 'I may be permitted to say that it might be as well if the Redruthians would not adopt such a high and mighty tone in their dealings with all and sundry. They should understand that, whatever their position in the county, the putting on of side [behaving in a superior manner] is calculated to put other people's backs up and cannot induce to the establishment of those friendly relations which all clubs should try to cultivate by all means in their power.'[32]

The stand-off with Camborne lasted a matter of weeks. In January 1894, it was reported that Camborne players were indignant about 'the inexcusable conduct of their captain and ex-captain in refusing to play important matches' and a meeting was called. The result was that a scratch team, minus some key players, made the journey to the ground of the old enemy. Predictably, given the weak Camborne side, Redruth won the encounter, but the thawing of relations was good for the Cornish game as a whole, as well as the bank balances of the two clubs.

Redruth's claim to be Cornwall's premier club took a knock the following month after an unexpected defeat at Falmouth by two tries to one on 3 February 1894. The victors were a club that had been gaining in strength over the previous few years and would top the unofficial merit table by the end of the decade. News of the win was rapturously received, with the *Cornish Echo* mischievously suggesting that the Reds needed more practice.

Behind the scenes, moves were under way to break the deadlock with Penzance. So serious was the situation that a Redruth representative took the train to Penzance to discuss fixtures face-to-face, his fare listed on expenses in the annual accounts. Some in Penzance were concerned about the future of rugby in the town if it proved too difficult to secure games, a problem that had dogged Redruth's early seasons and one compounded for Penzance by its location even further west. Not only had the club refused to play Redruth, but two Devon sides, Albions and Newton, previously regular visitors to Penzance, had also called off their games. It was, therefore, reported with some relief that Penzance had agreed to play the Reds on 3 March.

Redruth, meanwhile, had to prepare for their own visit by Albions, the champion club of Devon, for a fixture keenly awaited by local rugby enthusiasts. One Camborne supporter, writing to the *Cornish Telegraph*, said that after Redruth's strong performance against Llanelli, the Reds might be feeling confident of beating Albion, but his fellow townsmen would happily wager against them.

In the end, honours were even and the match went down as a scoreless draw. Several members of the Albion team reportedly lost their heads and their tempers, indulging in rough horseplay and delighting in what was described as 'showing their boxing abilities and skill at kicking shins'. It was suggested that, in future, Redruth ought perhaps to source a neutral official from the RFU, as the match referee had been seen dining with the Albion team before the game and indulging in a sing-song with them afterwards.

The match was the most lucrative for the club that season, bringing in more than £35 at the gate. The game against Llanelli, and another against Devon Wanderers over the Christmas period, had attracted similarly large crowds, but those two clubs had been paid a guarantee to come, which cut into the profit.

The relief at Penzance's change of heart over playing Redruth was short-lived. Despite optimistic reports of a thaw in relations between the clubs, the match scheduled for 3 March was called off, with Penzance declining to make the journey. It would not have escaped Redruth's notice that Penzance had fulfilled fixtures with both Camborne and Falmouth over the previous few weeks; the Redruth second XV did play Penzance at home on 24 February.

These local matches were important to Redruth. They boosted the club's profile, provided regular game time and generated gate money to help fund the expensive away trips to Devon. In the 1893/94 season, the first XV only played five home matches against local clubs; Camborne twice, Falmouth, Penryn and Truro. They also played two games against scratch opposition, one of them a well-attended invitational captained by Redruth player Arthur Teague. In total, these matches against Cornish opposition raised just short of £33 for the club. Out of a total season's gate money of almost £188, the lion's share came from the six home games against Devon clubs and Llanelli.

At the August 1894 annual general meeting, it was announced that, for the first time since its formation, Redruth had ended the season in the black. Gate money, subscriptions of just over £18 and 'sundry receipts' contributed to a total season's income a little over £214. The club spent almost £165, leaving a profit of £49, enough to wipe out debts from earlier years and leave a credit balance of £7. The decision was taken to engage a paid secretary in place of volunteers and James Evans was appointed.

Part of his role was to manage the club's expenses. The largest items of expenditure in the 1893/94 season had been travel (£57) and hotels (£33), which included paying for changing facilities at away matches. The balance sheet also showed payments of £3 7s, including gratuities, to the police for providing officers at the ground and a further £1 9s 6d to 'men watching hedges' to keep out those evading the admission fee at games.

A few years earlier, there had been lively discussions about the best way to stop spectators climbing in over the hedges, but it had not been until February 1891 that the decision had been taken to threaten all trespassers on to the Recreation Ground with prosecution. This would help deter the euphemistically named 'hedge tickets' and reduce the cost to the club of having police officers at home games, although the presence of police would still be needed on regular occasions.

In the future, the club would make vital income from a bar, but before the turn of the century there were few facilities at the Recreation Ground, which the club continued to share with Redruth Cricket Club. In April 1886, tenders had been invited for the erection of a pavilion on the site, but the rugby club had continued to use Tabbs Hotel as a base. Tenders to provide catering for events made it clear that only non-alcoholic drinks could be sold.

Gate receipts and subscriptions from members were the main sources of income and Redruth needed to ensure regular home games to attract crowds. There was one way to make matches at Redruth more attractive to both supporters and prospective opposition, and that was to field men who had been selected for the Cornwall county side and it was hoped, in time, for England.

By this time, Redruth had produced a number of outstanding players and the increasing press coverage of games ensured that their names were well known in Cornwall and beyond. Prominent players in the 1890s included Frank Woolf and Alexander Suter Grylls, younger brother of the club's founder, Henry Grylls, who captained both his club and the Cornwall side.

Others in that first Redruth generation to get their county caps were Walter and Tom Smith, Will Rowe, Charlie Pearce and Willie Blewett. They were followed by the likes of Jack Viant, Harry Phillips, Trevenan Peters, Nick James and Harry Carvolth. With so many Redruth players picked to play for Cornwall in the County Championship, then the pinnacle of English rugby, it was felt to be only a matter of time before the club would have a player selected for the England team, but the call did not come.

A number of reasons have been given for this failure by the RFU to acknowledge Cornish players during the 1890s, including geography and simple class distinction. A look at the England team that took on Wales in Cardiff on 7 January 1893 tells much about the national side of that period. Of the 15-man team, ten had attended fee-paying schools and eight of these players had gone on to Oxford or Cambridge. Eight played for fashionable London-based clubs, Richmond, Harlequins and Blackheath. Nine had careers in the professions or business. Only four could have been considered working class and three of those played for Yorkshire, the side that dominated the County Championship in the 1890s, winning in nine of the ten years.

The final years of the 19th century would prove significant for Redruth, as the club fought to establish its position as the most successful side in Cornwall. This was against a background of continuing decline in the Cornish mining industry, the loss of further players as men went overseas and the failure of neighbouring clubs, with the resulting loss of regular fixtures. It would prove to be a challenging time.

Chapter Three

Growing Rivalries 1895–1904

IN THE mid-1890s, Britain stood at almost the peak of its imperial power. The Industrial Revolution had transformed the nation, propelling it into an age of technological advancement and urbanisation, but social and economic disparities saw the working class grappling with harsh living conditions and labour struggles.

The expertise in hard rock mining that had developed in Cornwall from centuries of extracting tin and copper from granite bedrock was highly desirable and young men had long been going overseas to work in mines and goldfields across the world. Towards the end of the century, the gold rush on the Witwatersrand in the Transvaal was at its peak, contributing to a surge in emigration, and it is estimated that some ten per cent of Cornwall's population moved out of the county during the 1890s.

Rugby in Cornwall suffered from the exodus of these young men and Redruth, with its dependence on mining, was particularly affected. Newspapers were full of reports of players leaving Redruth for South Africa and there remains an area in Johannesburg, 50 miles from the Witwatersrand, known as New Redruth. These 'Cousin Jacks', as the emigrating Cornishmen were known, took with them their strong rugby tradition, along with the Cornish pasty and other elements of Cornish culture that can still be found there today.

Redruth was fortunate to have a good network of feeder teams in the area and a strong second XV which had grown in strength over the previous five years. These players were eager to step up and play for the chiefs when players left, enabling the club to continue to field full sides. Veteran player Frank Woolf had been re-elected as captain for the 1894/95 season, and his experience, along with that of other long-standing players, helped to mould the upcoming talent. More than 40 participants turned out for the season opener on 14 September 1894, a trial match between a captain's side and one selected by the club secretary. Despite the worries over departing players, the club published a full fixture list for both the first and second XVs.

Redruth's first away game of the season was at Falmouth and was played at such a fast pace that the referee was apparently unable to keep up. It ended without score, but the speed and rough play took their toll and, by the end, it was reported that several players had been knocked out. This most likely referred to players being winded, rather than left unconscious, but it is indicative of the robust style of rugby played throughout West Cornwall at the time.

There was much anticipation in Redruth when the club faced Penzance at the end of November. It was the first game between the two sides since Penzance had refused to play Redruth the season before and then subsequently pulled out of the rearranged fixture. The Reds won a high-speed, often physical encounter by the only try of the game. Afterwards, there were predictable mutterings about the decisions of the referee, in this case the Redruth vice president, Dr William (Willie) Hichens.

The row over clubs appointing their own referees rumbled on in the absence of any leadership from the Cornwall Rugby Union. Referees did not have to be qualified in any way, nor even to have played the game, although many of them had. For their home match against Falmouth on 21 December, Redruth decided to sidestep the issue by bringing in a man from St Austell, an option not open to every club because of the cost of paying expenses. The move appears to have been successful, as there was little, if any, dissent and Redruth were able to celebrate victory by two goals to one penalty goal.

The club suffered a blow in January 1895 when star winger Harry Carvolth was forced to move to Plymouth to find work. There he joined a newly formed club that would later become Plymouth Albion and continued to entertain the crowds. Vice-captain William James also departed, after eight years wearing a Redruth shirt, when he followed other former players to South Africa. While there, he contracted pulmonary tuberculosis and he returned to Redruth in 1906 a shell of the man he had been. He died three years later.

Even without some of its best players, Redruth lay top of the unofficial league table, which at that time comprised just three other clubs – Penzance, Camborne and Falmouth. Their reward was to host a Rest of Cornwall side at the Recreation Ground, but it was a game no one seems to have wanted. Redruth put out a second string and lost by a goal and two tries to nil. When the Penzance referee disallowed a Redruth try, nine of the side walked off, leaving skipper Frank Woolf and five other players to see out the last few minutes. The unfortunate official had to be escorted from the ground by the police after being manhandled by members of the crowd.

The club's fixture list for the start of the 1895/96 season lists 25 upcoming matches. Clearly it was felt that such a busy schedule would require more practice from the players and they were instructed to take part in regular sessions. In the past, these had been few and far between and often sparsely attended. While the communal running sessions which had been practised since the days of Henry Grylls were useful in keeping players fit, they did not allow the honing of ball skills. Players of the period relied on a combination of self-directed practice, informal guidance from experienced players and team collaboration to improve their game.

The RFU frowned on any sort of coaching on the basis that it did not fit in with the game's amateur ethos, but the lack of formal coaching did not mean a lack of expertise or strategic thinking, as demonstrated by the impact made by John Longdon. Rugby has always been a sport that values the knowledge and experience passed down from generation to generation, but it would be another 80 years before formal coaching became an intrinsic part of the game in England.

The first game of the season was away to Camborne on 12 October and it appears the additional practice sessions may have had an effect. The superior fitness of the Redruth side saw them win by the only try of the game after a determined Camborne performance. This was followed by a home win over Falmouth and a scoreless draw at Penzance, a game which was notable for having a marked absence of ill-feeling among either players or spectators. This happy state of affairs would not endure long.

The last match of 1895 saw Redruth travel to the County Ground for their first encounter against Exeter. It was a hard-fought contest, which the home side finally won by one unconverted try. The loss left the Reds with just four wins from nine matches in the first half of the season, a frustrating record after several successful years and one which showed the impact of losing so many experienced players.

Playing in the big away games and the usual busy Christmas schedule did help the new recruits bed in and results improved considerably in the new year, with wins over Dartmouth, Falmouth and Plymouth. They were beaten away at Albion, the Devon County Cup holders, when Redruth missed a few chances that allowed the home side to scrape home, but the return match at Redruth ended in a draw.

March saw Redruth defeat Falmouth, Penzance, Penryn and Camborne in successive matches, taking them once again to the top of the Cornwall table. The last match of the season was against Bridgend, who had travelled from South Wales for a tour of the South West. Their visit to the Recreation Ground on Easter Monday ended in a 6-6 draw, which allowed the Redruth team to hold their heads high and end the season in good spirits, as well as making a healthy contribution to the coffers. Redruth had paid Bridgend a guarantee of £12 10s to play, but took more than £22 on the gate.

The season had also seen fewer disputes over refereeing, thanks to the County Union finally having set up a Referees' Association. Neutral officials or, at least, officials with less obvious affiliations, now took charge of matches. It was hoped that these impartial referees would make decisions based solely on the merits of the game and the actions of the players, without any perceived favouritism, and so would enhance the integrity of the sport and help to maintain a level playing field. Unfortunately, it did not always work out like that.

The 1895 close season was to see one of the most significant developments in the game of rugby, with the foundation on 29 August of the Northern Rugby Football Union, later to be known as the Rugby Football League. It marked the official establishment of rugby league which, over the ensuing decade, developed as a separate code with its own laws. The Northern Union broke away because so many of their players were working class and could not afford to take time off to play for their local clubs unless they were compensated.

The same was true in Cornwall, as it was in Wales, but what became the 13-man code never found a foothold in either place. In Cornwall's case, that is almost certainly due to the county's relative isolation and the small number of clubs, which would have made a professional league uneconomic. In any case, as in Wales, there were ways and means of compensating players for lost wages without incurring the attention of the Rugby Football Union and, in Redruth's case, there were certainly understanding employers who could be flexible over working hours. As we shall see, only one serious attempt was ever made to bring rugby league to Cornwall and that never went past the discussion stage.

Nevertheless, the quest for higher wages and better job security continued to have an impact in Redruth and the team lost two more first XV players during the summer, with John Winn and Willy Veale leaving for Australia. The social aspect of rugby was important to a team rebuilding after so many changes and the rest of the players enjoyed a day out at Newquay, making the three-and-a-half-hour journey to the seaside in a horse-drawn brake, with a stop at Zelah for refreshments and to rest the horses. A game of football on the Newquay ground was followed by lunch and a swimming session in the afternoon. It was midnight before the party arrived home.

The club was in optimistic mood for the annual dinner at Redruth's Masonic Hall in September 1895. Around 100 members and guests sat down for the evening to hear Willie Hichens, now club president, announce that Redruth RFC was in a 'high position' in terms of winning matches and was also in a sound financial state. The success of the club's second XV meant that younger players were being developed to take the place of the men Redruth had lost to emigration.

Redruth issued a fixture card for the 1895/96 season showing games with Albion, Paignton, Dartmouth, Broughton and Bridgend, as well as fixtures against other Cornish clubs. The first of these was against Camborne at Rosewarne on 12 October 1895 and was described as rough, with Redruth winning by the only goal of the game. The on-field action was followed by the rival spectators hurling stones at each other. There followed a narrow home win over Falmouth in which the Redruth three-quarters proved a little too quick for their opponents.

Despite these early wins, it was clear from match reports that Redruth had hit something of a plateau and performances were not of the same standard as the previous season. There was concern that many players had not been turning up for practice sessions and some were not as fit as they might be. On 7 December, after a string of indifferent matches, Redruth were beaten on their own ground by Penzance in front of a disappointingly small crowd. A defeat by Plymouth followed just before Christmas.

Redruth did well enough against other Cornish clubs to start 1896 in second place in the table behind Penzance, who had played two games more. It was customary for sides to play each other four times during the season, but only the first two matches counted for points. The Reds did take heart with a fine performance away to Devon Albions. Despite losing by a goal and a try to nil, they pushed their hosts all the way to the end and were unlucky not to get on the scoreboard.

A fine win at Penzance in February showed that Redruth were upping their game and, coupled with wins over Camborne and Penryn, it took them briefly to the top of the table. However, they found themselves being barracked by their own supporters when they turned in a lacklustre performance against visiting Falmouth and the game ended in a scoreless draw. Although fiercely loyal, Redruth supporters always made it clear that they expected nothing but total commitment from their team.

Redruth retained the title of Cornish champions for 1895/96, having won four of their six qualifying games and drawn one. A draw against visiting Welsh side Bridgend on Easter Monday brought the season to an end. The Redruth A team, which played a full programme of fixtures with considerable success, won 13 of their 20 matches and drew five. The reserve side provided a number of players for the chiefs during the season, including five of the side that had lost to Plymouth.

Redruth was not just relying on the second XV for new players. In the late summer of 1896, Penzance came close to folding as a result of debts and the loss of their ground, and Redruth took advantage by snapping up one of their best players, a full-back named Jasper. He played in Redruth's first match of the 1896/97 season against Albion, which they lost 6-0. Jasper's defection drew much criticism from the football correspondent of *The Cornishman*, who wrote under the pseudonym 'Impartial'. His sobriquet appears wide of the mark where Redruth were concerned:

'It does not look sportsmanlike to say the least, and is quite contrary to the general doings of a town which boasts to be the best nursery of the rugger game in the county. I thought that such an action by the Cornish champions would be below their dignity.'[33]

In the event, Mr Jasper's stay at Redruth was to be short. Penzance managed to find a ground and he had moved back there by the end of October.

Penzance were not the only club facing difficulties. On 3 October 1896, Redruth took on a newly formed side from the Camborne School of Mines, winning by one goal to nil in front of more than 2,000 spectators. The large crowd reflected the fact that the new student team contained players who had previously turned out for the Camborne town club. It had a disastrous effect on the latter, whose name disappeared from the unofficial merit table for the whole of the 1896/97 season. Indeed, match reports over the ensuing months referred to the student side simply as Camborne.

The following month, Redruth's season was disrupted by an outbreak of smallpox in the town. Dartmouth cancelled Redruth's visit on the pretext that disease might travel with them, and Newton pulled out of a visit to Redruth the following week. In December, what should have been a Redruth home fixture against Exeter became an away match in Devon. The outbreak meant the game against Falmouth on 2 January was the first home match Redruth had played for two months. It ended in a scoreless draw.

A week later, on 9 January 1897, Redruth's home game against Penryn was their first under a new law requiring players to relinquish the ball when they were tackled. Before then, a tackled player was expected to hang on tight to the ball until the forwards arrived to try to heel it back. The crowd at the Recreation Ground would have been happy with the outcome, as Redruth won convincingly 14-5. The *West Briton's* football correspondent was less impressed and claimed the law change made the game more like association football.

Crowd trouble erupted again at Redruth when the club defeated visiting Falmouth in April. According to a newspaper report, as the crowd surged towards the exit, a number of fist fights broke out and blood flowed. It took the efforts of four police officers to restore order, including one Sgt Vanstone, who was reported to have waded into the crowd and dragged out one participant with considerable force.

A win over visitors Exeter in April 1897 was a high point, but otherwise it was an average season for Redruth. Their defeat by Penzance in the last game of the season saw the club finish third in the merit table, with Penzance crowned champions and Camborne School of Mines in second place. The club had also finished the season with a financial deficit of almost £40 and this would have been worse had it not been for a concert given by the Snowball Minstrel Group in Druids Hall, which raised more than £10 for club funds.

Redruth and a few other clubs had been pressing for a league system in Cornwall to formalise the merit table and provide a more reliable programme of fixtures, and the Cornwall Rugby Football Union (CRFU) had finally agreed to act. It announced that a senior and a junior league would be set up for the 1897/98 season and that money would be raised to provide a cup for each group. Redruth, along with Penzance, Falmouth, Camborne School of Mines, Penryn, Hayle, Tuckingmill and Troon had signalled their intention to join the senior league, while Redruth A would be in the junior division.

The new competition got under way with a Redruth reserve team facing Penzance Reserves in the first junior league match ever played in Cornwall. On the day, Penzance won by the only try of the game; however, the result would not stand. Redruth lodged a complaint with the CRFU that Penzance had fielded ineligible players. The Cornwall committee was tied on its decision, so the chairman's casting vote went in favour of Redruth, who were awarded the game and the two points for a win. The fact that the chairman was William Hichens, president of the Redruth club, did not go unnoticed in Penzance.

Violence flared again when Redruth entertained the naval students from the Royal Naval Engineering College side. A player named Shaw in the Keyham side was seen to kick Redruth's Goldsworthy in the head while the latter was lying on the ground. The referee refused to send him off and a mass brawl broke out on the pitch, with several players knocked unconscious. After the game, the Redruth crowd followed Shaw up Green Lane to the Coffee Tavern, where the sides changed their clothes, and it was only the efforts of the police that stopped him from being attacked.

Redruth finished runners-up to Penzance in the first season of the Cornwall Senior League, Penzance having won all ten of their games, while Redruth, in what had been an indifferent season, just five of theirs. The club had the consolation of seeing their reserve side pick up the Junior League Cup following a victory over Camborne Reserves in the final game of the season.

In the summer of 1898, the club launched an appeal for subscriptions to clear their deficit. Among the main subscribers were Arthur Strauss, who was the local Member of Parliament, Lord Clinton, the Redruth Brewery and Tabbs Hotel. Altogether, 57 names were listed, with sums given varying from 5 shillings (25p) to a guinea (£1.05).

One of the factors which had depleted the finances was the decision to award county games to other clubs. Redruth had always received a proportion of the gate money to help defray costs, but a County Championship game had not been held at the Recreation Ground for several years. The club had been lobbying the Cornwall committee and it seemed that their efforts had paid off when it was announced that Redruth would host the Cornwall match against Somerset.

The celebrations were short-lived. The decision was reversed when Redruth refused to give up a share of the gate receipts.

There were howls of protest when the county instead awarded the game to Camborne, meaning Redruth's fiercest rivals would have both Cornwall home games that season and the resulting benefits from 2,000 spectators coming to the town.

Redruth crammed four games into the Christmas 1898 period. A match against Camborne on Christmas Eve was followed by a Boxing Day clash with touring side Exeter Oaks and an away game at Falmouth the following day. There was another home match scheduled against Camborne on New Year's Eve. The reserve team had fixtures against Newlyn, Falmouth and Camborne over the same period. Considering the extremely physical nature of the game at the time, the toll on players must have been immense.

After a loss of form over the previous 12 months, Redruth were relieved to end the year in second place in the senior table, just behind Falmouth. The reserves were doing less well than the previous season, finishing the year in mid-table in their league. The Redruth supporters would have been delighted with the result of the final game of December, against Camborne, when the Reds scored four goals and two tries to nil.

Unfortunately, there was to be no conclusion to the league season. The official senior and junior leagues that had begun with much fanfare at the beginning of the 1897/98 season came to an abrupt end. The CRFU had started the competitions without gaining the necessary authority from the RFU. It was not until the league's second season was well under way that they somewhat belatedly asked for permission. The RFU turned them down flat.

The CRFU had no choice but to bow to the strictures placed on them by the loftier body and the clubs reluctantly accepted the decision. Two years later, clubs in the Bristol area set up their own combination, complete with league tables and cup competitions, in defiance of both the RFU and the two county bodies covering the city. Such unity of purpose was almost non-existent among Cornish clubs and there was too much overlap between the officials of the clubs and the CRFU to expect similar non-compliance.

In the absence of a formal league table, Redruth were declared the top club in Cornwall, which triggered a predictable outcry from Falmouth and Penzance. The Reds had failed to beat either team during the season, but had played and won more games than their rivals, elevating them to the top of the table. The furore ended in something of a farce when Redruth, as champions, took on a side representing the rest of the county. A sizeable Falmouth contingent had been selected to play for the Rest of Cornwall, but they all pulled out in protest just before the game and the Reds overwhelmed a much weaker team.

In the summer of 1899, the veteran Redruth captain, Frank Woolf, announced his retirement at the age of 45. More than 30 guineas was raised for a presentation, including the sum of £16 12s collected by former Redruth players in South Africa. Woolf had played for the club for an incredible 23 years and, although his regular playing days were over, he would continue to pull on a Redruth jersey for occasional matches through most of the next decade.

As the 1899/1900 season began, there were hopes that Redruth might cement their position as Cornwall's premier club after a number of indifferent campaigns. The continuing loss of players meant the team that started the season was much changed from the year before, but there were still plenty of fine players coming through the ranks, including some of those that had won the Junior League Cup two seasons before.

One season preview confidently stated that Redruth should be in a position to thrash any local team in the county and the chiefs looked ahead to a busy fixture list, including several matches across the border with Devonport Albion, Plymouth and Torquay. So many away matches in the calendar resulted in a stern note in the club minutes stipulating that players must adhere to the rule that they should all travel by the same train when going out of the county.

The minutes of the meetings of the newly appointed selection committee survive from 1899 onwards and list the players selected for each match. The first such entry was for the traditional season opener on 16 September between two Redruth teams. The two players at half-back for the first XV were James Davey and Alfred Thomas. They would, in time, be seen as one of Cornwall's finest-ever such pairings.

The half-back partnership in rugby is key to any successful team, the scrum-half and fly-half working together to orchestrate the team's plays and control the flow of the game. At scrum-half, Thomas was the engine, delivering quick and accurate passes from the scrum or the breakdowns; Davey was growing into a great fly-half, an adroit playmaker, a ferocious tackler and a thrilling attacking player.

James Davey, later known as Maffer, was born, the son of a miner, at Blights Row in Redruth on Christmas Day, 1880. He learned the game as a pupil at Trewirgie School and had first played for Redruth in October 1896, just two months short of his 16th birthday. One report said he was one of the most promising players among the juniors – fast, tricky and full of pluck. By 1898, Davey was regularly appearing in the Redruth first XV and getting mentions for his smart play in getting the ball out quickly to his three-quarters. As well as his speed of delivery, he was also making a name for himself as an expert at the drop goal.

On 30 September 1899, he and Thomas took part in the first of two county trials, with Davey scoring a drop goal and a try from 25 yards out. Davey and Thomas were selected for the Possibles against the Probables in the final county trial at Redruth. Such was the performance of the two men that both won their first caps for Cornwall in the away game against Devon at Newton Abbot the following month. James Davey, who was still only 18, would go on to win another 34 caps for Cornwall and be capped twice for his country.

Redruth ended 1899 with a scoreless draw away at Penryn. They had been due to play Newlyn on 23 December, but just seven Newlyn players had turned up, only two of whom could actually play football. According to the minutes, this behaviour had caused a loss of gate and insult to the club, and they wrote a strongly worded letter of complaint, which caused some amusement at the CRFU committee meeting held on 15 January. A Newlyn representative offered the excuse that many players had missed the train.

The Cornwall committee decided, after an acrimonious discussion and in the absence of a proper league structure, that Redruth should be declared champions of Cornwall. This was in breach of a previous decision to take the results of the first two games played between any of the clubs. The season had not yet finished, and Falmouth had won more games, so it is difficult to see how they reached this conclusion. The reported minutes fail to explain their rationale and the Falmouth club's case was strengthened further when they hosted Redruth a week later and beat them by two tries to nil.

Redruth ended the 1899/1900 season having played 30 games, winning 14, drawing nine and losing seven. The captain of the chiefs, John Hewitt Thomas, was the leading try scorer with 23, followed by James Davey on 16. Redruth Reserves had been undefeated, scoring 372 points with just 32 points against.

The minutes of Redruth committee meetings from this period give a fascinating insight into the organisation of the club. On 27 August 1900, it was noted that practices were held on five evenings a week and that players not arriving on time were locked out of the ground. During the season, there was a run of up to four miles each Tuesday evening, while Wednesday evenings were for general training, including skipping rope practice. Players were warned that a failure to attend these sessions would result in them being asked to resign.

The management of the club's finances was equally robust. A quote to convey the team to away games from a Mr Trethowan was accepted at a charge of one shilling a head. It was stipulated by the club that three horses must be used. The club had also set up an insurance fund to provide support to injured players, whether they had sustained their injury on the playing field or elsewhere, and a note was made that Mr Prisk would receive ten shillings in respect of an injured arm.

The minutes also include the names of players selected for individual matches, the time they should leave for away games and a stern warning that anyone who could not make the departure time must inform the secretary on Friday evening. At one meeting, the club resolved to write to Mr Wickett of the Redruth Brewery, asking him to ensure that customers of the Farmers Arms in North Street, which the brewery owned, were stopped from standing on the pub roof to watch games, avoiding the admission fee.

It is not clear whether this appeal was successful, but one imagines the pub roof would have been a popular place to be on Boxing Day 1900 when Redruth hosted Camborne. At a committee meeting the previous March, it had been decided that Camborne should be offered Feast Monday at Camborne and Boxing Day at Redruth as the fixtures for the 1900/01 season. It was the first time since 1885 they had met on what would eventually become the traditional day for the fixture and only the fourth Boxing Day clash since the formation of Camborne in 1877. Redruth won by a try to nil in what was described in one paper as 'a battle royal'. It would be another decade before Camborne would leave the Recreation Ground victorious in this fixture.

Redruth's win over Penzance on 28 December put them top of the table, just ahead of Falmouth, while the Redruth second XV also led their table, six points ahead of Camborne. Early 1901 saw a short hiatus as matches were cancelled out of respect following the death of Queen Victoria in late January, and her subsequent funeral, although the CRFU was asked to extend the season to allow the matches to be rearranged.

No sooner had play restarted than there was a return to refereeing controversy, this time at Redruth's home game against

Torquay Athletic on 16 February. On occasions, it was still the practice for home clubs to nominate a referee, and Torquay had agreed to the two names submitted in advance by the Redruth committee. However, on arriving at the ground, the visitors discovered that the official in charge was Willie Hichens. This did not go down well with the *Torquay Times and South Devon Advertiser*:

> 'It is almost impossible for a local man, however impartial he might desire to be, not to display his weakness for the club he supports, but quite apart from this, Dr. Hitchings [sic], who is a heavily built man, was much too slow in his movements to be able to closely follow a present day rugby game, and there were consequently many things which happened, wherein he displayed either an ignorance of the rules, or proved that he had been unable to see what really took place.'[34]

Torquay complained that Redruth's first try, scored by James Davey, had come after Torquay had touched the ball down in their own goal area and Davey had then rushed up and fallen on it. Redruth's second try, according to the report, was scored when the player concerned only crossed the line after colliding with the referee and knocking him over. The fact that Torquay, one of Devon's strongest teams at the time, lost by 11 points to eight may have added to the sense of grievance.

Redruth would go on to be named that season's Cornish champions a few weeks later but, before the official confirmation, they faced a team representing the Rest of Cornwall in a game at the Recreation Ground on 20 February 1901. Tries from James Davey and Thomas Lidgey were enough to win the match for Redruth, with the Rest of Cornwall scoring a single try. The gate money totalled £17, of which £13 went to the county, the fine weather on the day contributing to the large attendance.

On 6 March 1901, Redruth were officially named at the CRFU meeting as champions of Cornwall, with the club's second XV the champion reserve side. This time there was no argument; the final table showed Redruth seven points clear of Falmouth, with Camborne in third place. These three clubs, together with Penryn, Penzance and Camborne Students, were the only sides in that year's table. After a quarter of a century, the heart of Cornish rugby remained confined to an area west of Truro.

Three days later, Redruth travelled to Penzance, with whom relations were still testy. The Reds won 8-4 in a game marred by crowd trouble. A subsequent meeting of the CRFU committee discussed a complaint from the Redruth secretary, James Evans, who had been acting as touch judge at the game. He alleged that, after Redruth's first score, the crowd had begun abusing him and complaining that Redruth had brought their own referee. Evans said that, shortly after Redruth had scored again, stones and pieces of turf had been hurled at him by Penzance supporters.

There was also an allegation that Evans had been threatened by a Penzance supporter carrying a stick. The committee decided that, as Penzance had been cautioned for a similar incident in the past, the entrance fee for their next home game should be doubled to sixpence (2½p), with half of the gate money going to the County Union. They were also ordered to compensate Redruth in the sum of 13s (65p) for failing to turn up for a reserves game at Redruth on the same afternoon.

While this was going on, James Evans, as secretary, was asked to go back to Penzance to discuss a match they had cancelled, and subsequently to write to Penzance to remonstrate with them over the unsportsmanlike manner in which they had treated Redruth. At the beginning of the following season, he felt compelled to tender his resignation and an effort by two committee members to reinstate him failed.

None of the alleged crowd incidents appeared in the match reports in the local press, perhaps because they were not out of the ordinary. Indeed, it was the CRFU which was criticised in the *Royal Cornwall Gazette* for levying the penalty on Penzance. It complained that the county should not be making money out of a club's misfortune and that such measures would do nothing to curb the growing tendency towards rowdyism in Cornwall.

The Reds started the 1901/02 campaign in fine form, with a 9-0 win over visitors Penzance and a defeat of Falmouth by the same scoreline. The latter game was marred by yet more crowd trouble. The referee, a Mr Thorne, told a subsequent CRFU meeting that he had had to stop the game on occasions because of the foul language being hurled at him by Falmouth supporters, who had accused him of being a cheat. This had followed his dismissal of a Falmouth player named Hughes for the offence of assaulting the Redruth half-back, Alfred Thomas, as the latter lay on the ground; 'the foulest blow I have ever seen on the football field'. Thorne stated that he had had to be escorted out of the ground after the game.

The Falmouth president, J.H. Lake, admitted that the game had been a little rough but claimed that Hughes had only punched Thomas because the Redruth player was kicking at him. After much wrangling, Hughes was suspended for a month. When the committee came to discuss the crowd trouble, Mr Lake stated that he could not expect Falmouth supporters to be quiet when Redruth were being given advantages by the referee. After more debate, the committee ruled that Falmouth should double its gate prices for the next four matches.

Soon afterwards, a letter appeared in the *Cornish Echo* from someone signing themselves 'An Old International' who said he had been visiting Falmouth from up country and had gone along to watch the match:

> 'I can honestly say that had the spectators behaved as they did on, and especially off, the field on any ground in Middlesex or Kent, the ground would have been suspended for at least a month. Cornwall

county rugby football won't improve if the executive committee do not uphold our referees and insist on the good behaviour of players and supporters.'[35]

Obviously, the gentleman concerned was used to a more genteel style of game than was common in the rugby hotbed of West Cornwall.

Redruth continued to display their determination to hang on to the title of top side in Cornwall with a tremendous display against visitors Penryn in late October. The Reds scored 13 unanswered points in the first half, finally running out winners, 20-0, with a performance that would have thrilled the home crowd. At this stage of the season, Redruth remained unbeaten by any other Cornish side and sat six points clear at the top of the table. Meanwhile, the Redruth reserve side set what was considered at the time to be a Cornish record win when they hosted Penzance Reserves, winning by 60-0.

The senior side maintained their unbeaten Cornish record with wins over Penzance, Penryn and Falmouth. The Redruth committee minutes noted that a policeman should be engaged for the match against Falmouth, presumably because of the incidents at the Falmouth ground the previous month, but it was far from being the only game of the season with a police presence. The Redruth accounts show a total of £8 paid for police officers during the 1901/02 season.

In the game at Redruth on Boxing Day against Camborne, honours were even at half-time after a try for the home side from Job and a Camborne penalty. However, the Reds cut loose in the second half with two more tries from Job, a try and a drop goal from Davey and a try by J.H. Thomas, converted by Eathorne, to give the Reds a 21-3 win. This put Redruth well clear at the top of the unofficial league table.

During this period, the potential for trouble bubbled under the surface, both on and off the pitch. A visit by Plymouth in early January 1902 saw it come to the surface. Redruth were awarded a try in Hellfire Corner, a score Plymouth disputed on the grounds that a Redruth player had been offside. They also complained that their players had been impeded by members of the crowd invading the pitch. The referee, Mr Lawry from Penzance, allowed it. Redruth supporters then lined the road from the ground back to the hotel where Plymouth were staying and shouted abuse at their players. It was asserted by the Plymouth press that the team would not again be found playing on the Redruth ground.

There was more trouble when Redruth travelled to Camborne a week later. Two players were sent off for fighting and a columnist in the *West Briton and Cornwall Advertiser* deplored the actions of players and crowd at the game. He criticised the two sets of supporters for cheering particularly rough play and accused them of being delighted when a brawl involving most of the players broke out in front of the grandstand. He complained that the scenes were painful to the many who had attended hoping to see a friendly game. Given the history between the two clubs, it was highly likely that a friendly game was the last thing anyone expected or wanted. Redruth won 10-3.

In March 1902, Redruth were again confirmed Cornish champions. They had lost just two of the 18 games they had played against other Cornish clubs, racking up 33 points in the table, twice that of second-placed Camborne. The club's AGM in July noted that, in addition to the good performances on the field, the finances were in a healthy state. Henry Downing, who had taken over as secretary from James Evans in 1901, was re-elected and would continue to serve in that post until the outbreak of war in 1914. The meeting also discussed the idea of forming a juvenile football team for boys under 16 as a recruiting ground for the club, a forerunner of today's mini juniors.

The 1902/03 season began with James Davey taking over as captain of the chiefs from John H. Thomas. Soon after came a startling report that a representative from an unnamed Lancashire rugby league club had approached both Davey and

Alfred Thomas with an invitation to play professional rugby in the north of England. According to a newspaper article in October 1902, the two had been offered £75 each, easily two year's wages for labouring men at the time. Both players turned down the offer. The report made it clear that this was not the first time they had been approached.

Over the following years, some Cornish players would make the long journey north and turn professional, either because they were recruited directly or they had gone to find work and ended up playing for a local side. What is probably more surprising is that relatively few Cornish players made the trip.

At the same time, a 19-year-old miner called John Charles Solomon, better known as Barney, joined Redruth Reserves. He would become a regular selection at full-back throughout his first two seasons. A couple of years later, he would be joined by his little brother, Bert, and they would go on to make Redruth history.

Another legendary Redruth player, Arthur Teague, was welcomed back into the chiefs for the Boxing Day clash with Camborne, following his return from several years abroad. Teague was something of an all-rounder, having turned down the opportunity to play association football for Cornwall. The Reds beat Camborne 9-0, with Teague scoring a try. The game was the first for which Camborne supporters could travel to Redruth on the new tramway system which linked the two towns and which had been opened just a few weeks earlier.

At the beginning of 1903, Redruth could celebrate once again being top of the Cornwall table, four points ahead of Penzance, while the Redruth Reserves also headed their league. They were further cheered with a home win over Plymouth in the first game of the new year, with a Tom Lidgey try giving the Reds a 3-0 victory. The Devon side had obviously forgotten they had vowed not to play at Redruth again.

The *Western Morning News* report noted that the rough and tumble was notably absent and that the running and passing were the highlights of the game, with Redruth having a lighter and more mobile pack than had been seen in the past, a break from the traditional Cornish rugby built on a game dominated by forwards. However, the paper did take a swipe at the Redruth ground:

'It is of peculiar construction which visiting teams find so much difficulty in grappling with. The touchlines are unknown quantities, except to the home team, of course. The ground has an awkward slope to one corner and on the stand side it takes an ambulatory course which in wet weather gives it the not infrequent puddles which so often turn games into mudlarks.'[36]

The following week saw another attack on the state of the Redruth ground after a visit by Devonport Albion. Before this match, the two sides had met 17 times, with Albion winning every game. This time it ended in a 3-3 draw, with the visitors unable to cross the Redruth line, frustrated by muddy conditions and torrential rain. The correspondent for the *Western Evening Herald* described the encounter as neither great nor pretty.

Arrangements to improve the ground were in hand. For many years, the club had been asking the Recreation Ground Company, still the owners of the leasehold, to carry out the necessary work, but its committee had refused to consider the matter. The club solved the problem by buying 200 shares in the company, giving them a controlling interest, and work was scheduled for the summer. The plans included the demolition of the old grandstand and the construction of a much larger one on the opposite side of the pitch, where the grandstand is today. The ground entrance would be improved and new turnstiles installed. The pitch did get some levelling but the slope into Hellfire Corner remains to this day.

In March 1903, Redruth travelled to Camborne for one of the first games in Cornwall held to raise funds for a good cause, in this case the nursing associations of the two towns. The game was played at a furious pace and Redruth ran out 12-6 winners. The gate money, a total of £32 7s, was divided between the two associations. Redruth were unbeaten by any Cornish club that season and finished top of the table, eight points clear of Falmouth. Redruth Reserves also maintained their position as Cornwall's best second XV, winning 13 games out of 16.

Less than six months after turning down the invitation to move to Lancashire, James Davey and his half-back partner Alfred Thomas announced they were leaving Cornwall to find work in the South African goldfields. The three-quarter line stalwart Tom Lidgey would go with them on a path already taken by many former Redruth players, including Veale and Viant, who had been forced to look abroad for work by worsening unemployment. On 28 April, the Redruth club held a 'smoker' at Tabbs Hotel, which was attended by a large gathering of officials, players and supporters. Davey and Thomas were presented with gold watch chains and Lidgey with a gold medal as a token of their contribution to the club.

Both Thomas and Davey would continue to play rugby in South Africa, joining four former Redruth players at the Crown Reef club, the leading side in the Transvaal. Davey made such an impression that he was asked to captain Transvaal in the Currie Cup. He would return to play rugby in Cornwall in 1907, but Arthur Thomas's playing career came to an end when he suffered a serious injury while playing for the Transvaal side. The loss of this talented half-back pairing left a void at the heart of the Redruth team which would be hard to fill.

The Reds opened 1903/04 on 20 September with an 11-5 away win over Falmouth, their success reportedly due to the weight and power of the Redruth pack. One irritated Falmouth supporter wrote to the local paper to complain that he had hired a cab to be at the ground for 3pm, only to have to wait 45 minutes for kick-off, as Redruth had not yet turned up. He was apparently told this was quite normal, as Redruth were always late. Meanwhile, back at Redruth, the club's reserves had no difficulty overwhelming their Falmouth equivalents 36-5. Young Barney Solomon, who was growing more confident at full-back in his second season in the reserves, was largely untroubled, but dealt with what little came his way.

Shortly afterwards, Redruth's trip to Penzance ended in a 12-5 defeat, with a columnist suggesting that the loss of the Davey-Thomas combination at half-back was a telling factor. The unexpected result was reported to have created great astonishment among supporters. Penzance rubbed salt into the wound the following week when they travelled up to Redruth and won 5-0. A home defeat against Falmouth, the first time the latter had won on the Redruth ground for several years, added to the misery.

Better than expected performances, away to Plymouth and at home to a strong Devon Albion side, did bring some consolation, but there was little doubt that the team were not matching the performance levels of the previous season. Spirits were lifted on Boxing Day 1903, with a win over the old enemy, Camborne. Redruth kicked two penalty goals to Camborne's drop goal, in front of a crowd of around 3,000, raising £80 on the gate.

The club began 1904 with a 9-0 home win over Plymouth at the Recreation Ground, the visitors arriving at Redruth without having lost a game all season. The committee's hopes of another record gate to further boost the coffers were dashed, however, when torrential rain began an hour before the game, putting off all but the most enthusiastic supporters. No doubt the home game against Albion Reserves the following week reminded the faint-hearted what they had missed. A thrilling win was further enlivened when no fewer than six of the visiting side had their jerseys torn off their backs during play, prompting one wag in the Redruth crowd to suggest they had picked them up at a jumble sale on the way down.

In late January, there was sad news for the club when Alexander Suter Grylls died from pulmonary tuberculosis at the age of only 35. Suter, as he was known, had captained both Redruth and Cornwall before serving on the Redruth committee. He had also served as the honorary treasurer of the Cornwall Rugby Union, which sent its condolences and a wreath. An account of the club's history from 1890 to the First World War, written by John Prater, a local printer and committee member, describes Suter as one of the best forwards the county had produced. Prater insists that he would have played for his country had the rugby authorities only paid the same attention to Cornwall as they would a few years later.

Redruth finished the 1903/04 season with a series of better results than those they had started with, although Penzance took the honours as the top team in the Cornish table. The Reds' return to form came just in time for an exciting Easter Monday visit to the Recreation Ground by London Harlequins, one of England's best-known and most successful sides.

Playing for them at half-back was a young Adrian Stoop in only his third ocason for a club whose ground would one day carry his name. He would go on to play 182 times for Harlequins and 15 times for England, later playing in the same England team as Redruth's Bert Solomon. The illustrious opposition found the Redruth defence hard to break down and were defeated by 30-3. A Harlequins player declared that Redruth were the best side they had faced all season.

Around this time, Redruth's former half-back pairing of James 'Maffer' Davey and Arthur Thomas were featured in an article in a South African newspaper, which was reproduced in the *Cornubian and Redruth Times*. The article claimed that Thomas and Davey were, without doubt, the best in South Africa and, had their team been eligible to take part in the South African senior competition, the miners would have been more than able to hold their own.

The siren call of the South African Witwatersrand claimed another Redruth star player that summer; Dickie Eathorne, who had played full-back for both the club and for Cornwall. Dick, who worked as a blacksmith, had joined Redruth at the age of 17 and had taken the place of his brother, Jack, at full-back in his first season. He had won his first county cap the following year and had narrowly missed being selected for the South in an England trial.

The *Cornubian and Redruth Times* speculated that, if only the great Herbert Gamlin had not been England full-back at the time, then Dick Eathorne might well have been in line for an international cap. The paper went on to imagine that, if a South African side should ever tour England, a Redruth quartet of Eathorne, Arthur Thomas, Maffer Davey and Tom Lidgey could well turn out for the Springboks. However, as in the case of Davey, it is highly unlikely that they would have met the residency qualifications.

As strong a player as he was, Eathorne's departure overseas opened the door for some changes at full-back, a position he had all but made his own since claiming it from his brother. Initially, it was Joe Williams who would fill the role but by early December, it was clear that Barney Solomon would be selected to play for the chiefs. His first match would begin a new chapter in the history of Redruth Rugby Club, not just because of his own participation, but because there would be two Solomons on the field that day.

Chapter Four

The Making of a Legend
1904–1907

SOME TIME in late 1904, the Redruth chairman, Willie
Hichens, was approached by Frank Eade, the manager of a
junior team, Treleigh Rangers, which played at a small hamlet
on the edge of Redruth. Eade brought news of a promising
young player he felt might be considered for the Redruth chiefs.
Accordingly, members of the club committee travelled the short
distance to watch the 19-year-old in action. His name was Bert
Solomon.

More than 120 years after the Redruth committee watched
the young Bert play at Treleigh, there are few followers of
Cornish rugby who would dispute the claim that he was one
of the most gifted players that Cornwall ever produced and,
at his peak, the best centre three-quarter in the country. He
displayed a natural talent that would eventually take him, via the
Cornwall side, to international honours with England. The fact
that even Camborne supporters would speak of Solomon with
respect and admiration underlines the impact this shy working-
class man had on football in the duchy.

Bert was the second son of Josiah Solomon and his second
wife, Catherine, known as Kate. The family originated at St
Columb Minor and his grandfather, James, who was a sawyer,
moved to Redruth in the mid-19th century. Josiah, a mine
carpenter, married his first wife, Louisa, when they were very
young and she had died three years later having given birth

to their only child, Joseph. In 1883, Josiah married Catherine Mackman (or McMann), two months after the birth of their first son, John Charles, who would become known as Barney. Bertie was born two years later, on 21 February 1885, in Sandow's Row, Redruth, just a stone's throw from the Recreation Ground.

The young Bertie went to Treleigh School, where he struggled with reading and writing, an issue blamed on poor eyesight. Bert's son, Stoyle, would later explain that the condition had deteriorated and, by 1910, his father had completely lost the sight in one eye. Escaping the poorly lit schoolrooms, he would run and play ball with his friends, showing an early aptitude for rugby and an eagerness to be outdoors.

That enthusiasm got the better of him when, at the age of 17, he and eight friends were warned by PC Hocking for playing football outside Bert's house in North Street. According to Hocking's evidence in court, they had stopped when they had seen him, but had started again as soon as he had disappeared around the corner. The magistrates fined each lad 1s, plus 4s 3p in costs. This must have made a considerable dent in the wages Bert earned working as a lard refiner at the local bacon factory, where he would use his strength to lift heavy pig carcasses up on to hooks. He would remain at the factory for the rest of his working life.

By the start of the 1904/05 season, Bert had been playing at Treleigh Rangers for up to two seasons. Perhaps he had been encouraged to play there instead of in the streets, where his exuberance could be so costly. Or perhaps he had seen his older brother play for the Redruth reserves and wanted to emulate him. Although he always struggled to read newspapers, he would have followed the fortunes of the local rugby teams, feeling the sense of anticipation of the new season, described by the *Cornish Echo*'s football correspondent in terms which would be equally relevant at the start of any modern campaign:

'The football season is on us again, bringing with it endless hopes and fears for the long-suffering secretaries, savage joy and bitter disappointment for the spectators, and hard knocks and varying praise and blame for the players.'[37]

The newspaper was published in Falmouth and it was there that Redruth travelled on 24 September for their first Cornish table match, with Joe Williams at full-back in place of the departed Eathorne. The game ended in an unexciting scoreless draw. The return match a week later at the Recreation Ground generated much more excitement, albeit for the wrong reasons.

An early exchange of punches set the tone for the afternoon, but the referee failed to send off the two players involved. The sides turned around at half-time with Falmouth 5-3 ahead, but Redruth took the lead two minutes into the second half, inspiring Falmouth to indulge in some rough play as they tried to fight their way back into the game.

Shortly before full time, a punch was thrown at Joe Williams and hundreds of outraged Redruth supporters invaded the pitch to take part in a mass brawl. It took a while for the officials to restore order. *The Cornishman*, in theory a neutral voice as a Penzance newspaper, claimed that the blame lay mainly with Falmouth, who were doing everything possible to spoil the game, while Redruth were doing everything possible to play football. Redruth were awarded the win, 6-5.

At the next meeting of the county committee, the referee, a man from Camborne named Tippett, reported the Redruth supporters for rowdyism. The committee decided that some blame should be attached to the referee for failing to send off the two players who had been fighting early in the first half. Redruth offered to fence off the ground to prevent a repetition of the pitch invasion, but it was decided that the club should face the sanction of doubling their gate fees for a period of one month. Doubling admission was by now the

CRFU's established punishment for disorderly conduct by a club's supporters, with the union receiving the proceeds of the extra admission fee.

Joe Williams's abilities in the full-back position were called into question in a couple of newspaper articles that autumn, which suggested there were weaknesses in his defensive game. However, he remained the first choice for the chiefs throughout September, October and November 1904, with Barney Solomon continuing to play full-back for the reserves. Younger brother Bert was, by now, getting brief mentions in the newspapers when scoring for Treleigh Rangers.

In early December 1904, the Redruth committee met in their usual room at Tabbs Hotel. Willie Hichens was in the chair and there were 11 other members, including the secretary. They had two important items on the agenda. One was team selections for the upcoming games against Camborne School of Mines, the other was the scoring system the club would support in the ongoing English Rugby Union review of the matter. The committee decided unanimously to support the awarding of three points for a penalty goal, two for a goal from a try (conversion) and three for any other goal.

We cannot know how the conversation about team selection went that day. Willie Hichens had been to see Bert Solomon play and was no doubt keen to put him straight into the chiefs team. But Bert was shy and uncomfortable around people he did not know and this would be a big step up for him. It would also mean giving a first-team place to the younger brother when the elder had given good service for two years without receiving the same honour. In the end, it was decided that both brothers would travel to Camborne and would make their first XV debut on the same day.

And so, on 10 December 1904, Bert Solomon appeared for the first time in a Redruth jersey, playing against Camborne School of Mines at Penponds. His performance on the field had the journalist from *The Cornishman* enthralled:

'It would be unfair to individualise the players on either side, seeing they all did well. Attention, however, might be called to the capital display which Redruth's new recruit, Solomon, gave at centre three-quarter. Until Saturday he was practically unknown to the football world, having played only for Treleigh Rangers. The youngster has a fine turn of speed, kicks strongly, accepts his passes well, and tackles effectively.'[38]

Among the crowd was Redruth's former captain, Frank Woolf, now aged 49 but still turning out to play at every opportunity. He must have been delighted that such a talent had joined his club and made such an impression. Indeed, he was present at the committee meeting three days later at which the teams for the following week were selected virtually unchanged. The chiefs side would remain consistent for most of the season, but for some changes in the forwards and the unfortunate loss of the captain, Fred Daniell, through suspension.

On Christmas Eve 1904, Redruth faced St Ives, knowing that a win and a draw in their last two matches of the year would be enough to see them declared Cornish champions. St Ives had heavily defeated them earlier in the season and, for the first 40 minutes, it looked as if they might repeat the performance. In the second half, Redruth upped their game, eventually winning 8-3, with Bert Solomon, at centre, once again being singled out in the match report.

Bert further distinguished himself when he scored the winning try during Redruth's 11-0 home defeat of Camborne on Boxing Day, a result that made the Reds Cornish champions before the season was half over. It was an impressive recovery following the disappointments of the previous year. With Norman Job and Willy Paull – and his brother, Barney, at full-back – Bert was already considered one of the outstanding performers in the team.

Redruth Football Club 1875, (l-r) back row: C.Beringer, A.Thomas, C.Williams, ? Hall, F.W.Woolf, G.Peter, L.Peter, A.Williams, P.Preston, W.M.Willimott (capt), R.Tregaskis; front row: J.Penberthy, H.Grylls, E.Bonds, ? Taylor, H.Edwards, J.W.Everett, A.H.Meadows.

Welsh back John Longdon brought new flair to Redruth's three-quarters.

John Hewitt 'Breechy' Thomas (l) and veteran forward Frank Woolf. The latter played for more than three decades.
Paddy Bradley collection

Redruth away to Camborne at North Roskear on 12 October 1895. It was not uncommon for spectators to throw stones at each other after the match.

Bert Solomon: Ever the enigma.

William Mitchell Grylls, the first Cornish-born England international.

Bert Solomon shrugs off three Durham defenders to score his second try in the 1908 County Championship final at Redruth.

James 'Maffer' Davey: with two England caps and a Lions tour, he was one of Cornwall's most outstanding fly-halves.

Henry Grylls, co-founder of Redruth RFC.

Redruth at home in 1910. Police officers were a common sight at home games when crowds could be volatile.

Players setting off for their annual outing in 1911. Two years later the RFU banned the club from paying for these trips.

Redruth players take the field against Devon side Albion on 9 March 1912. It was a rare win for Redruth over their strong opponents.

A record crowd watch Redruth run out to face Camborne on 5 April 1920. Redruth won 3-0 thanks to a try from Fred Pappin.

Falmouth visit the Recreation Ground on 13 November 1920. Redruth wear letters on their shirts rather than numbers. Redruth won 5-3.

Gordon Robins, a schoolboy county player considered one of the best flankers of his generation.

Douglas Roberts, a Trewirgie School pupil, won a schoolboy England cap against Wales in 1932.
Kresen Kernow collection

Having assured themselves of victory in the Cornish table, Redruth seemed to go off the boil. They lost against Falmouth on 27 December and then went down away to Devon Albion on New Year's Eve, although no one had really expected them to win that one. What was unexpected was a 13-0 defeat away to Newton in the first week of January, a side that had not been in the best of form for a few years. It was a game that triggered a feud between the county committees of Devon and Cornwall.

A penalty try had been awarded to the home side after a player was fouled while dribbling a ball forward, close to the goal line. The Redruth players protested and, according to a report, one of them had called the referee 'a cheat'. The Redruth captain, Fred Daniell, was alleged to have refused to confirm the player's identity and then to have led all but four of the Redruth players off the field, although they did eventually return to complete the match. The Devon committee sent the report to their Cornwall counterparts.

It received short shrift. The Cornwall committee chairman was Dr Willie Hichens, Redruth's president. He told the meeting that, while it was accepted that the referee had sent off the player, who had by now been confirmed as Nick Rich, he had no right to report the rest of the Redruth team for leaving the pitch because he had not ordered them to go. Dr Hichens said that he always found that when a Cornish team was defeated, the referee was always in the wrong. After much wrangling, it was decided not to act on the referee's complaint.

By this time, the matter had excited the attention of newspapers across the country, with accounts in the London press. The Devon committee referred its complaint to the RFU, which inevitably wrote to the Cornwall committee criticising it for its failure and instructing it to sort things out and report back. The CRFU found itself backed into a corner, largely through its own failure to properly deal with the matter in the first place.

At a subsequent meeting, Fred Daniell, the Redruth captain, was suspended from the game for a month. Rich was excluded for the rest of the season, although not before the Redruth representatives had argued for much lighter sentences for both men. This action appeared to have mollified the committee at Newton, as Easter that year would see them travel to Redruth, signifying that there were no hard feelings over the trouble at the previous encounter.

Back on the field, Redruth's poor form continued with an 11-7 defeat at St Ives, but they pulled things back with an entertaining win over Camborne on 21 January 1905. In the best tradition of sport heroics, Redruth had fallen 3-0 behind and then lost two players, Johns and Williams, with injuries. In the second half, a 50-yard dash by Redruth's Norman Job had resulted in a try, which was converted, and Redruth added to the winning margin with a second try scored by Raymond Gray and converted by William Grylls, making it 10-3 to Redruth. This was the third defeat in a row Redruth had inflicted on their nearest rivals.

In February 1905, it was announced that William Mitchell Grylls, the son of the club's founder, Henry, had been selected for the England team to face Ireland in Cork, in what was then called the Home Nations Championship. In doing so, he became both the first Redruth player and the first Cornish-born player to win an international cap.

England selectors had previously called up two players listed as being from Cornwall, Gerald Gordon-Smith in 1900 and John 'Jumbo' Milton in 1904. However, neither player came from a Cornish background. Gordon-Smith hailed from Hampshire and Milton was born in South Africa. Both were only resident in the duchy because they were studying at the Camborne School of Mines.

Grylls had previously played in an England trial but had been overlooked on that occasion. However, the crushing 25-0 defeat inflicted by Wales on England at Cardiff in January

1905 had encouraged the selectors to seek new blood. Grylls, who played in the second row, had a reputation as a fast and mobile forward and he was called up to bolster the England pack. Regrettably, his presence did not improve the England performance; they lost 17-3 to a rampaging Irish side.

Grylls had been playing most of his rugby for the Royal Military Academy at Sandhurst, where he was in officer training, but he had continued to turn out for Redruth when he came home on leave. Had it not been for his army service, he might well have achieved more international honours but, after being commissioned, he was posted to India, where he remained for more than two decades, rising to the rank of Lieutenant Colonel. He remained a keen sportsman, continuing to play cricket and hockey while overseas.

One England selector felt Ireland had triumphed because the England team had been forced to make the tiring journey all the way to Cork. He suggested, perhaps tongue in cheek, that the next home game with Ireland should be played at Redruth, on the grounds that it would be regarded as a kind of exploring expedition by those who considered it their duty to go and see the contest. Redruth's perceived remoteness from the centre of the game would be a running theme, still causing comment and debate in the newspapers almost 90 years later when the New Zealand All Blacks played the South-West at the Recreation Ground in 1993.

Soon after Grylls gained his international cap in February, his young team-mate, Bert Solomon, was selected for Cornwall for the first time. The call came in late March, just a month after his 20th birthday and a scant three months after making his senior debut for Redruth. Usually in the three-quarter line, he was unexpectedly picked at fly-half for a play-off match against Devon to determine who topped the South-West table. However, Solomon's name was absent from the final teamsheet, which showed John Jackett at fly-half. It is not clear why Solomon failed to take part in the game, but it was held on a

Wednesday afternoon, which might have made it difficult for him to get time off work.

Solomon was in the Redruth side that entertained Devon Albion at the Recreation Ground a few days later. The visitors eventually ran out 12-9 winners, snatching victory with a late drop goal, but this was the closest Redruth had come to beating their formidable opponents. It was felt that Redruth could well have forced a draw, but for a fine Albion tackle on a speeding Solomon towards the end. The game was further enlivened when the referee blew up and went over to lecture the Redruth crowd over what was later described as a 'trifling matter'. *The Cornishman* felt the referee's tirade was unfair and that, having paid their sixpence, the supporters had a perfect right to cheer their side when the occasion demanded it.

Had the crowd merely been cheering, it is unlikely that they would have invited the referee's attention. In the wake of this game, a note appears in the Redruth minutes that a Mr Hawken should be contacted to see if he wished to prosecute the person who had allegedly thrown a stone at him during the match. The club offered to pay all his legal expenses. A week later, the secretary was asked to thank Mr Hocking [sic] for the tone of his recent letter and advise him that they had decided to take his advice and not prosecute in this case.

A few days later, Redruth's run of good form took them to a 19-0 victory away at Camborne School of Mines. The Mines had been one of Cornwall's top sides for several years, chiefly because many of the students had played the game at school before coming to Cornwall to study. On this day, the students had no answer to the Redruth attack. Fred Daniell was back after his month's suspension for the fracas at Newton, but the loudest cheer of the day came when the veteran Frank Woolf, having been drafted in at the last minute, crossed the line for a try, leading the pack at the age of 51.

Bert Solomon was playing out on the wing, instead of his customary place at centre. It could be a cold and lonely position in those forward-dominated days and, although he scored one of Redruth's tries, he looked uncomfortable so far from the action. Interestingly, the selection committee minutes show him at fly-half, perhaps to accommodate Daniell's return to the three-quarter line, but changes were clearly made on the day. Back at Redruth, the reserve team also won convincingly 22-4, making it a bad day for the Mines.

Redruth's final few weeks of the 1904/05 season saw them inflict a heavy 27-4 defeat on Camborne, the fourth time the Reds had beaten their neighbours that season. Sadly, victory celebrations were muted when the news came that Norman Job, who had been carried off the field, had been taken to hospital with a fractured left hip. The club would later present the Miners' Hospital with an operating table in acknowledgement of their help in treating Job's injury.

There followed a loss at home to visitors Torquay Athletic, but comfortable wins over Penzance and Falmouth ended what had been a good season for the club. Redruth's newly capped international, William Grylls, came back from Sandhurst and was greeted with a huge cheer when he arrived at the ground in his England blazer to finish the season with his home club.

Redruth, once again, ended the campaign as Cornwall's champion club. The AGM, held at Tabbs Hotel in August 1905, heard that the first XV had won 17 from 33 games played and lost 15. The reserves had won 17 out of their 24 games. The club was in a strong financial position and had finished the season with a cash surplus.

The president, Willie Hichens, who had recently stepped down from his position at the CRFU, announced he was resigning after 15 years and he was elected Redruth's first life member in recognition of his service. Sydney Lanyon was elected as the new president, while Henry Downing was re-elected as secretary. Willie Hichens was also given a permanent seat on the Redruth RFC general committee, a relatively new body set up to separate general matters from team selection.

The task of choosing players for future matches was given to a new selection committee, initially comprising three playing and three non-playing members.

A look at the fixtures for that 1904/05 season shows the absence of a number of the clubs that had featured in previous years. Rugby was no longer being played at Penryn, Hayle, Truro, Bodmin or St Austell and it had been reported that both St Ives and Penzance were facing financial difficulties. Redruth had only played five other Cornish clubs and it was clear that rugby in Cornwall, certainly at senior level, was still confined to the far west. Meanwhile, association football was increasing in popularity and there was little sign that the CRFU was doing much about it.

Redruth, too, faced challenges. There was concern about the number of experienced players retiring from the game, particularly in the scrum, where county player Howard Gray was just one of the older generation who had decided to call it a day. While the reserves had been boosted by players joining from junior clubs such as Lanner, Redruth Rangers and Treleigh, high levels of emigration from the area continued to deplete the pool of skilled players who had played at senior level. Fortunately, there was more strength in the backs, with Nick Rich once again available following his suspension, Norman Job recovering from his hip injury and Willy Paull, Bert Solomon, Fred Daniell and J.H. Thomas all in good form.

Despite bad weather disrupting early practice games, Redruth were optimistic at the start of the 1905/06 season. Their first competitive game was a tough one, away to Devon Albion on 16 September. The Reds may have hoped their opponents would be weakened, with eight of Albion's first-choice players on duty with Devon, who were playing a touring New Zealand side. Albion showed no sign of being under strength and inflicted on Redruth the worst defeat in their 30-year history, 43-8. The Reds played most of the second half with 14 men. Bert Solomon, who had scored a try before the break, left the field feeling ill.

Two days later, the touring New Zealand team arrived by train at Redruth to stay at Tabbs Hotel, their headquarters for the match against Cornwall. Their scheduled games against Devon and Cornwall had created great excitement in the South West. It was New Zealand's first international tour and the one in which they acquired the nickname 'All Blacks', because of the colour of their playing outfits. The match against Cornwall was at Camborne, although several newspapers erroneously reported it as being at Redruth, most likely due to the town being their base and metropolitan confusion over Cornish geography.

The tourists were in fine spirits, having demolished Devon 55-4 on the previous Saturday in their opening game of the tour. Among the enthusiastic crowd that greeted them were Redruth's Willie Hichens, Sidney Lanyon and William Grylls. The New Zealanders spent the week practising at the Redruth ground and touring the local area, including making a visit to Dolcoath mine, where a few of their number were brave enough to descend to the lower levels.

Surprisingly, no Redruth players were selected in the Cornwall team to face the tourists at Camborne, although Bert Solomon, Norman Job and Arthur Lawry were named as reserves. Cornwall fared little better than Devon, going down 41-0 to a rampaging New Zealand side. The tour would pass into rugby legend and establish New Zealand as a major force in the international game. Now known in New Zealand as the Originals, they won 34 out of the 35 games they played between September 1905 and January 1906, losing only to Wales. As well as introducing the now familiar black shirts, they brought with them the opening haka, to the surprise and mystification of the Cornish crowd.

After the excitement of the illustrious visitors, Redruth returned to action with a 52-3 thrashing of Penzance at the Recreation Ground. Bert Solomon delighted the home supporters by scoring five tries.

It would be their last good result for some considerable time. They lost away to Falmouth a week later and then by a narrow 7-6 margin against Camborne School of Mines, although they were short of several first-choice players for the latter. One writer tipped Falmouth as possible Cornish champions, claiming it appeared to him that Redruth hardly appeared to be as good as three or four years before and that the players struck him as not being imbued with the keenness and enthusiasm of their predecessors.

A large crowd turned up at the Recreation Ground on 14 October for the visit of Torquay Athletic, but the supporters went home disappointed after the Reds lost 11-9. The Redruth three-quarters were taken to task for bad handling and missed passes, with the match report claiming that no one had done the right thing at the right time. Morale did not improve when Redruth made the trip to Plymouth and were soundly beaten 40-0 in a match in which Redruth were completely outclassed. The Reds may have regretted agreeing to move the match, which was originally to be played at the Recreation Ground.

A rather dull scoreless draw with Camborne School of Mines followed, a restive crowd inciting the players to liven up the game with some moves not included in the laws. *The Cornishman* took the moral high ground, thundering: 'It would be as well if this unruly part of the crowd could be prevailed upon to play the game.'

One bright spot for followers of Redruth came when Bert Solomon was chosen to start in the three-quarter line for Cornwall's County Championship match against Somerset. Some other key players had pulled out, but it was a vote of confidence in his abilities and a recognition that it had perhaps been an error to select him at fly-half on the previous occasion. Cornwall won 6-4.

Bert was back in action two days later in the Redruth side that faced Camborne on Feast Monday. Camborne Feast was a traditional celebration held on the Sunday nearest to Martinmas

(11 November). A match on the following day would eventually become a regular fixture between the two teams, with the return match usually being on Boxing Day. As Redruth had beaten Camborne all four times they had played the previous season, they must have hoped that this game would see them prevail, but it was not to be. Camborne won 3-0 and Redruth suffered more bad luck when Willy Paull broke his collarbone and they had to play the second half with 14 men.

The Redruth faithful were not easily discouraged and the club saw the biggest gate of the season for a hard-fought home game against Falmouth on 2 December. Falmouth won the encounter 9-3, which virtually ensured they would be crowned the champion club of Cornwall. To add to Redruth's woes, their reserve side, who had travelled to Falmouth, were beaten 8-0. As they approached the end of 1905, Redruth found themselves in the unusual position of being close to the foot of the Cornwall table, only a winless Penzance keeping them from the bottom.

A trip to Devonport Albion took their minds off the Cornwall table, but a 19-3 loss did nothing to relieve frustrations over their lack of scoring success. The home match against Camborne on Boxing Day gave the Reds a boost with a much needed 16-0 win, a score in double figures providing some hope of a change of fortune, but it lasted just two days until their away game at Falmouth where they were defeated 20-0.

Redruth began 1906 by beating a struggling Penzance, but that did little to improve their position in the table and they went on to lose to Camborne, St Ives and Torquay Athletic. They arrived at Torquay with only 14 players after Bert Solomon missed the train from Redruth and they were defeated 20-0. Solomon was also absent for the return match with St Ives at Redruth, but both teams were fielding second-choice players and the Reds were able to end their losing streak with a comfortable 15-3 win. The veteran Frank Woolf was once again encouraged to don a Redruth jersey for the occasion.

A one-point win over Camborne School of Mines at Penponds was followed by a decisive 15-0 victory over the usually strong Royal Naval Engineering College, visiting from Devonport. The *West Briton* singled out Bert Solomon for what was described as a zig-zag, dodging run which baffled the defence and enabled him to touchdown under the posts, his brother Barney, at full-back, making sure of the conversion.

This was Bert Solomon, one minute missing the train for an important game, the next selling the most outrageous dummies to a bewildered defence and scoring a brilliant try. His name is missing from a number of games Redruth played in that disappointing 1905/06 season, at a time when he should have been an automatic selection for every match.

There has been much analysis of his complex and sometimes contradictory nature. With his skill and daring, he could light up any game in which he played, but he would alternately delight and frustrate Redruth supporters, performing brilliantly in one game and playing the role of spectator in the next. Sometimes, he would turn up at the ground after the kick-off or even fail to turn up at all. By this time, Bert had begun keeping racing pigeons and if they had not returned to their loft, he would stay at home until they did. Willie Hichens, who had brought Bert from Treleigh, would go to his house to beg him to arrive on time for an important match.

No one disputed his value to the side. When he was good, he was very, very good and a host of stories have been told about his brilliance on the field. It was said that he could sell a dummy so skilfully that a team-mate would dive over the line convinced Solomon had passed him the ball. On other occasions, it was claimed that a referee had blown up for what he thought was Solomon throwing a forward pass, only to see Bert crossing the line himself. Once, it is said, he scored a try that was so brilliant that the opposition players stood on their own goal line and applauded him.

He possessed an electric ability to accelerate away. He kept the Redruth crowd on tenterhooks with periods of seeming indifference to the game around him, then suddenly he would receive the ball and sprint for the line. When he turned up for his one and only international cap, it was said that an England three-quarter, possibly Adrian Stoop, had asked: 'How do you like your passes, old man, waist-high or breast-high?' Bert is alleged to have replied: 'Just thraw the ball out, I'll catch 'un.'

There are so many legends surrounding him that it is difficult to know how much is true and how much is layer upon layer of anecdote and hyperbole. The writer Tom Salmon concludes that it is impossible to understand what drove him:

> 'Bert Solomon was a totally enigmatic and wayward fellow with all the failings and strengths that are the delight and despair of those who vainly try and comprehend the Cornish. He was also a naturally brilliant footballer.'[39]

This sentiment was expressed more pithily by the Cornish writer and historian Francis Edwards: 'Sounds like he could have been an awkward bugger in the true Cornish tradition.'

Redruth had no choice but to plough on, with or without their mercurial talent. Easter 1906 was to be a busy weekend. They had arranged games against Falmouth, Devon Albion Reserves and Newton Abbot. The fixture against Newton was on Good Friday and, as a result, drew criticism for the fact that in the South West only Redruth and Newton played on the 'sacred day'. There was a call to the Cornwall Union to follow the example of Devon and ban all games on Good Friday:

> 'Seeing that the Redruth club claim to be the pioneers of rugby in Cornwall one would expect that with the sound financial basis they stand on, and with such respectable support that they have, they would not take

advantage of such an occasion to increase their coffers, as I see no other reason for matches on such a day.'[40]

A large number of spectators ignored these entreaties and turned up to watch the match, which Redruth lost 16-5. The match report in the *West Briton* noted that the decisions of the referee were not well-liked by the home supporters and he had, at intervals, had a warm time. A thick skin was a prerequisite for any referee who took charge of a Redruth home match and remains a necessary characteristic to this day.

Redruth did manage a win on 14 April, a 14-8 victory over visiting Falmouth, the new Cornish champions, but it did little to improve their record for the season; they had won just 11 of their 32 games. One more match remained, a home game against Camborne to raise funds for the Redruth and Camborne district nursing associations. In what was described as an uninteresting match, Camborne, who fielded two St Ives players and one from Cambridge, won 9-3, their first win at Redruth in four years.

The minutes of Redruth's AGM, held on 31 August 1906, are extremely sparse, but newspaper reports indicate that behind the few terse sentences was a good deal of discussion and hand-wringing about the previous season's discouraging results and the knock-on effect on finances. The club's cash surplus had halved since the previous season. According to the president, Sydney Lanyon, this was mainly because of the 'non-success' of the teams, which he attributed to a lack of practice and training.

Lanyon urged the players to show more enthusiasm for the game, telling them they were treated second to none. He also gave them some reason for optimism, saying that now that one or two prominent players had returned from South Africa, and with others likely to return by the time the season started, the outlook was far more promising. Former captain Frank Woolf also urged players to attend training, insisting that it was essential to hold at least two practice sessions a week.

South Africa was much in the thoughts of the Redruth players. The Mines Football Club, captained by Maffer Davey, had just won the Transvaal football competition for the very first time. Arthur Thomas had played for the Mines side, along with other Redruth players including Dickie Eathorne, Rich, Job and Edward Pearce. *The Cornishman* proudly reproduced an article from the *Sunday Times of Johannesburg* describing Davey as perhaps the most notable figure in Transvaal rugby football. He had already played for Transvaal in one Currie Cup competition and would be selected again for the 1906 Cup, along with team-mate Dick Eathorne.

The return of Arthur 'Spud' Thomas and Frank Curtis from South Africa was, therefore, cause for some excitement and *The Cornishman* expressed the hope that it might see Redruth return to winning ways in the 1906/07 season:

> 'The Reds are again lifting their diminished heads from the dust with renewed hope and enterprise and anyone who knows these same Reds will pause before prophesying renewed disaster for them.'[41]

Unfortunately, hopes of an early revival of form were dashed in the opening game of the season, which Redruth lost 26-6 away to Plymouth. This was followed by an 18-3 loss to Newton. The match report suggested, somewhat ominously, that while the score slightly flattered the home side, the Redruth players did not seem to be in good training.

Wins over Penzance and at the Royal Naval Engineering College in Devonport lifted the mood and an entertaining home win over St Ives on 13 October saw Bert Solomon at the centre of some exciting back play.

Next up was an away game at Falmouth, reigning Cornish champions. It was always likely to be a tough encounter, but the Falmouth pack were dominant throughout and Redruth lost 17-4. Two Redruth players, Bray and Knight, were reported to the

CRFU for what was described as 'obscene and very disgusting language' aimed at the referee. One witness reported that some ladies in the stand had indeed been disgusted and had vowed not to attend another match. Both players were suspended, Bray for two months and Knight for one.

There was some comfort when Penzance, who were struggling even more than Redruth, made a second visit to the Recreation Ground in late October. The match ended in a decisive 37-3 win for the Reds, who showed that they could score five goals and four tries without the assistance of Bert Solomon, who was absent from the side. Such was Redruth's territorial advantage that the home supporters changed ends at half-time for a better view of the action.

Solomon nevertheless retained his place in the Cornwall side selected to face Somerset at Penzance, with Redruth forwards Howard Gray and Tom Roskrow also called up. However, Solomon was replaced by his Redruth team-mate Frank Carbis before kick-off. Cornwall won 3-0.

A crowd of more than 3,000 turned out to watch Redruth win the annual Feast Monday match against Camborne 15-6. The visit of an unbeaten Falmouth side to the Recreation Ground in early December resulted in a closer result than the meeting between the two sides earlier that season, but the score was still 8-3 to Falmouth at the close. The result left Falmouth top of the table, with Redruth four points behind.

There was great excitement at Redruth with the imminent arrival of the South African touring side on their first visit to the British Isles. Just like the visit of New Zealand the year before, this inaugural tour would prove to be a landmark in the team's history. It would coin the name Springboks and establish South Africa as a rugby heavyweight.

During the tour, they played the four home nations and France, as well as clubs, counties and invitational sides. Like the All Blacks 'Originals', they lost only once during the tour, this time to Scotland.

The match against Cornwall was even more significant for Redruth than the previous year's game against New Zealand. Not only was it to be held at the Recreation Ground, but three Redruth players would line up to represent their county; Bert Solomon, Frank Carbis and Tom Roskrow. In addition, many people in the town had friends and relatives who had emigrated to South Africa and some had distinguished themselves in local rugby teams, so people felt a kinship with the visitors. This brought more than 10,000 people to the Recreation Ground on 22 December 1906, the highest attendance ever before seen at a Cornish ground. They were rewarded with a thrilling, fast-paced game, with Cornwall eventually losing by only 9-3, one of the closest games on the whole tour.

The run of better form for the Reds continued during the second half of the season. March was brightened with a win over visitors Torquay Athletic, followed by a 22-6 victory against Newton during the Easter weekend. Next was a gruelling contest against Falmouth, unbeaten by any Cornish club that season. Eventually, Redruth ground out a win, but it would not count in the championship table, which awarded points only for the first two encounters between teams in each season. A cold, wet April saw them beat both Camborne and Plymouth Albion at home and, while the club had not yet returned to the sort of form that had won them the Cornish championship in the past, things had certainly improved since the disappointments of the previous season.

Members were in a more optimistic mood at the club's AGM, held at Tabbs Hotel in July 1907. The chiefs had won 22 of the 32 matches they had played and the cash surplus of £95 was more than double the amount at the same time the previous year. The committee voted to reward the players with an outing and, after considerable discussion, it was agreed to organise a trip to Newquay.

Within the space of a few years, the Redruth players had gone from being county champions to tasting the bitter disappointment of coming second to bottom in the table. They had fought back and felt the thrill of hard-won victories over respected opposition. At a time when the only way to follow rugby at a distance was through newspaper reports, they had been able to watch two strong international sides play, in the flesh, on their doorstep.

South Africa had played at their very own ground and been held to nine points by a county team which included members of their own club. It is hard to overestimate the impact that this would have had at a time when there were few opportunities to watch top-flight rugby being played in the far South West. The players knew there were lessons to learn and they were eager to learn them. What was needed next was some experienced leadership and for Bert Solomon to deliver on the promise he had shown. Had they but known, both were on the horizon.

Chapter Five

Glory for Cornwall 1907–1914

THE WEATHER on Saturday 21 September 1907 was unseasonably warm and a large crowd had come to the Recreation Ground to see Redruth play the visiting Plymouth side, St Chad's, in a season opener. Word had gone out that the former county half-back James 'Maffer' Davey was back from South Africa. Before kick-off, the Redruth players gathered around to elect their captain for the season and Davey was the only possible candidate.

Redruth lost the toss and started down the slope. Within minutes of the starting whistle, Bert Solomon had scored a drop goal. Shortly afterwards, his brother, Barney, scored a penalty. By half-time, Redruth were 20 points up and showed no sign of letting up. Carbis, Barney Solomon, Willy Job and Bray all scored tries and, right at the end of the match, Bert Solomon made a solo run of 40 yards up the sloping field to score again. Newspaper reports praised the flowing passing between the backs and made note of Maffer Davey's skill in feeding the ball out to the three-quarters and the promise shown by the new half-back pairing of Davey and Nick Rich. Redruth won 42-0 with four goals, one drop goal, one penalty goal and five tries.

A week later, Redruth ran in nine tries at home against Royal Navy Harlequins, four of them scored by Bert Solomon, and won 37-0. There were four further matches during September and October 1907, including victories against Albion Reserves and the touring Devon Ramblers, but Redruth lost 9-0 at home to a strong Plymouth side and a trip to Newton ended in a 6-0 defeat.

Redruth's first match of the season against a Cornish side was a short trip to Falmouth, which resulted in a 3-3 draw. Maffer Davey was unavailable and it was felt his presence would have given Redruth the advantage. The side did continue to play the running game which had given them such a sparkling start to the season. Making good use of the backs was a significant change of approach for a club that had taken so long to move on from the dominance of forward play.

The Feast Monday match at Camborne attracted more than 4,000 spectators and was won 6-0 by Redruth after tries from Davey and Howard Gray. It was clear that Redruth were superior in every department and their tactic of moving the ball wide was more than equal to Camborne's kick-and-rush approach.

Spirits were high after a 3-0 victory away at St Ives brought a satisfactory end to the home club's undefeated run, but then came a 14-5 defeat by Plymouth. Redruth were still to record their first victory against the Devon side, but the result might have been closer had Redruth not played nearly the whole of the second half with a seven-man scrum after Paull injured his hip and had to go off.

Three Redruth players, Bert Solomon, James Davey and Arthur 'Chummy' Lawry were selected for Cornwall in the second County Championship round against Devon in Plymouth in early December. It was a dull, wet day and Cornwall spirits were further dampened by a 17-8 defeat. However, the performances of Solomon and Davey caught the eye of the English Rugby Union selectors and both were chosen to play for the South West in an England trial match against a side representing London.

Redruth's 27-0 defeat of the Camborne School of Mines in mid-December put them in pole position to lift the Cornish championship again, with all but one of their remaining matches to be played at home. They had scored 51 points against Cornish clubs so far that season and conceded only three. A second win over St Ives and a 16-3 defeat of Camborne on Boxing Day further strengthened their position. The club also gained approval in the local press for agreeing to play a match against a re-formed Truro side and donate half of the gate money to the visitors.

Bert Solomon, Maffer Davey and Arthur Lawry were again the only three Redruth players selected for the Cornwall side to face Gloucestershire at Redruth on 11 January 1908. The grandstand quickly sold out and extra banking was built around the ground to accommodate the overflow of spectators. Although two days of frost had hardened the ground, the Welsh referee decided the pitch was playable and Cornwall were anxious to start. However, Gloucestershire refused to play, despite having made the long trip down, and the match was postponed. By this time, thousands of people were on their way to Redruth, many on special trains laid on by the Great Western Railway.

Redruth secured the championship of Cornwall on 18 January 1908 with a 9-3 home win over the previous holders, Falmouth. Newspaper reports were almost unanimous in stating that it was one of the most exciting games held at Redruth that season. There was a notable contrast in styles between Redruth, who continued to spin the ball wide, and Falmouth, who relied on their forwards to retain possession. Redruth's tactics had now delivered them 100 points over the season, with just nine scored against them.

Not everyone enjoyed the afternoon. The football columnist for the Falmouth-based *Cornish Echo*, who called himself 'Rufus', declared that he had been left despondent by the actions of Redruth and its supporters at the match:

> 'Many of the homesters developed unnecessarily rough
> and in some cases brutal tactics, while a large body of
> the home supporters did nothing better than excite

their players and howl madly at the referee when he chanced to decide against the Reds. Several of those standing around the ropes continued, without caution, to hurl pieces of turf and orange peel at the Falmouth linesman and the language they directed at him can best be described as un-English.'[42]

Having made sure that the Cornish championship was in the bag, Redruth experimented with some team changes for their away game at Falmouth and fell to an 8-3 defeat. They lost again the following week, by 8-0, against Devon Albion. The result was not too disappointing, given the strength of the opposition and the fact that the Reds were without James Davey and had to call up two players from the reserves. One of those players was Richard Solomon, unrelated to Barney and Bert, the first time these three Solomons appeared together in the Redruth team.

The rearranged Cornwall game against Gloucestershire finally kicked off at Redruth on 25 January in front of 4,000 spectators. Redruth's Richard Davey came into the side to join his team-mates Bert Solomon, Maffer Davey and Arthur Lawry. Gloucestershire, who started as favourites, raced to an early ten-point lead but, just before half-time, Bert Solomon crossed to put Cornwall on the board. The second half was all Cornwall and they closed out Gloucestershire to take victory 34-10 in front of an ecstatic crowd. Solomon contributed two tries and Lawry scored one. The result meant there was a tie at the top of the championship table and Cornwall, Gloucestershire and Devon would have to play again.

The first replay was against Devon at Redruth on 13 February. A crowd of 6,000 saw Solomon score an audacious try which quickly became legendary. Dean, the Devon Albion player he had faced just a few days earlier, received the ball from his fellow half-back, then passed the ball straight to a grateful Solomon, who dummied to Bennetts before doubling through on his own and scoring behind the posts. Cornwall won 21-3.

The Devon back, Lilicrap, who had boasted that he would never be fooled by Solomon's dummy, was forced to eat his words.

Solomon had a knee injury for the Gloucestershire replay, so the backs were rearranged and Redruth's veteran full-back, Eathorne, joined the team, with Lawry and the two Daveys making up the Redruth contingent travelling to Kingsholm. Lawry was injured 12 minutes into the game, but the Cornish pack was strong and they still managed to dig out a 15-3 victory with seven forwards, setting up a home semi-final against Middlesex, which, it was announced, would be played at Redruth on 12 March.

The decision to allow Redruth to host the match came after a huge row at a CRFU meeting. The Camborne and Falmouth representatives both demanded the match should be played on their respective grounds, with the latter claiming that the fixture was needed to boost support for rugby in the town. Redruth's Willie Hichens, obviously with tongue firmly in cheek, declared that his club did not want the fixture because of the amount of work needed to organise such a game. However, he said that he would support Redruth for the sake of the county. Hichens also claimed that John Jackett, the Falmouth and Cornwall captain, favoured Redruth, as he knew every inch of the ground and that was important in a county match. With Camborne's ground still undergoing work, there was a large majority for Redruth.

In the weeks before the County Championship semi-final, Redruth's selection committee continued to experiment with new combinations, giving their county players a chance to rest and prepare for the big match. The Reds took a side largely comprised of reserve players to Truro, winning easily 23-3 against opponents still gaining experience. The following home game against Falmouth was played in a blizzard in front of a sparse crowd and without Bert Solomon, James Davey, Dick Eathorne, John Lawry or Prisk. Redruth were defeated 16-8.

Finally, the long-awaited day of the county semi-final against Middlesex arrived. Victory would see Cornwall face

Durham, the county which had won the championship five times in the previous eight years. Some 8,000 spectators arrived at the Recreation Ground on a Thursday afternoon. Hundreds of them had booked their places in the grandstand before the venue had even been confirmed. The visitors arrived with a team packed with players from clubs such as Harlequins, Richmond and Rosslyn Park, but had been forced to make seven changes from the side originally announced.

Cornwall scored first, a fine run by James Davey sending Jose over, but Middlesex swiftly drew level and the home crowd feared that Cornwall were not matching the performances delivered in their previous games. Early in the second half, a Cornwall try was disallowed when the linesman, Redruth's own Dr Willie Hichens, judged that a player had a foot in touch. In the end, the strength of Cornwall's forwards won the day, especially the giant powerhouse international 'Jumbo' Milton from the Camborne School of Mines, with two more tries in the final quarter pushing Cornwall to a 19-3 win.

Davey's performance saw him selected to play for England in their forthcoming Calcutta Cup match against Scotland after the England selectors convened a meeting on the train home from Redruth. The half-back had already been named as part of the Anglo-Welsh team, forerunner of the Lions, for a tour to New Zealand. He became the second Redruth player, after William Grylls, to win an England cap.

Following the victory, the CRFU held a special meeting at Redruth to decide the venue for the final against Durham. The two Camborne representatives proposed the match should take place on their ground but, in an unusual move for the time, the players had been asked for their view and, according to the county secretary, Dennis Lawry, had chosen Redruth. The Camborne delegate threatened that his club would leave the CRFU if it did not get the game, a statement that Redruth's Willie Hichens described as a puerile argument that was an insult to common sense. He received a round of applause.

Because of his selection for England, Maffer Davey, perhaps wisely, decided to opt out of Redruth's next home game against Devon Albion. He was probably glad not to have been involved. Two days of heavy rain had left pools of water on a pitch that was largely comprised of mud. It all ended in a scoreless draw, but the Reds would have been happy to finish level against a side they had never defeated.

The night before the 1908 County Championship final saw more heavy rain pouring down on to the Redruth ground, but by morning the skies had cleared and the pitch was declared to be in good shape. Redruth itself was decorated with ribbons, flags and flowers, all displaying the black and gold of Cornwall. Spectators arrived in the town on foot, by bicycle and by the many special trains laid on for the occasion. Contemporary reports estimated that, by kick-off, up to 18,000 people were jammed into the Recreation Ground. Every available rooftop in sight of the pitch was occupied. The Redruth club had built temporary grandstands all around the ground and these were filled more than an hour before the game got under way. It was said that Bert Solomon himself had been among the volunteers erecting the stands the night before.

Bert was the last player to emerge on to the pitch and by then the roar of the crowd could be heard four miles away in Camborne. With him in the team were three other Redruth players; James Davey, Richard Davey and Arthur Lawry. The posts were adorned at one end with the toy monkey of Durham and at the other by a large hanging pasty. The teams took their positions, Cornwall playing uphill towards the Camborne end, and the whistle blew.

Soon afterwards, a surge in the crowd caused some railings behind the benches allocated to the press to collapse and play was halted. It only served to increase the anticipation and when play resumed, Solomon took a pass from Bennetts and went over for Cornwall's first try. It was Solomon again who skilfully intercepted a Durham pass, accelerated away and sent Bennetts over for Cornwall's second. The sides turned round at half-time with Cornwall 8-3 ahead.

There was more to come from Solomon in the second half. A clever pass from Maffer Davey saw Bert dash for the line, sell an outrageous dummy and crash over himself at the Piggy Lane end with three Durham players clinging to him. It was a sign of Solomon's ability to fool the defence that Bennetts was himself tackled by two Durham defenders who were convinced he had received a pass from Solomon. Maffer Davey scored Cornwall's fourth try, with Nick Tregurtha of St Ives contributing a fifth just before full time. It finished Cornwall 17 Durham 3.

Bert Solomon's performance on that day confirmed the belief of many in Cornish rugby that he was the finest player Cornwall had ever produced:

> 'Bert Solomon was the outstanding star. He played the game of his life. It is a pity that the internationals are over because on Saturday's form he is the finest centre in England. By his quickness in seizing opportunities he frequently turned a breakdown in the enemy's attack to good advantage while his speed was too much for his opponents.'[43]

Following the game, the crowd carried Bert shoulder-high through the streets of Redruth, an event that must have been profoundly embarrassing for such a modest man. He had already suffered some embarrassment during the game when, running in to score what might well have been his third try, his shorts had come off. Whether this was due to a rotten leather belt or a Durham tackle is not clear. With many ladies in the crowd, including his mother, Kate, Bert had lain face down on the turf until a new pair of shorts could be secured.

Among the vast crowd that day was a young man named Bill Osborne, from Four Lanes near Redruth. He would spend a lifetime following Cornish rugby and, many years later at the age of 103, he would be at Twickenham, with three generations of his family, to cheer on the black and gold. That day, in April 1991, would be the next time Cornwall would lift the County Championship, 83 years after winning it for the first time in 1908 on the Redruth ground.

Cornwall's victory against a strong Durham side again raised the question of why so few Cornish players had been selected for international honours. At the traditional after-match dinner, held at Redruth's Masonic Hall, Willie Hichens, who had been given the task of thanking the referee, deviated from his prepared remarks to make that very point: 'It is a total mystery,' he said, 'that while Cornwall has beaten all the other counties in England, not by small margins but by big ones, only one of their team has been chosen to play against Scotland and he only at the last minute'.

Perhaps the answer lay in an article that had appeared in the *Morning Post* a couple of weeks earlier. The anonymous writer suggested that the England selectors should look at the performance of the clubs and the universities rather than at the county sides when picking a team. The message was quite clearly that England places should go to university men and those turning out for the fashionable sides such as Harlequins, Richmond and Blackheath, the right sort of men to represent their country. Given that the English selectors came from the same background, it is little wonder that players from the more remote areas of the country were seldom considered. It would take years for this attitude to change.

With Cornwall as county champions and Redruth already crowned the top side in Cornwall, the final weeks of the season were something of an anti-climax. One bright spot was a gathering at Redruth's Dunstanville Hotel on 8 April to mark the imminent departure of Maffer Davey for the Anglo-Welsh tour of New Zealand and Australia. Davey was presented with a gold ring, a case of pipes, a writing case and a box of cigars. There was obviously some concern that, having already spent time in South Africa, he might be tempted to remain in New Zealand. The meeting chairman, Sidney Lanyon, said he hoped Davey would return and, when he did, he should stick to his mother team at Redruth.

Maffer told the gathering he would rather play Durham again than be standing before them making a speech, but he was quick to reassure those present that he had no intention of remaining in New Zealand: 'I have played for Cornwall for many years but this is the proudest year of my life and I am glad to think that I am a Cornishman.' It was widely reported that Bert Solomon was also invited to take part in the Anglo-Welsh tour, but that he declined to leave his home and family for so long, even with the promise of his friend and mentor, James Davey, at his side.

On the pitch, Redruth saw out April with home games against Camborne School of Mines and Newton, and a busy Easter weekend of fixtures against Cardiff Northerns, Bridgwater and Albion Reserves, while Redruth's second XV faced matches against Four Lanes, Lanner and two encounters with Camborne reserves. The match against Devon side Newton was particularly physical, the *West Briton* reporter considering that several players were lucky not to have been sent off. Once again, Bert Solomon was the outstanding figure, scoring a 40-yard try and dominating the game with his personality.

Having handsomely beaten Camborne School of Mines and Newton, Redruth faced the touring side Cardiff Northerns at the Recreation Ground, winning by 33-0. The following day, they beat Bridgwater 28-0, although the Somerset side was at a disadvantage, having arrived with just 13 players. The club closed the season with a 15-3 win over Camborne in front of what was described as only a small crowd.

The England cap won by Maffer Davey earlier in the year against Scotland arrived in the post at his home in Redruth, just as he was preparing for the first match of the Anglo-Welsh tour in New Zealand. On the way south, the ship had docked at Cape Town where officials from the local rugby side had asked the captain to delay departure so that Davey could play in a forthcoming match. The tour manager, George Garnett, had been understandably reluctant to release his player and the ship had left on time.

The summer saw the club in buoyant mood at the July AGM, able to celebrate both success on the field and a stronger financial position than any club in Cornwall. The following week, the players went to Lands End for their annual outing, taking the early train to Penzance, then being conveyed the rest of the way in Jersey cars, a type of horse-drawn waggon.

The 1908/09 season started with a disappointing defeat away to Plymouth in a game which, according to several newspaper reports, Plymouth were fortunate to have won. The club was also disheartened by the news that the Recreation Ground would not be hosting either of the two opening matches in the County Championship and neither would it be hosting a touring Australian side who were due to play Cornwall in October. Following the earlier row at the CRFU over the decision to award the 1908 final against Durham to Redruth, it was decided that the County Championship matches would be held at Falmouth and Camborne, with the latter also the venue for the game against Australia.

Redruth's bid to retain the Cornish championship got under way with a 14-3 win away at Penzance. The side had been boosted by the return of John Scoble from South Africa, playing at fly-half in place of Maffer Davey, who was still on tour with the Anglo-Welsh side.

The following week, it was announced that three Redruth players – Frank Smith, Bert Solomon and Arthur Lawry – had been selected to play for Cornwall against the touring Australians. Barney Solomon and Len Browett were named as reserves. The Australians won 18-5. With nicknames having by then become the order of the day for touring sides, the English press had attempted to christen this Australian team the Rabbits, but the players thought it inappropriate and chose to be called the Wallabies instead, a name they have used ever since.

Redruth had a narrow 5-0 home win over St Ives on 10 October in one of the toughest games seen at the Recreation Ground that season. On the same day, the Anglo-Welsh rugby side returned to Britain, docking in Liverpool. True to his word, Maffer Davey had returned home, although four other members of the team had elected to remain overseas. *The Cornubian* wasted no time in obtaining an interview with the returning hero, sending a reporter to waylay him in Redruth's Fore Street for a chat.

Davey had made five appearances for the touring side, one in a Test match against New Zealand, and had scored five tries. He reiterated his intention to refuse any offers to turn professional, but he would not be drawn on whether he would rejoin Redruth. Asked whether he would be turning out for his home team against Albion Reserves that coming Saturday, he simply said: 'I cannot say.' According to the club minutes, he was selected for the game.

Davey was also named in the Cornish side picked, as county champions, to represent Great Britain at the Olympic Games being held at White City in London. Matches were scheduled against France and the touring Australian side, which had recently beaten Cornwall. However, France pulled out at the last minute, leaving Great Britain and Australia to compete in what was effectively a final. Redruth's Barney Solomon was a last-minute replacement for Barrie Bennetts in the Great Britain side which lined up against the Australians in heavy drizzle on 26 October. Just 3,000 people were present at the vast White City Stadium, which had a 68,000 seating capacity. A third of those had made the long journey up from Cornwall.

The game was completely one-sided, with the Australians winning 32-3. Cornwall's only score was a try by Bert Solomon following a well-worked move by Maffer Davey that had opened up the Australian defence. The only consolation was the award of a silver medal.

Bert Solomon and Len Browett are the only two Redruth players listed among the Cornwall team in their opening game in defence of the County Championship at Falmouth in early November. Maffer Davey was also in the team, but is listed as playing for Coventry, a side he occasionally represented while working in the Midlands. Cornwall beat Somerset 16-0 in front of a crowd of about 4,000 and Solomon dazzled, receiving the ball from Davey then baffling the opposition and scoring the best try of the match.

Two days later, on Monday 9 November, Redruth played their traditional Feast Monday match against Camborne. It was more eagerly awaited even than the county game, with the Reds putting out a strong team, including Frank Smith at full-back, both Solomon brothers at centre, flanked by Brewett and Carbis on the wings, and Rich and Davey as half-backs. Redruth won 14-8, but that was not the headline in that week's *Cornubian* newspaper. 'Redruth v Camborne, Annual Feast Encounter,' it read. 'Bert Solomon's Collar Bone Broken.'

According to Allen Buckley's biography of Solomon, the Camborne full-back, Arthur Stephens, had promised his supporters before the game that, no matter who else might score for Redruth, Solomon would not. As Solomon received a pass from Maffer Davey, he leaped in the air to try and avoid the advancing Stephens and both men came together and crashed awkwardly to the ground. It was said the sound of Solomon's collarbone cracking could be heard in the grandstand. It would keep him out of the game for several weeks and a meeting of the club's finance committee was convened the next day to vote through a payment to Solomon of £1 a week from the insurance fund while he recovered.

At the end of November, it was announced that Davey had been selected for the South of England side to take on the North in an international trial match. Although Maffer had been working in the Midlands and had turned out for Coventry from time to time, he still played for Redruth when he could. He was selected for the Camborne game on Boxing Day and the match against Albion on 2 January. A report in *The Cornubian*, following the Boxing Day clash with Camborne, which Redruth won 20-5, suggested that he had made a commitment to Redruth for the rest of the season. Two weeks later, Davey won his second England cap in the Home Nations match against Wales at Cardiff, which England lost 8-0.

Lawry, Davey and Browett were the three Redruth players who travelled with the rest of the Cornwall team up to Stroud to face Gloucestershire in the third County Championship group match on 9 January. Cornwall were without Bert Solomon, who failed to arrive at the station. A report in *Lake's Falmouth Packet* said that someone was sent to his house, only to be told that he had decided not to travel. According to the paper, it was gone noon on Friday when Len Browett was approached to take Solomon's place and he hurriedly left to catch the 12.55pm train to Gloucestershire:

> 'It will come as a surprise to the public if Solomon is called upon again for the season, for however good a player may be, it cannot be expected that the county will again run the risk of being placed in such a humiliating position.'[44]

Realistically, this game would have been less than nine weeks after Solomon's injury, so he may not have been fully fit. It seemed that the Cornwall selectors, who, it must be remembered, included Bert's greatest cheerleader, Dr Willie Hichens, did not feel humiliated or perhaps took a more pragmatic view. Solomon was named in the Cornwall side for the replay against Gloucestershire at Redruth on 28 January.

In the same week, the England selectors announced that Solomon had been asked to make himself available to play for

England against France, although he did not make the final XV. However, he took part in both County Championship play-offs against Gloucestershire and Devon. Cornwall won both to top the group and set up a semi-final clash against the Midland Counties.

The proposal to play this game at Redruth set up the now routine row at the CRFU committee meeting. The Camborne representatives argued that five out of the seven previous big games had taken place at Redruth. Willie Hichens, the Redruth representative, pointed out that Camborne had failed to bid for the Gloucestershire replay, so they had no cause to complain. After further wrangling, it was decided the game would be played at Redruth.

The match set the stage for a classic Bert Solomon performance. Cornwall fell behind in the first half, but two glorious tries from Solomon after the break helped them to a 26-8 victory to set up a second consecutive final against Durham, this time in West Hartlepool. Sadly, the result would be very different from the previous year, and the Durham forwards won the day 12-0.

Back at the club, the Redruth first XV had retained their position as Cornwall's champion club. The reserves had also held on to their crown as the champion junior club following a hard-fought match against Troon on 20 February. A drop goal from Thomas, the Redruth full-back, was the only score in the game. There were now two players by the name of Solomon playing for the reserves, with Barney and Bert's little brother, Jimmy 'Dickus' Solomon, having joined during the season, meaning that, with Richard Solomon also in the reserves, selection sheets would frequently feature the name four times. A younger Solomon brother, William, still only 13 in 1909, would also later play for the club. In 1910, he would win the lads race at the town's sports day, showing he was already in preparation to pull on a rugby jersey.

Redruth racked up their fourth victory of the season over Camborne, winning a home game 20-8, but not before blows had been exchanged. Camborne took exception to what they thought was a late tackle by Bert Solomon on Stutheridge and Solomon was grabbed around the neck by a Camborne three-quarter named Bath, who refused to let him go until the referee intervened.

Redruth played three fixtures over the 1909 Easter weekend. The now regular arrival of touring sides in Cornwall saw Redruth host Ebbw Vale reserves on Good Friday, winning 17-3. On Easter Saturday, they defeated the visiting Albion reserves 14-3. Easter Monday featured a match against old foes Newton, in what seems to have been a rough affair. Redruth ran out 8-5 winners, but Gray of Redruth and Mason of Newton were both sent off following a set-to shortly after half-time.

On 22 April, *The Cornubian* published a full list of Redruth's results for the 1908/09 season. The chiefs had played 32 games, won 20, lost ten and drawn two with 419 points scored and 170 conceded. The highest-scoring game had been the 33-0 defeat of Penzance back in September. The reserves had not lost a game all season, winning 24 of 29 and drawing five. Their best result was a 71-0 drubbing of Camborne School of Mines.

The club faced major challenges at the beginning of the 1909/10 season, with a number of changes in the playing line-up. Several men had decided to stand down, including Prisk and Howard Gray. However, Harry Rich had returned to the club after a number of years in the Transvaal and there were many players vying for a place in the reserves, which boded well for the future. The club, unlike some other Cornish sides, had also managed to retain fixtures with some of the best Devon teams, the first of which, at home to Newton, was won 6-3.

Maffer Davey missed the beginning of the season. He had been caught up in an RFU investigation into suspected financial irregularities at Coventry RFC, for whom he had played on a few occasions. These revolved around expenses paid to the players for travel and subsistence, and some players had been suspended. Davey was instructed to travel up to London to give an account of himself to the RFU investigating committee. *The Sportsman* reported his insistence that the explanation he had given was satisfactory. One other Redruth player involved was Dickie Eathorne, who had also played for Coventry, but the RFU committee was told that he was in South Africa.

The findings of the investigation into the Coventry affair saw the club being suspended from competition for the season. Two Coventry officials were expelled from the Rugby Union and Maffer Davey and another player were suspended 'during the pleasure of the Union'. Dickie Eathorne was suspended pending his appearance before the committee, although whether this news reached him in the Transvaal is not clear.

Athletic News reported the affair with a strong dose of scepticism, offering the opinion that Davey's decision to leave Redruth was inexplicable and giving a strong hint that his employment at the Rex Motorcycle Works might have been arranged so he could play for Coventry.

The absence of Davey did not stop Redruth securing a rare victory over visiting Devonport Albion in October, but only one of their players, Bert Solomon, was selected for Cornwall in the forthcoming County Championship competition. Frank Smith, Tom Lawry and Len Browett were named among the reserves. Smith and Lawry did make the starting line-up after Jackett and Turle dropped out, but Cornwall lost 6-3 in the game at Bath.

Redruth were finding the defence of their Cornwall title tough going. The changes in the side seemed to have disrupted the team, which was not functioning as well as it had the season before. They were also faced with stronger opposition with both St Ives and Camborne delivering improved performances. Redruth's 6-0 defeat at the hands of St Ives in mid-November was said by the *West Briton* to be the first win the visitors had ever secured at the Recreation Ground.

The match report in the same paper suggested that opponents were getting the measure of Bert Solomon, who was given little room to show his talent. There was more misery on Feast Monday when the club went down 8-6 against Camborne. It had been a long time since the Reds had lost to their closest rivals and there was, understandably, much jubilation in the Town camp.

The affair of 'Maffer Davey' and Coventry rumbled on. A meeting of the CRFU committee on 22 November heard that Willie Hichens had written to the RFU asking for a clear reason for Davey's continuing suspension, but no reply had been received. He told the committee that the whole matter revolved around allegations that Davey had stayed at a hotel in Coventry at the club's expense and that it was only justice to the man that he should know why he had been sanctioned.

Redruth secured a welcome 20-0 victory at Penzance in late November, despite being without either Bert Solomon or Arthur Lawry, both of whom were injured. Bert's injury meant that he was also unable to play in the England trial being held at Birkenhead on 11 December. He was selected for another England trial at Twickenham on 18 December and, judging by newspaper reports, was one of the best players on the field.

Solomon's presence at the England trial meant he was not available for Redruth when they took on Falmouth on the same day in what was seen as a significant fixture in the battle for the Cornish championship. The Reds' 19-3 win would have done much to boost Redruth confidence after what had been a slow start to the season. Bert was also unavailable for the Boxing Day match against Camborne, having been selected for Cornwall to face Somerset in a County Championship play-off, but Redruth beat the visitors 9-0, retaining their 100 per cent record in the fixture.

Solomon played in yet another England trial when he was selected for the Rest against England at Twickenham on 8 January 1910. England's complicated selection process, involving multiple trials, was coming under criticism from commentators who felt it was unhelpful to have the team undecided right up until a few weeks before the Home Nations Championship started.

Redruth's away game at Falmouth ended in chaos when the referee sent off a Falmouth player midway through the second half. This incensed the Falmouth crowd, which began hurling abuse at the referee, and the bad feeling spilled over to the players. The referee blew up and declared the game over, at which point he was knocked over by the crowd and crushed against the rails. Eventually, he was forced to leave in a cab after it was noticed that a large proportion of the Falmouth supporters were waiting for him outside the ground. Falmouth had been leading 3-0 when the game had been brought to a premature end.

Meanwhile, Bert Solomon did not disappoint in his final England trial, playing for the Rest. The England selectors had picked the whole of the England back division from Harlequins and they were amazed when their first-choice team was beaten 19-10 by the Rest. As far as the press was concerned, Solomon was the man of the hour. The opinion of the *Leeds Mercury* that he was the best centre three-quarter playing in England was echoed in many other papers.

The result left the England selectors scratching their heads and it was not until late afternoon on the following Monday that the team to play Wales was announced. Eight players who had turned out for the Rest were named in the side, among them B. Solomon (Cornwall and Redruth). On the same day as his triumph at Twickenham, his club were in action at home to Penzance, winning 22-0 without him.

Whatever class differences can be experienced by sportsmen and women today are nothing compared with those 100 years ago. It is difficult to imagine the state of mind of Bert Solomon when he found himself thrust into a team largely comprised of professional men. The Gloucester forward, Harry Berry, was the only other player who had not been to a fee-paying school. Bert was a working-class man from the far end of Cornwall who laboured in a bacon factory and whose leisure time, when he was not playing rugby, was spent with his racing pigeons and on his allotment.

He spoke with a thick West Cornwall accent and he could barely read and write. In his biography of Solomon, Allen Buckley says that Willie Hichens and the Cornwall secretary, Dennis Lawry, spent a great deal of time talking him around and calming him down. It was Lawry who travelled with him on the train to Twickenham, after a large crowd had gathered at Redruth Station to see him off, fresh pasties tucked away in his kitbag.

On the day of the match, Solomon did his talking in the way he knew best. There are conflicting reports about his part in England's first try, which caught the Welsh defence napping. It has been suggested it was he who span the ball out to the England wing, Fred Chapman, who then became the first man to score an international try on the new Twickenham ground. However, there is no doubting Solomon's role in England's second try. With England attacking the Welsh half, a ruck formed and Dai Gent, the England scrum-half, sent the ball to Solomon. Bert accelerated forward, sent two Welsh defenders the wrong way, dummied around the Welsh full-back Jack Bancroft and crossed the line to score, to the delight of the England fans and the small body of Cornish supporters that had come to watch the game. England won 11-6 in their first defeat of Wales in more than a decade.

What happened after the whistle would be incomprehensible to anyone who did not know Bert Solomon. It is said he muttered the words 'I'm finished' and then refused to attend the traditional post-match dinner, fearing, some later said, that he would not know what to do or say in a gathering of public school men at which the menus were written in French. With the ink barely dry on effusive newspaper plaudits – one dubbing him 'as crafty as a Welsh centre' and another describing his try as 'the greatest effort of the match' – he walked away, not just from Twickenham but, to all intents and purposes, from competitive rugby.

He was named in the England team to face Ireland, but turned down the offer. He did the same with requests to play in two subsequent home internationals. He had already refused an invitation to join the 1908 Anglo-Welsh tour of New Zealand and Australia, and it was said he had also declined an offer of £400 to move up north and turn professional.

It was not quite the end of Solomon's days as a rugby player. He appeared in the County Championship play-off between Cornwall and Gloucestershire at Redruth on 3 February. Cornwall were defeated 12-11 but Solomon scored a try and conversion. He also continued to play for Redruth, scoring a try in a 17-3 victory over Camborne School of Mines.

Redruth put in a disappointing display in a home game against Camborne in mid-March, narrowly winning 6-4. It was clear that the gap between the two sides in terms of performance had narrowed considerably. Bert did not play in that game, but he did feature in the match against Albion reserves on Easter Saturday, which the Reds won 3-0, and in the Bank Holiday Monday match against Falmouth, won 13-5 by the Reds. James Solomon was granted his Redruth first XV cap for that weekend and all three brothers were on the field for the Falmouth game.

The CRFU had waited three months for a response to their request that Maffer Davey's suspension should be lifted. In March, the RFU replied to state 'that no good purpose could be served by reopening the matter'. It was the end of the rugby career of one of the most gifted players of his generation, demonstrating once again the zero tolerance attitude the RFU had for anyone suspected of taking any sort of financial reward from the game.

Redruth's match away to Penzance on 2 April saw Bert Solomon run in two tries, the first within three minutes, for a 17-3 win. The return game, a week later, was the last of the regular season and was won by Redruth in handsome style, 36-0. *The Cornubian* correspondent found it too one-sided to be interesting, but declared that Bert Solomon, who again scored twice, was the best man on the field. He had paired well with brother, Barney, although the latter did not have his kicking boots on and missed an easy conversion. Yet another Solomon, Tom, was one of two Redruth reserves players loaned to Penzance to make up their numbers. In spite of this positive end to the season, Redruth failed to retain the Cornwall championship, the honours going, for the first time in many years, to Camborne.

On 16 April, Redruth and Camborne met for the fifth time that season, this time for their annual charity match on behalf of the local hospitals, nursing and ambulance associations. Both teams fielded almost their first-choice sides and, for Redruth, Barney and Bert Solomon were in their now customary positions together at the centre of the three-quarter line. However, according to *The Cornubian:* 'The game was far too keenly and closely contested to be a good one, the home backs evidently determined to give Bert Solomon no room to move, and succeeded fairly well.'

This was Bert Solomon's final game for Redruth and the last in which he would play regular competitive rugby. He would return to the rugby field for special occasions or charity matches, including a game in 1920 in which the entire three-quarter line was made up of Solomon brothers, but he would never again play a serious game. He was selected to play for Cornwall against Glamorgan on 22 April 1910, but he failed to take part. Stevens, Howard Gray and Harry Rich were the three Redruth players in the county side for that game at Camborne, which Cornwall lost 3-0.

As the new season started, Bert Solomon's absence from the Redruth team was put down to sickness. Rumours abounded that he would soon return, but the only Solomon to appear regularly for the chiefs in the first few games was Tom. Members of the committee may have believed Bert just needed to take a break.

Redruth's fixture list for 1910/11 showed 35 games lined up. The dearth of senior sides in Cornwall was highlighted by the fact that Redruth would only face five local clubs. Camborne, Falmouth, St Ives and Camborne School of Mines had been regular opponents in the past and would play four games each against the Reds over the season. Penryn was now listed as a senior side, having re-formed a couple of years previously, and they were due to play Redruth twice. Penzance was a conspicuous absentee. The remainder of the fixtures were against the usual Devon sides; Newton, Plymouth, Albion and Torquay. Touring sides due to visit the Recreation Ground were London Welsh, Old Merchant Taylors and Cardiff Centrals.

The club's AGM had heard that, while the finances were still in good shape, the bank balance had fallen over the previous 12 months and concern was expressed about the level of expenditure. Much of this was caused by the expense of travelling to away games and the costs of bringing touring sides to the Recreation Ground. It may have been concerns over money which prompted the club to end the practice of allowing ladies to watch matches without paying.

On a positive note, two players, Carter and Burgoyne, had joined from Camborne, while Willie Menhennet, described as a finely built forward, had returned from the Transvaal. An unexpected surprise had been the move of the Penzance back, Barrie Bennetts, to Redruth, making his debut for the Reds on 1 October against Plymouth Reserves. Bennetts was a regular in the Cornish side and had twice played for England in 1909. The Reds narrowly lost the Plymouth game, and the earlier away match against Albion, but they did manage a 3-0 win at Torquay.

Redruth's first game of the season against a Cornish side was a 53-0 demolition of Camborne School of Mines. The student club was a shadow of what it had been when it had boasted two England internationals and had more than held its own in the Cornwall championship. Because of this, the Reds took the chance to blood some new players, including a man named Stephens, who had been playing for the junior side, Redruth Midgets.

Barrie Bennetts, who had been injured in his appearance for the Reds in early October, was named in a much-changed Redruth side that travelled the short distance to Camborne for the annual Feast Monday game. It was a disappointing performance by Redruth and they lost 9-3.

There was some surprise in the local press when Falmouth came to Redruth and defeated them 8-6. Concern was expressed in match reports that the Redruth half-backs, Tom Solomon and Truran, were struggling to make an impression, meaning that the three-quarters were not getting enough quick ball. It was evident that Maffer Davey was greatly missed and the newer players in the side were taking time to settle.

They did get back on track with a 12-0 defeat of St Ives but were defeated at home by Camborne on Boxing Day, 9-3. Not only was this the first time that Camborne had won the Boxing Day fixture, which had been played 13 times since 1871, the result also gave Town the championship of Cornwall. The following day's 6-3 defeat of Falmouth provided little consolation.

Redruth's first game in 1911 was at home to Penryn, the side that had lost to the Reds reserves earlier in the season. The result was a 43-8 win for Redruth, perhaps a sign that the new Borough side was still finding its feet. Redruth's third game of the season against Camborne resulted in a third defeat and the general view of the press was that their three-quarters were well below form. There was better news when the club entertained Plymouth on 28 January and the Reds pulled off a rare win, 8-0, against the Devon side.

In March, it was announced that John Hewitt 'Breechy' Thomas, one of Redruth and Cornwall's star players of the late 1890s and early 1900s, had died from pneumonia. He had started playing for the club at the age of 17, going on to captain Redruth and become an England trialist. Following his retirement as a player, he had taken up refereeing. Hundreds of people turned out for the funeral at St Euny Church, including representatives from the Redruth club.

In an echo of the past, Redruth were criticised for failing to arrive on time for their match at Falmouth on 18 March. According to the *Cornish Echo*, the game was scheduled to kick-off at 3.15pm, but Redruth failed to arrive until 4pm. The report claimed that the Reds were again becoming notorious for turning up late and urged the CRFU to put a heavy foot down on such practices. The game commenced in pouring rain and it had become so dark towards the end that the referee blew up ten minutes before time. The sorry affair ended in a scoreless draw.

The game, in a way, summed up Redruth's season, the only chink of light being a 3-0 defeat of visiting Camborne on 1 April and the usual entertaining matches over Easter. The highlight of the Easter weekend was the first visit of London Welsh, one of the country's top club sides, who arrived with a team boasting two Welsh internationals and a Cambridge Blue. Redruth turned on a performance that had been lacking for much of the season and beat their visitors 14-3.

For all that, it was a disappointing season, which Redruth ended having won 22 of their 37 matches, scoring 418 points with 142 against. The club's performance against Devon sides was, according to the secretary, Henry Downing, the best ever. However, it must have been a concern to the club that of the 18 sides they had played during the season, only five had been Cornish. Redruth spent more time in Devon than any other club in Cornwall, which impacted heavily on the cost of maintaining the teams.

With the economic situation in the area continuing to worsen, more players were opting to leave Cornwall, either to go elsewhere in the British Isles or to move abroad. The previous season, only five senior teams had competed in the Cornish championship and, of those, Hayle, St Ives and Falmouth were receiving financial support from the CRFU. Penzance seemed to have folded altogether.

It was against this rather dismal background that Redruth started the 1911/12 season with a trip to Devon Albion, the home side winning 13-6. Redruth finished with 14 men after George Richards had been given his marching orders for, as the referee reported later to the CRFU, mauling after the whistle and attempting to strike an opposition player. Nevertheless, the football correspondent of the *Western Evening Herald* felt that Redruth had given a good account of themselves and that Albion might well find things difficult in the return fixture.

The first game against a Cornish club saw them entertain Hayle at the end of September, the visitors back in the ranks of senior Cornish clubs for the first time in two decades. Clearly they were still finding their feet, as the Reds romped home 30-3. They followed this up with a 9-5 win at Falmouth the following week. 'Rufus', the football correspondent of *Lake's Falmouth Packet and Cornwall Advertiser,* claimed that Redruth's Willie Menhennett was guilty of objectionable tactics, although, disappointingly, he did not elaborate with any details.

Noses in Falmouth were put out of joint when it was announced that Dick Jackett, brother of the England and Cornwall full-back Edward, had requested a transfer to Redruth. Falmouth representatives on the CRFU committee, when considering the proposed transfer, complained that Redruth should not be using players from outside their area; there was a real concern that too much talent would be appearing for just two clubs, Redruth and Camborne. When it was suggested that, if Redruth did not have him Camborne would, the move was agreed.

Jackett's first game for his new side was the annual Feast Monday match at Camborne, in front of a record crowd of 4,000. According to *The Cornubian*, Redruth had most of the territorial advantage but failed to create enough opportunities. The result was a scoreless draw and the fact that both sides were so evenly matched suggested that the fight for the title of Cornish champions would be a close one. There was, accordingly, great anticipation for the return fixture on Boxing Day. Redruth kept their title hopes alive with another defeat of Camborne School of Mines, 26-0, before beating Plymouth by a single try, scored by Barrie Bennetts towards the end of the first half.

Having complained about Redruth's late arrival earlier in the season, Falmouth turned up nearly an hour late for the return match on 16 December. The result was that the spectators could not see the ball at all in the final quarter. The match was drawn 3-3.

A 25-5 win at Hayle a week later set Redruth up for the home clash with Camborne on Boxing Day. The ground had been soaked by a storm that morning, conditions that obviously suited the Reds, and they won 8-0. A collection was taken at the ground for the widow of a young Camborne forward, 24-year-old William Bassett, who had died in the Miner's Hospital after being severely injured in an underground explosion at South Crofty mine.

In January came the news that Bert Solomon had travelled to Guy's Hospital in London for a course of treatment said to be aimed at restoring him to full health. He was seen off at the station by Luke Smith and a number of other friends from the rugby club. The reason for the treatment is not known. Bert had always suffered with a sight problem – he was virtually blind in one eye by 1910 – but this may well have been a more serious condition for him to travel all the way to London. Unfortunately, Guy's Hospital patient records for that year have not survived.

Redruth's 14-3 win over St Ives on 20 January kept them well clear of Camborne at the top of the truncated Cornish table, although a 37-3 home win over Falmouth was marred by a leg injury to Barrie Bennetts which would see him out of action for several weeks. Redruth's continuing good form was shown when they had a rare win over Devon Albion at the Recreation Ground, beating the visitors 11-4 in front of 3,000 spectators. The *Western Daily Mercury* felt that rarely had Redruth performed so finely and that, if their form could be maintained, their halcyon days should speedily return. A 6-0 win at St Ives in late March saw Redruth, once again, crowned Cornish champions.

With Redruth having taken the championship from Camborne, a keenly fought contest was anticipated when Town travelled to Redruth on 13 April 1912 for their fourth encounter of the season. This would be a deciding match for the season, as they had won one game each and drawn the third, but the large crowd could not have been prepared for the events that took place towards the end of the second half.

The atmosphere was nasty even before kick-off. There was little love lost between the Cornish and the many Irish immigrants who had come to work in the local mines and factories, as had been shown by anti-Irish riots in Camborne in the past. The family of Camborne's Tom Morrissey had come from Tipperary and, even before the game started, he was subjected to what we would today term racist abuse from the home crowd. This continued throughout the game.

Morrissey was no shrinking violet. He had only just got back from a two-week suspension for rough play. Understandably sensitive about the abuse, he turned his back on the crowd, dropped his shorts and presented his bare backside to the grandstand. Several ladies left the ground while the Rector of Redruth, H.W. Sedgwick, declared himself so shocked that he resolved never to watch rugby there again.

The mayhem continued when Camborne's Sam Carter allegedly saw Redruth's Willie Menhennett doing something unpleasant to Morrissey in the scrum. Carter grabbed Menhennett, pulled him to his feet, and planted a massive punch just above his eye, knocking him senseless. This led to several hundred spectators surging on to the pitch. Carter then turned to the referee, Dennis Lawry, and threatened that something unpleasant would happen if he was ordered off. He apologised almost immediately and was allowed to remain on the pitch. Remarkably, the game continued. At the final whistle, Menhennett and Morrissey were still trading punches on the pitch, where they were joined by hundreds of spectators for a mass brawl.

The CRFU meeting on 25 April heard claims and counter claims over the assault on Menhennett. After much deliberation, the committee decided to suspend Menhennett for a month, Carter for three months and Morrissey for two years, on account of him having had two previous misconduct complaints against him. Morrissey and Carter, who did not attend the hearing, shrugged off the decision and made their way north to turn professional with Rochdale Hornets.

In retaliation, Redruth decided to cancel the annual charity match which had been arranged at Camborne the following week. Camborne's response was to send a telegram to Redruth cancelling all fixtures between the two clubs in the 1912/13 season unless the charity game went ahead. Neither club gave way.

The threat of professional rugby never really went away during this period and the feud between Redruth and Camborne saw it come back into the press. Redruth was forced to deny that it had been involved in negotiations to set up a Western League of professional rugby clubs, to emulate the Northern Union. Newspaper reports suggested that Bridgwater, Exeter, Plymouth and Redruth were among the clubs being approached. At Redruth's AGM, in August 1912, the club secretary, Henry Downing, confirmed that he had received communications on the matter, but had refused to reply to any of them. To loud applause, he announced that Redruth was quite outside the movement. He also refused to comment on the aftermath of the recent game against Camborne.

It was also announced, with some excitement, that the Welsh-born England international, Dai Gent, who had played alongside Bert Solomon when England had defeated Wales in 1910, had signed for Redruth. As he worked in Plymouth and lived in Saltash, his appearances would be sporadic and it was not long before he moved to Sussex and became the rugby correspondent for the *Sunday Times*.

There were some new names in the Redruth fixture list for the 1912/13 season. Early on, Redruth played St Day, the first time the two clubs had met since the village side had been formed in the 1890s. Not surprisingly, the Reds won comfortably, 31-5. Hayle, who were playing their first season as a senior club since being re-formed, gave the Reds an early fright by going 10-0 up in the first ten minutes. Cries of 'Wake up Reds!' sprang up in the crowd, an entreaty still heard at current matches. The supplications of the supporters were eventually heeded; Redruth got into their stride and won 39-10. Devon club Brixham made their first visit to the Recreation Ground in late September, but returned home empty-handed after a 46-5 defeat.

Willie Hichens told the September meeting of the CRFU committee that he had tried to heal the breach with Camborne by offering them fixtures, but had been met with a peremptory refusal. Hichens told the committee that Redruth needed to know whether Camborne would come around, as, if they did not, Redruth would look to play a big Welsh team on Boxing Day. At the same meeting, it was confirmed that Redruth would host the game between Cornwall and the touring South Africans on October 10. Six Redruth players, Frank Smith, Barrie Bennetts, Martin, Nick Rich, Howard Gray and Dick Jackett had been selected for Cornwall.

More than 8,000 spectators packed into the Redruth ground for the game. In the first half, Frank Smith kicked a Cornwall penalty and, when the two teams were level at 3-3 at half-time, they dared to hope for an upset. Unfortunately, injuries to Nick Tregurtha and Barrie Bennetts, who had to leave the field, saw the visitors take advantage and run in four more tries. It was 15-6 to the Boks at the close.

Two wins over Camborne School of Mines were the only reported games between Redruth and other Cornish clubs in the period running up to Christmas. The rift with Camborne, the continuing absence of Penzance from competitive rugby and suggestions in the local papers that Falmouth was no longer functioning, meant there were few opponents in Cornwall for the Reds to play at senior level.

Redruth entertained Newton on the Saturday before Christmas, winning 14-3. The normal Boxing Day fixture against Camborne had fallen victim to the ongoing dispute between the two clubs, so Redruth played host to United Services, winning 12-4 in the teeth of a howling gale and driving rain.

Two days later, they travelled to Hayle, where the match ended 3-3.

A one-point defeat away at Devonport started 1913, followed up by a shorter journey down to Newlyn, the fishing village just south of Penzance. Matches against Newlyn were normally reserve games for the Reds, but their improvement in performance, coupled with a lack of senior Cornish teams, had seen changes in the Redruth fixture list. Redruth won a tough encounter 12-0. They followed this up with what had now become a regular demolition of Camborne School of Mines. In the third encounter between the two sides, Redruth scored 25 points with no reply.

The impasse with Camborne continued. There were complaints in Camborne that the club had arranged no Easter matches and the hope was expressed that the disagreement would soon end. Redruth had arranged a Good Friday fixture with Penryn, with a return game the following week, and there was to be a second trip to Devon to face Newton. The *Western Morning News* complained that matches were so uncertain that the original fixture cards had become so much waste paper. Redruth were crowned Cornish champions again but, without Falmouth and Penzance and with no matches with Camborne, there was not a great deal of opposition. Only St Ives were showing any sort of form.

Finally, signs came of a thaw in relations with Camborne. A meeting of the CRFU on 13 May heard that Town were now willing to discuss playing Redruth again. It is almost certain that money, or a lack of it, was the driving force behind a peace deal. Both clubs had suffered financially by missing out on the income from the large crowds that attended their games.

Representatives from both clubs met at the Commercial Hotel in Camborne on 1 September and agreed to resume fixtures in the 1913/14 season. In a change from previous practice, it was agreed that the Feast Monday game at Camborne would continue, but that the Boxing Day match would alternate between the two grounds, with Easter Monday being added as a regular fixture to be played at Redruth. One other fixture would be added, so the clubs would benefit from a total of four games in the season.

The meeting also agreed that the referees and touch judges should be appointed by another county union and that the income from the four games would be pooled. The proposals were agreed at the Camborne AGM on Monday, 8 September and at a Redruth general committee meeting the following day.

The lack of competition in Cornwall worsened in October 1913 with the news that Penryn had announced it could no longer carry on. The Borough side had been restarted at least twice in the previous 30 years and the Penryn secretary told the press that a lack of fixtures in the previous season was to blame for a financial crisis. Meanwhile, Redruth had to be content with games against Lanner and visitors St Peters, before the first serious opposition of Devon Albion arrived at the Recreation Ground on 18 October. The lack of competitive rugby showed on both sides, but an estimated crowd of 5,000 watched Redruth win 5-0.

A similar-sized crowd flocked to Camborne for the resumption of the annual Feast Monday game. Camborne had more of the game territorially and the match became a tussle for forward domination, so Redruth were lucky to win the match 3-0 thanks to an unconverted try scored by Trethowan.

Camborne gained revenge when they visited Redruth two weeks later, winning 5-0. The game was as closely fought as the previous match, with the Camborne defence proving more than equal to a string of Redruth attacks. To underline the peace that had been agreed between the clubs, the Redruth committee entertained both sets of players to a dinner in the evening.

The patching up of the feud between Redruth and Camborne gave both clubs a boost, but there was still a shortage of top-flight opposition in Cornwall and matches against Devon clubs were ad hoc arrangements outside any formal structure. Willie Hichens was at a meeting in Exeter on 22 November 1913 where it was agreed that a Western League should be formed for the principal clubs in Cornwall, Devon, Somerset and Gloucestershire in order to improve the quality of rugby in the region. Hichens was elected president of the new body, which had received permission to set up the competition from the English Rugby Union.

A note in the Redruth committee minutes from December 1913 underlines the close watch the RFU kept on players receiving any kind of reward. Twickenham had written to the CRFU telling them to inform both Redruth and Camborne that the practice of using club funds to treat players to a summer outing must be stopped.

Redruth's visit to Camborne on Boxing Day was just as tough an encounter as the previous two games between the sides. Redruth led 3-0 at half-time thanks to a penalty kicked by Barney Solomon and, after the break, Will Rich crossed for a try, which Stapleton converted. Camborne scored one unconverted try in the second half, leaving Redruth 8-3 winners.

There were mixed results in early 1914; wins against St Ives and away to Torquay, but a 31-3 thrashing at the hands of Albion, away. Redruth's home game with Torquay on 21

March ended in a 3-5 defeat, but might have gone differently had Reginald Carah not stopped running when he was just yards from the line and certain to score. Someone in the crowd had blown a whistle and the player had pulled up, believing it had come from the referee. There are times when playing to the whistle is not such a good idea, particularly when it is not the whistle carried by the referee.

The Easter weekend brought three wins for the Reds. They overcame touring side Streatham on Good Friday, beat Albion Reserves on Easter Saturday and, far more importantly for the Redruth faithful, narrowly defeated visitors Camborne on Easter Monday. A drop goal from Martin in the final minutes of the game put them ahead 7-4. Luckily for the Reds, a drop goal was worth four points in 1914.

The 1913/14 season was a good one. Both the chiefs and the reserves topped their respective tables and only one team, Camborne, had beaten Redruth on their home ground. The senior side scored a record 508 points, with just 103 against, and won 23 of their 28 games. The reserves lost just five of their 24 games. The secretary announced that fixtures had been confirmed with all the leading Devon clubs for the 1914/15 season and that the club had a firm platform for further success in the coming campaign.

It was not to be. The United Kingdom declared war on Germany on 4 August 1914, just five days after Redruth's AGM. Three weeks later, the CRFU met to plan how to keep the game in Cornwall going. The popular belief at the time was that the war would all be over by Christmas, so those sitting around the table set out to plan a damage limitation exercise, hoping to get rugby through the following four months. The immediate problem was the dwindling number of players, as reservists were called up for service and other young men flocked to the colours.

The committee heard that 14 players from St Ives, eight from Hayle and three from Redruth had already signed up and that there was little chance of Camborne School of Mines getting a side together. It was decided that individual clubs should be left to arrange what games they could. By the beginning of September, it was clear that any attempt to hold matches was doomed to failure. On 15 September 1914 the Redruth committee took the decision that no further games would be played that season. In fact, it would be five long and bloody years before club rugby resumed.

Chapter Six

A Time of War and a Time of Slump 1914–1925

THE CHRISTMAS truce of 1914, in which men from the British Expeditionary Force on the Western Front played association football against their German counterparts, is a legendary episode in the early days of the Great War. It is less often reported that rugby, too, was played on the battlefield, although not, as far as we know, against the Germans.

One of Redruth's players, John Westcott (Jack) Solomon from Illogan wrote home in May 1915 to describe one match at the front between teams representing Devon and Cornwall. Before they could play, they had to fill in a 'Jack Johnson' hole, a large shell crater, and Solomon wrote that there was a chance that a few more would be made during the match, but fortunately the Germans left them alone: 'Perhaps they did not want to spoil our game.' He provided a full list of the players, including a fellow Redruth man named Bosanko, men from Bodmin, Newquay and Camborne among others, as well as the name of Sgt Phillips, who refereed. Camborne Rugby Club is believed to have sent out the ball.

Solomon said that the Devon men had won by two tries, but they hoped to have their own back the following week. In another letter, he wrote: 'There is nothing like a good game of football to brighten up the chaps' spirits. While the match is in progress you take no notice of the roar of the cannon, and think you are only out here for the game.' Jack Solomon, who was serving in the Royal Army Medical Corps, died from disease, on the Somme, just a year later. His brother, Richard, also played for Redruth.

In the early days of the conflict, rugby back at home continued sporadically. Occasional games were held to raise money for the war effort. The traditional match between Redruth and Camborne went ahead on Feast Monday 1914, with the proceeds from the gate being donated to the Patriotic Fund, set up to provide for dependants of soldiers who had been killed or injured in the service of their country. Both clubs fielded weakened sides, but £60 was raised on the gate.

Two weeks later, the Redruth committee met to discuss raising funds to maintain the club's ground during the conflict and to ensure that the club would be able to retain it after the war. It was agreed that the Recreation Ground committee, on which the club still had members, should be paid £25 as a year's rent. This was the last entry in the club minute book until 1919.

Later in the war, miners from East Pool played some matches at the Rec, mainly against service sides. These games, which carried on until late spring 1919, kept the game of rugby alive in the town and attracted large crowds to the ground. Redruth players, many of whom were in reserved occupations, also took part in scratch games between a Cornwall XV and sides made up of Australian and New Zealand troops who had remained in the country after the end of the war.

Dr Willie Hichens died in January 1915 at the age of just 50. He had become almost synonymous with the Redruth club and a towering figure in Cornish rugby as a whole. Hichens had learned his rugby while at Epsom College and had continued to be involved in the sport when returning to work as a doctor in Redruth, in partnership with his father and his brother, Frank. Hichens had served as Redruth's president between 1893 and 1903 and was the club's representative on the CRFU.

On occasion, he had been known to take the whistle at Redruth games, although some of his decisions had not been popular with opposition supporters. He had gone on to serve as president of the CRFU for 15 years, during which time his forthright remarks, often in support of his home club, had enlivened many a committee meeting. There was a large turnout for the funeral, including the staff of the West Cornwall Miners' Hospital, where he had worked, local mine captains and representatives of all the local sporting bodies, including Camborne Rugby Club.

Three months after the Armistice, in February 1919, Redruth players and members gathered once more and a decision was taken to resume playing the following September. Sydney Lanyon was re-elected as president and the role of secretary went to Hugh Downing, the son of the club's former secretary, Henry Downing. Henry, a former headmaster of Treleigh School, had died two years before. The committee agreed that posters should be put up around the town announcing the club was restarting. Subscriptions for vice-presidents were set at 15s (75p) and 7s/6d (37p) for members. In order to boost the club's depleted finances, the first three games of the season would be designated 'all pay'.

The side that reassembled for the first practice session on 2 September 1919, under the captainship of Tom Roscrow, had been severely weakened. Among those players who had died in service were Percy Lidgey and Leonard Trethowan, both killed in action in Flanders in 1918, as well as Jack Solomon. The total might have been higher but mining was a reserved occupation, as was farming, and men working in those industries were dissuaded from volunteering for the armed forces.

Away from the conflict, the club had also lost James Paull, a former winger, who had lost his arm following a mining accident at Tresavean. Nick Rich, a skilled fly-half, had died after an operation for appendicitis. In addition, a number of players who had been active in 1914 felt they were past their best. The East Pool miners, whose matches had provided entertainment at the Recreation Ground during the war, provided the nucleus of a new team, together with former players Bernard Smith, Sidney Thomas, Harry Ham, Willie Beard and Jack Richards.

Redruth's first game after a five-year break was on Saturday, 13 September 1919 against touring side Corinthians. They wore new shirts for the occasion, which bore letters, rather than numbers, to identify the players. This system would become common in Wales and was used by some English clubs, such as Bristol and Leicester, right up until the 1990s. The Reds defeated Corinthians 38-0.

A month later, they played a side from the Holman factory in Camborne. The Redruth Reserves were also in action that day, travelling to Newlyn where they lost 6-3. The fact that Redruth had two sides up and running within a few weeks of the season starting suggests that a number of younger players had been eager to come forward to play for the club. Plymouth Albion had a team ready to visit the Recreation Ground on 1 November, but Redruth were able to despatch them convincingly 17-0.

At the game, the Redruth Town Band organised a collection for the families of the 31 miners killed, and many more injured, in the Levant Mine disaster, which had happened at Pendeen in the far west of Cornwall ten days before. A man engine, a device of reciprocating ladders and platforms designed to raise men up the shaft, had collapsed. A large group of miners had been coming back up to the surface after finishing their work and, although some were able to step off the engine, many were carried back down the shaft with it. Miners from East Pool were among those who helped in the five-day operation to dig out the men.

The resumption of the Feast Monday game against Camborne on 10 November attracted more than 4,000 spectators, with Camborne winning 5-3. Redruth travelled to St Ives on the following Saturday, snatching a 6-3 win in what was described as a disappointing game.

Harry Ham and Tommy Harris were the only Redruth players selected for Cornwall's County Championship game against Somerset, played at Redruth on 29 November. The home side lost 8-3. Both players featured in Cornwall's final match against Gloucestershire, but any hopes of further progression in the championship ended with an 18-8 defeat at Kingsholm.

The economic situation in the mining area continued to worsen after the war and there was another exodus of players and potential recruits, like the one which had plagued the club at the turn of the century. Several promising men of this period, including Fred Pappin, a brilliant three-quarter, were forced to find work abroad. A handful of others, such as Tommy Harris, took the difficult decision to go north. Harris joined Rochdale Hornets, where he took part in the Challenge Cup Final of 1920 against Hull, still the only such final Rochdale has won. It was reported that he received a cheque for £300 to turn professional.

As Christmas approached, Redruth went down 3-0 at Hayle and then, on 27 December, were held to a 3-3 draw away to Falmouth. Both clubs had been in the doldrums prior to the war, but their performances indicated that the Reds would now face more challenging opposition from fellow Cornish clubs. In between was the traditional game against Camborne on Boxing Day, played in Redruth in floods of rain and gale force winds. The only score of the game was a penalty by the Redruth full-back, Frank Smith, giving the home side a 3-0 victory.

The 1920s began with a surprise 6-5 defeat away to Newlyn, with the opposition forwards dominating the game. Results continued to be mixed, with wins at Hayle and against a Holman side, plus an 11-8 win against a Royal Navy XV at Devonport. There was also a 3-0 defeat at Camborne and a disappointing loss at Falmouth. The Reds then came back with wins against a re-formed Penryn, Holman, Camborne School of Mines and United Services, Devonport.

Redruth faced Camborne on Easter Monday, 1920 in accordance with the agreement made before the war. More than 6,000 spectators were at the Recreation Ground and they enjoyed a hectic and full-blooded encounter which Redruth won

3-0. The attendance was a record for a local game in Cornwall, surpassed only by County Championship clashes and matches against international touring sides.

There was another red letter day at the Rec on 29 April when Bert Solomon ran out on to the pitch for the first time in a decade. Together with his brothers – Barney, William 'Jocky' and Jimmy 'Dickus' – he was part of what was dubbed an 'Old Crocks' side in a charity match against a Redruth XV. Bert, now in his mid-30s, had to be content with converting the only try scored by his side in the game. 'Jocky' was only around 23 at that point, with his best playing years ahead, but the prospect of having four Solomon brothers on the same side was clearly too good to resist.

The local economy was a cause for continuing concern, with no sign of a peace dividend in the local industries – in fact, the reverse. The war had raised the demand for Cornish ore, but now it was falling and Cornwall was facing increased competition from overseas mines, particularly in South America and Malaysia.

In 1920, the Dolcoath mine, the largest and deepest in Cornwall, ceased operating. The impact of its closure was starkly underlined at a meeting held in Camborne on 28 August. It was reported that 300 young men from the Camborne-Redruth area had gone abroad and it was believed a further 300 would shortly follow them. Devastating for an already impoverished area, this also amounted to the loss of a generation of potential players for the rugby clubs of the two towns.

In an effort to invigorate rugby in the duchy, and having obtained permission from the RFU, the Cornwall Rugby Football Union proposed setting up a new cup competition. It would be run on a league rather than a knockout basis, with a junior and senior table. Redruth had been expected to sign up as one of the senior clubs, but the committee, in contrast to its attitude in previous years, opposed a league system and refused to join. Weeks later, Camborne announced they were pulling out of the competition because of the loss of three of their best players. Without Cornwall's two strongest sides, the status of the competition was much weakened. Falmouth were champions of the senior section that season, but it had little meaning. The truncated league staggered on for the next couple of years before being abandoned.

It was against this background that Redruth opened their 1920/21 season with an away game against a revived Penzance side. The chiefs won comfortably by 19 points to nil. The reserves had been due to host their opposite numbers on the same day, but Penzance were unable to field a side. Instead, the second XV played North Country, a district side that had been set up by the former Redruth player, Willy Job.

Redruth beat United Services 26-6 on 25 September and this was followed up by a 17-0 home win over Hayle. The Reds almost pulled off a surprise win at Beacon Park against Plymouth Albion, only a last-minute try saving the home side from defeat. A hard-fought game away to St Ives ended in a draw.

Five Redruth players – Bernard Smith, Tom Ham, Fred Trevarthen, Tom Harris and Jack Richards – were selected for Cornwall's opening County Championship game with Somerset at Bridgwater on 6 November. This meant it was a much-weakened Redruth side that hosted Penzance on the same day, but the Reds still ran out comfortable winners, 32-3. Redruth Reserves made it a double on the day when they travelled west to beat Penzance Reserves 29-0. Redruth were, therefore, providing a third of the county side and still had enough strength in depth to beat Penzance handsomely and field a strong reserve side. Few other clubs in Cornwall could have done that at the time.

One club that could go toe-to-toe with Redruth was Camborne. The Feast Monday match there, a forward-dominated tussle, ended in a 3-3 draw. A few weeks later, the Boxing Day match was also held at Camborne for the first time following the agreement struck before the war. This time, the

Reds were no match for the speed of Camborne play and they lost 11-5 in front of 4,000 spectators.

The new year began with a 3-0 win over visitors Newton, the first Redruth victory over a Devon side that season, but there was a narrow 9-7 defeat on a windswept St Ives ground at the end of January. They bounced back for an 11-6 home victory over Plymouth Albion, which saw the Reds playing some of their best rugby in months.

The Easter weekend saw Redruth lose to Camborne School of Mines on Good Friday, but they defeated a touring side from Cardiff the following day. On Easter Monday, according to the agreement between the two clubs, they would host Camborne.

Earlier in the season, the Redruth committee had decided to give the unemployed free entry to games. It had reduced the amount of money taken at the gate, but made rugby accessible to people who needed every shilling to put food on the table. Redruth saw no reason for the Camborne game to be an exception; indeed, it was the most popular fixture of the season, so why not give the struggling local community a treat? However, the gate for games against Camborne was shared between the two clubs and it was feared that Town would refuse the concession.

The secretary was instructed to inform Camborne that if they insisted on charging, posters would be put around the town to tell the unemployed that the privilege of free entry had been overturned at the diktat of the Camborne committee. They would also have to pay half the cost of the extra police presence. Six officers were asked to police the game. There is no record of a Camborne response, but they turned up to play the game on a wet Easter Monday. Redruth won 3-0.

It is clear from the club minutes that extensive use of police officers was still common at Redruth home games. At one meeting, concern was raised that boys were sneaking into the ground through a side gate and the local police sergeant was asked to station a constable there. The practice of hiring police officers, and of paying them gratuities, was commonplace and payments are recorded in the club's accounts. It was also sometimes useful to have police officers available to escort from the ground those referees whose decisions had not found favour with the home crowd.

The record for the season showed that the first XV had won 24 of their 38 games, with six drawn and eight lost, only one of which was at home. The club ended the season with a small loss, due to heavy travelling expenses and to the policy towards unemployed spectators. This concession was estimated to have cost them £150 and it was dropped for the 1921/22 season in favour of half-price admission.

A decision was also taken that the full-back, sometimes referred to in newspaper reports as 'the custodian', would wear a white jersey. This may have been an echo of football's goalkeeping jerseys, which had been mandated to be a different colour from those of the rest of the team since 1909. Since the same rules applied to a rugby full-back as to every other player, it was soon realised that the change provided no benefits; indeed, it might help an attacking team avoid the last line of defence. The innovation only lasted for a single season.

Sidney Lanyon stood down as club president at the end of the 1920/21 season. He had served the club for more than 40 years, initially as one of Redruth's early players, then combining the roles of honorary treasurer and president between 1893 and 1914. He had balanced his roles with the rugby club with his ownership of the Redruth gasworks and his duties as a county councillor. Luke Smith, a former player, was elected as the new club president and Lanyon was made a life member. Sadly, his life membership was to be brief; club members were saddened to hear of his death less than a year later on 15 April 1922.

At the end of July, it was announced that Redruth and Camborne had agreed to cancel the previous agreement with regard to holiday fixtures and that the four games between the two sides would take place on Saturdays. It had also been agreed that the gates would no longer be shared. The decisions are not minuted and it is not clear why the agreement drawn up after the row between the two clubs in 1913 was discarded, but Redruth had already been making enquiries of Cardiff's Grangetown RFC about arranging a match for Easter Monday.

The season opened with a 6-0 win away to Newlyn before an 11-3 win at home over Hayle. A draw at home to Penryn maintained the unbeaten run for September, which the club continued into October by beating Devonport Services 9-0. The Redruth three-quarters had been the weaker part of the side in the previous season, but match reports suggested their performance had improved considerably. They carried this form into the away game at Hayle, played in unseasonal sunshine. The Reds came home with a 7-3 win.

The relationship with Camborne was about to be tested again. The previous season had seen the introduction of a programme which was on sale on matchdays. The Redruth club relied on a local printer to produce the programmes and gave him carte blanche to provide the content. Some of the proceeds went to the local hospital and the Redruth committee thought they were being charitable by selling the programmes at the ground.

In the edition produced for the home game against Newton on 22 October, someone writing under the pseudonym 'Old Crock' criticised the behaviour of some of the Camborne players in the previous week's game. Camborne officials made a formal complaint at an emergency meeting of the CRFU. The Redruth representative apologised and had to confess, not without some embarrassment, that the club did not vet its own programme.

This was not enough to satisfy the Camborne representative at the next monthly meeting of the full CRFU committee. Redruth was accused of allowing scathing remarks about Town players to be published, having a detrimental effect on the Camborne club. The representative from Penryn then weighed in to say such remarks had been made about his club in a previous Redruth programme. After much discussion, the Camborne representative agreed to accept the explanation given by Redruth, who promised to check all future programme material before it was published.

The row does not appear to have soured relations on the field, because Redruth's away game with Camborne, which ended in a 6-6 draw, was described as a sporting game and one of the best between the two clubs for a long time. More sporting spirit was reported when Redruth beat Penzance 21-0 at the Recreation Ground. Redruth approached Christmas with wins over Camborne School of Mines and a 22-7 Christmas Eve win over visitors Teignmouth. Boxing Day saw a 38-0 home victory over Plymouth CYMS.

The continuing shortage of senior rugby sides in Cornwall was highlighted by the Redruth fixture list for the second half of the 1921/22 season. A 5-0 home win over Falmouth was the first of four games which would be played between these two sides before Easter. There were two further matches against Camborne to add to the two already played, as well as encounters with Camborne School of Mines, Hayle, St Ives, Penryn and Newlyn.

With just eight clubs in regular competition, all of them west of Truro, concern was expressed at the January meeting of the CRFU over the standard of play in Cornish rugby. This was impacting their ability to raise a competitive County Championship side for what was, then, the most important domestic competition in England.

The degree to which rugby in Cornwall had fallen behind the rest of the country was underlined when Bristol made their first-ever visit to Redruth on 23 January 1922. Bristol were reckoned to be one of the top five sides in England and it showed in their performance. The two packs were fairly evenly matched, but Redruth had no answer to the speed and skill of the Bristol backs and fell to an 18-8 defeat. Redruth's first-ever visit to Teignmouth in March also ended in defeat, 6-0, but they did salvage some pride at the end of the month, beating visitors Plymouth Albion 10-6.

At the AGM in July 1922, it was reported that Redruth had played 38 games in the season, winning 23 and drawing five. The reserve side had won 17 of their 28 games, drawing four. A number of new fixtures had been added, including matches against Pontypool, Bristol University and London University. While the club had made a profit, concern was expressed that the offer of reduced admission to those who were unemployed was being abused. If it continued, the club would be forced to withdraw the concession.

Redruth launched the 1922/23 season with a 26-3 home win over Hayle and a narrow 6-5 victory down at Penzance. The match against Camborne on 7 October was disappointing. Although Redruth won 4-3, the Redruth backs hardly handled the ball and were never given the chance to cut loose and play entertaining rugby. Thirty years after John Longdon's efforts to encourage the running game at Redruth, and half that since the glory days of Bert Solomon's balletic runs, it would seem that the game was reverting to the old-fashioned forward tussles of the past.

Redruth's short unbeaten run ended on 30 October when 4,000 spectators watched them go down 16-10 to visitors Pontypool. Ironically, the man who did more than most to secure the win for the Welsh side was a Plymouth Albion half-back named Uren, who had been picked up by Pontypool on the way down to fill a gap in the the team.

Three weeks later, the reputation of rugby in the South West of England took a bashing as a result of an incident during a Redruth away game at Falmouth. The game had been unremarkable for most of the match, although it had been fiercely fought. Then, 15 minutes before full time, the referee blew his whistle, just as two Redruth players were trying to relieve a Falmouth forward of the ball. The official, a Mr Jackson from Camborne, decided the match was not being played in a sporting spirit and ordered both sides off the pitch.

Neither team was clear why the match had been halted, but news of the debacle appeared in papers as far away as Northumberland. The *Shields Daily News* felt the status of the game was being lowered by the conduct of certain teams in the West of England. The *Westminster Gazette* lauded Mr Jackson as a hero, a view that was probably not shared by either players or supporters at the game. The return match at Redruth was eagerly anticipated, but ended disappointingly in a scoreless draw. The only excitement was the sending-off of a Falmouth player near the end of the game for kicking an opponent.

The underlying bad feeling between Redruth and Falmouth had reached a new low and the Redruth committee announced that they were cancelling the remaining two games of the season between the sides. Camborne had already announced they had cancelled their fixtures with Falmouth. *The Cornubian* newspaper said the decision appeared to show there was an unsportsmanlike element prevailing in the Falmouth team, going on to say that Redruth, in contrast, had always been noted for its fair play.

Inevitably, the matter was brought up at the next meeting of the CRFU. The Redruth captain, Harry Ham, told the committee that the game had been 'a bit hot' and that he had needed to speak to the Falmouth captain about the behaviour of some of the opposition forwards. The committee decided to censure both clubs for the behaviour of their packs. Falmouth then raised a complaint about Redruth's decision to cancel their remaining fixtures, but the committee decided it had no power to intervene. Redruth's representative, the former county back Frank Smith, told the meeting that he thought that Camborne and Redruth were an example to the county at this particular time. If there was a response to this it was not recorded.

Redruth reached the halfway point of the season having lost just four of the 21 games they had played. The Boxing Day game was against a team representing Devon Public Schools, which failed to draw the sort of crowds that might have been expected if Camborne had been the visitors. On 30 December, Redruth played host to Exeter, a club with a reputation for having one of the finest packs in Devon. Heavy rain affected the size of the crowd, but those present saw Redruth win 6-3 on very soft ground.

There was a distinct falling off in performance during the second half of the season, partly due to players leaving the club. The shortage of first-choice players was exacerbated in the final weeks of the season by a series of injuries which saw several reserve players drafted into the chiefs. When the results for the 1922/23 season were tallied up, they were disappointing. Of the 41 matches played, only 24 had been won and five drawn. Equally worrying, the club was about £112 in debt.

During the immediate post-war period, the club had struggled to achieve the level of success it had enjoyed previously and the problem of recruiting and retaining talent was one which the club decided it had to address. It reached an agreement with junior clubs Redruth Highway and North Country that the Reds would have first choice of any promising players that emerged, in return for financial support. Two members from the junior clubs would also sit on the Redruth general committee and the clubs would be allowed to take turns to play at the Recreation Ground – if the field was not otherwise required. This was a very early example of the feeder system which is common in modern day rugby and appears to have been the first such formal agreement set up in Cornwall.

The club was also struggling to arrange games with sides from outside the rugby bubble of West Cornwall, seen as essential if the standard of the game was to improve. The secretary, Hugh Downing, apologised for what he described as the meagre fixture list, compared with Camborne's. He explained that if Devon clubs wanted to play a Cornish side, they tended to approach Camborne, which was now seen as the foremost club in the duchy. He told the Redruth committee that he had written to every big first-class team in England and Wales, but it was becoming difficult to persuade them to agree to matches. Downing suggested that he might have to try to fill the diary two seasons in advance and joked that, if the situation did not improve, he would be arranging fixtures for their children.

While geography played a part, there was also the issue of money. It was customary for clubs from up country to ask for a guarantee of a minimum payment from the gate to cover their expenses, which reduced the income for the club. Redruth minutes suggest that the average payment was around £20, although, on some occasions, it was double that. A match against Bristol in January 1922 was arranged for a guarantee of £60, but in another case a Cardiff team was told that Redruth could not offer more than £25 because of unemployment in the area.

One other factor hampering the growth of the game was the continuing popularity of association football in Cornwall. This was partly due to most elementary schools only playing association, believing the more physical nature of the rugby code unsuitable for youngsters. Trewirgie School in Redruth was one of the rare exceptions. There was also a suggestion that parents found rugby more expensive, as jerseys were much more likely to be torn than in the round ball game.

Some progress was made in persuading elementary schools in the area to adopt the rugby code at a meeting held in October 1924. Teachers from five schools in the Redruth area – Trewirgie, Treleigh, Lanner, Illogan and Carnkie – declared that they were willing to play the game, but said they might have difficulty in finding grounds and the money to pay for jerseys. The CRFU indicated it would give consideration to requests for financial assistance for jerseys and equipment, and hope was expressed that the clubs might be able to help with grounds. It would not be until the beginning of the school year in autumn 1925 that elementary schools began to teach rugby on a regular basis.

In that summer of 1923, it cannot have escaped the attention of many at the Redruth rugby club that they were just two years away from marking their 50th anniversary and, without an injection of talent and capital, it was beginning to look as if there would be little to celebrate. The sense that the club was losing its way had been made worse by the death in May of the Redruth president, Luke Smith.

Luke had been born in Lancashire, but his family had moved to Redruth by the time he was nine. His father eventually employed more than 200 people in what had become a large and successful shoe and boot-making business. Luke had begun playing for Redruth within six years of its foundation and gained his county cap in the first-ever Cornwall side in 1883. He had later joined the Redruth committee, before being elected club president in 1920.

Smith had been elected a life member of the CRFU committee in January 1923, just a few months before his death at the age of 61. Luke's sons, Frank and Bernard, also became noted players with Redruth and Frank became the club's representative at the CRFU. No fewer than 27 officials, members and players from the Redruth club joined dozens of other mourners at the funeral at St Euny Church.

The disappointments of the previous season were discussed by the Redruth Rugby Supporters' Club at its meeting in September. This was a completely separate organisation from the rugby club and ran social events to raise money to support the playing side and other local charities. In the early 1920s, it was hoping to raise funds for changing rooms at the club, but this was looking like a distant dream. Members also helped out on the gate on matchdays and ran sweepstakes.

The supporters' club had donated generously to the Redruth rugby club before and, in July, the rugby club secretary had written to them with a rough balance sheet to ask if they could render further financial help. However, social events had been poorly attended and many members were aggrieved that the playing side largely ignored them. There were serious discussions about winding up the supporters' club but, after much wrangling, they decided to continue, thanks in large part to the rugby club secretary, Henry Downing, who did his best to soothe the disgruntled supporters.

The 1923/24 season began with Captain Leslie Carkeek as president. It might be helpful to point out that anyone with the title 'captain' in West Cornwall was, like Carkeek, more likely to be a mine manager than a member of the armed forces. The season started with a clear focus on improving the balance sheet and it was decided that, henceforth, the unemployed would have to pay full price to enter the ground, although young players who attended practice would be allowed to buy season tickets at half price. A discount was negotiated with the Coffee Tavern for team teas and changing facilities, and the club also decided that it would take charge of producing and selling the match programme itself.

Results in the first half of the season were mixed. On a number of occasions, the chiefs had to draw on the reserves to make up the numbers and the back division often turned out with very young players who lacked match experience. The fixture list was made up of the traditional mix of Cornish clubs and those from across the River Tamar, and the club had managed to encourage the leading Welsh side Llanelli down for a game in March, which promised a large crowd but was a heavy drain on the club's bank account.

A former Redruth player, Albert Gregor, was killed in an explosion at South Crofty mine on 2 November 1923. Gregor had been an outstanding winger and had been capped twice for Cornwall in 1921. He had recently transferred from Redruth to Camborne Rugby Club. An inquest heard that he had been working 225 fathoms down in Robinson's shaft, where he had been charging a newly drilled hole with dynamite, which had then exploded. The deputy coroner, Barrie Bennetts, a former Redruth player, delivered a verdict of accidental death.

In January 1924, there was news from the United States that Harry Phillips had died, one of the outstanding Redruth players of the 1890s. Described as one of the most reliable three-quarters the club had ever possessed, he was part of a side which had dominated Cornish rugby in the last decade of the 19th century. A powerfully built man, he was renowned as a fierce tackler and had formed a strong combination with Jack Viant in the Redruth side. He had been capped seven times for Cornwall between 1888 and 1892. Like many Cornishmen, he had emigrated in search of work, leaving his home at Plain-an-Gwarry for the so-called 'Copper Country' in Michigan, where he had lived among a sizeable community of Cornish exiles.

Games between Redruth and Camborne had been relatively incident-free over the previous two seasons, thanks in part to the use of seasoned referees from Devon. In February 1924, hostilities resumed in earnest when Camborne came to Redruth seemingly intent on confrontation. One incident saw Roy Jennings, one of Redruth's rising stars, kicked in the stomach by a Camborne player after he had taken a free kick. Three other Redruth players were incapacitated in separate incidents over which the referee failed to act. Camborne won the contest 10-8.

There was a general air of gloom at the Redruth AGM in July 1924. It had been one of the worst seasons in memory for the chiefs; they had won just 23 games out of 42 and lost all but one of the others. To make matters worse, for the first time ever, Camborne had won all four of the games they had played against Redruth. The only chink of light was that the reserves had done better, winning 19 of their 27 games.

The club had recovered a little financially, but was still £60 in debt to the bank. Gate money remained poor and they were now subsidising the junior clubs at North Country and Redruth Highway. Guarantees paid to secure the visits of up-country sides were a significant cost and the treasurer questioned whether it was worth continuing this practice, as the gates often failed to match the money that was paid out. The club had managed to sell 8,500 programmes, but their publishing was at that point being run as a separate enterprise.

The summer provided a diversion from all the despondency when the Redruth Rugby Club hosted the inaugural Cornwall Wrestling Association tournament at the Recreation Ground on 7 June. The sport was being revived in the county after a break of some 30 years. The great and good of Cornwall attended, Sir Edward Nicholl presented two dazzling gold belts and the rugby club committee officiated.

Cornish wrestling is as far removed from the theatrical pantomime of WWE as it is possible to get. Two combatants, wearing canvas jackets, stand face-to-face and attempt to throw each other on to the ground on their backs. The former Redruth star Bert Solomon, still only 40, was among those from across Cornwall taking part in that first contest, but probably the most famous champion of that era was Francis Gregory.

Gregory played rugby for Redruth before going north, where he played for Wigan and Warrington and won an England rugby league cap. He won the Cornish Wrestling Championship no fewer than nine times between 1928 and 1936. He later changed his name to Francis St Clair Gregory and fought Mike Marino in the first televised professional wrestling match shown on British television on 9 November 1955. His two sons, Roy and Tony St Clair, also became well known as television wrestlers, often fighting as a tag team.

The journey north was still an uncommon choice for Redruth players, but emigration in search of work continued to impact the club and a number of older players also decided to retire at the end of the 1923/24 season, putting further pressure on the selectors. At the first general meeting of the following season, in August 1924, the committee rejected an ill-timed attempt to prohibit anyone from playing for Redruth unless they lived in the town. The chairman, Captain

Carkeek, felt that encouraging players from other clubs was bringing professionalism into the sport. Frank Smith pointed out, with some justification, that compelling players to turn out for one particular club would probably finish rugby altogether and eventually the selection committee was given discretion to select players from among those who turned up for practice.

We can imagine that many members must have walked home that night wondering if their club was going to survive. As it turned out, the 1923/24 season was to be the club's lowest ebb. Redruth's 50th anniversary in 1925 would be a curtain-raiser to a 14-year period when the Reds would return to form and dominate Cornish rugby in a way no other club had done before. A string of new stars including Roy Jennings, Harold Curnow, Les Semmens and Wilfred Johns would follow in the footsteps of previous legends like Francis Woolf, John Everett, Harry Phillips and Bert Solomon.

The Redruth fixture list for the 1924/25 season contained a total of 41 games, 17 of them against sides from outside Cornwall. This was normal for the period between the wars; the chiefs would usually play more than 40 matches in a season, significantly more than in the modern era. It is remarkable that the amateur sides of the 1920s could commit themselves to this gruelling regime, especially considering the difficulties of travelling and the long, hard hours worked by some of the players. The Easter weekend often had three games scheduled in the space of four days and there would be a similarly busy period between Christmas and New Year.

Early practice sessions in the late summer of 1924 were well attended and the players were looking forward to the first game of the season against visitors Exeter. There was great enthusiasm among the younger players wanting to make their mark, some of them having been drafted in from the previous season's reserve side. Although Redruth were unable to throw off their old habit of failing to open out from the scrum, they were able to put in a solid performance against a strong Exeter side and won a close match 6-5, with tries from Jennings and Solomon.

The following week, Redruth Midgets, a club that had been in existence for some years, appeared at the Recreation Ground branded as Redruth Third XV in a game against North Country.

James Tregellas and John Tredinnick had brought the side together, while the veteran full-back Harry Ham had been involved in coaching sessions. Some expressed the hope that perhaps Maffer Davey and Bert Solomon, both still living in Redruth, might be persuaded to take up coaching duties and offer some inspiration to the young players. Unfortunately, it seems that neither gentleman responded to the offer.

Harry Ham, Roy Jennings and Jack Richards were all selected in the Probables side to face the Possibles in a trial match to determine the Cornwall side to meet the visiting All Blacks on 18 September. William 'Jocky' Solomon was picked for the Possibles. Ham, Jennings and Richards all made the final team to face New Zealand at Camborne, with Richards as captain. There were seven Camborne players in the side, showing just how much the club was in the ascendancy.

Any thoughts that Cornwall might be able to pull off a surprise against the visitors were swiftly blown away as the All Blacks romped home 25-0. The only slight consolation was that it was an improvement on the 1905 match. Only Roy Jennings and Jack Richards featured in any of the season's Cornwall County Championship sides and the last game of the group, played in a rainstorm at Redruth, saw Gloucestershire run out winners and leave Cornwall with the wooden spoon.

Early wins over Exeter, Hayle, St Ives and Penryn gave the Reds a good start to the 1924/25 season. The match against Penryn had to be suspended for a time after a Redruth try was disallowed and the spectators expressed their disappointment in the traditional manner by invading the pitch.

Meanwhile, news had come through that the former Redruth player, Tommy Harris, who had gone north in 1920 to join Rochdale Hornets, had won his first England rugby league cap. Redruth supporters showed a great deal of pride in his achievement, in contrast to the attitude of many of the game's officials, who refused even to acknowledge that the 13-a-side game existed.

Despite Redruth putting in improved performances compared with the previous year, victory over arch-rivals Camborne eluded them. They arrived at Camborne on 27 November with a much-weakened team and the game turned into the sort of brawl that had been common between the two sides in the past. An early tussle between Camborne's Parnell and Redruth's 'Jocky' Solomon saw both players being spoken to by the referee. In another incident, Parnell and his team-mate, Biddick, narrowly avoided being sent off. The Reds played the second half with 14 men and, although they turned in a far better performance than in recent matches between the two sides, they still lost 7-0.

A surprise announcement the week before Christmas revealed that the Boxing Day clash between Redruth and Camborne would be reinstated after a gap of three years. This was to be in addition to the normal four games between the two sides and it was to continue into the future, when it would alternate between the two grounds. There was also a proposal that the Feast Monday match be reinstated. It was clear that both clubs had suffered from losing the money these two holiday games brought in. The 1924 Boxing Day game took place at Camborne, with the home side winning 9-3.

One of the other notable games of that season was on 12 March, when Redruth hosted Plymouth Albion. The players suffered a tough 80 minutes in a physical game which resulted in injuries to a number of Redruth players. Plymouth's reputation as a first-class side in Devon was not on display that afternoon and Redruth were unlucky not to win. The match ended in a 3-3 draw. However, bad feelings do not seem to have lingered after the game, the Redruth players being the first to contribute to a new fundraising initiative which would eventually allow Albion to purchase their ground at Beacon Park.

There was jubilation at Redruth on 4 April when the home side finally defeated Camborne, 11-10, Redruth's first victory over their rivals in almost two years. The game seems to have been played in good spirit, with no reports of the rough play that had blighted previous matches. The Redruth players wore black armbands and the flag at the club was flown at half mast in memory of Alfred Ham, a former Redruth player who had died of pneumonia at the age of 37.

After the disappointments of the previous season, there was a mood of optimism at the Redruth AGM in July 1925. The chiefs had still only won 22 of the 41 games they played, fewer victories than in either of the two previous poor seasons. But they had drawn five and had won ten of their final 12 matches of the season. The reserves had won 17 of their 28 matches and drawn five.

Captain Carkeek pointed out that the club would be celebrating its 50th anniversary during the coming season and hoped that prestigious sides from up-country could be persuaded to travel to Redruth to help celebrate the occasion. Redruth's playing side had not only been boosted by youngsters coming through from the reserves and local junior sides, but Fred Pappin had returned from America and rejoined the side at full-back.

In January 1926, Redruth issued a souvenir booklet to mark 50 years of the club's existence. As well as an account of the club's foundation, written by Henry Grylls, there was also a summary of the 1890–1914 period, provided by John Prater, a committee member. The final section, covering 1919 to 1925, was written by Jack Richards, a former club captain and later Redruth club president, who ended on a positive note:

> 'Since the war, Redruth have always been able to field a
> good pack of forwards, but the backs have not been up
> to the same standard and it has been an uphill struggle

to endeavour to provide open and attractive football. However, it looks as if the efforts of the club in this direction are to be rewarded as today we have certainly an exceedingly good back division which always does its best to provide good entertainment with bright bits of clever rugby.'[45]

This detailed history, written not by historians but by men who were deeply involved in the founding and running of the club, is probably unique in Cornish rugby.

The booklet, perhaps unsurprisingly, concentrated on players, and an unknown correspondent in the *Cornish Post and Mining News* felt that the role of the club's officials had been ignored. He singled out the long-serving treasurer, Sydney Howard Lanyon, claiming, with some justification, that he had carried the club on his back for a number of years. He also paid tribute to Dr Willie Hichens, saying that he had toiled and planned and worked for the club for much of his adult life.

The writer went on to say that the labours of these two men, along with others, had placed the club in a secure financial position for the future. There is no doubt that the calibre of the club's officials played a vital part in providing the platform for the successes about to come. As the club celebrated 50 years of existence, it was poised on the edge of a golden era.

Chapter Seven

The Roy Jennings Era 1926–1939

ON 11 March 1926, the Redruth first XV ran out on to the Recreation Ground in front of a large crowd for a match to commemorate their golden jubilee season. They faced a strong Cornwall XV selected by the CRFU president, Dr Lawry. The Reds, under the captaincy of Roy Jennings, won a keenly contested match 15-3. The jubilee game was followed by a dinner at Temperance Hall to which the teams, CRFU officials and representatives of each senior club in Cornwall were invited. Redruth were keen that their landmark year should be recognised and celebrated as the achievement it undoubtedly was.

The first half of Redruth's 50th season was somewhat indifferent, but fortunes picked up after the Christmas break. A 13-6 win over Camborne gave players and supporters a boost, although the match was plagued by a series of on-field confrontations and one of the Camborne players was sent off. During the rest of January and February, there were wins over Hayle, St Ives, Newlyn and Penzance. The 17-6 victory over Penzance came in large part from the boot of Roy Jennings, who had added two penalties and a conversion to the scoresheet, and it was clear his kicking skills were gaining attention.

Jennings was elected captain by his team-mates at the start of the 1925/26 season, just days after turning 20. He had already been capped for Cornwall and was seen as one of the brightest hopes of the new generation. Born Milroy Jennings in Redruth on 17 August 1905, the son of a saddler, he had initially gone to East End School. Later he had attended Taunton School, an independent non-conformist boarding school, where he had been given the opportunity to play rugby and cricket in a highly competitive environment. When home from school, he had played a few games with the Redruth Reserves in early 1923 at the age of just 17. It had not been long before he was promoted to the chiefs, initially playing as a wing forward, then later at centre three-quarter.

He had already won seven caps for Cornwall when, in spring 1926, he was appointed captain of the county side to face the French club Stade Francais at Camborne on 18 March. There were seven Camborne players in the side and only Jennings, Hollow and Harry Ham from Redruth and there was some muttering in the 6,000-strong crowd that the team should have been captained by a Town man. Stade had beaten Devon the previous day, but had been forced to make nine changes to the team and Cornwall won comfortably, 23-8. Jennings missed two conversions, but scored a third.

Fortunately, the match finished peacefully, despite the clear animosity in the crowd towards Jennings. Five days earlier, he had been knocked out by a Camborne player in the first half of a game between the two clubs at Camborne. The standard of play had deteriorated and the Devon referee had sent off Camborne's Warren and Redruth's Richard Triniman after a number of clashes. A fight had later broken out between Williams of Redruth and Wakeham of Camborne, but the referee had only sent off the Camborne player. Things had become so heated that the referee had blown up ten minutes from time. The Redruth committee called an emergency meeting the following Monday and decided, unanimously, to cancel the following season's fixtures with Camborne, saying it was in the interests of rugby. They had also voted to ban indefinitely one of the Camborne vice-presidents, a Mr E.G. Vine, from the Redruth ground for hurling abuse at Jennings.

A meeting of the CRFU a month later decided to suspend Triniman, Wakeham and Warren for two months, while Mr

Vine was banned from all matches in Cornwall for 12 months. Camborne were also ordered to post notices on their ground warning spectators of the consequences of bad behaviour. The Redruth secretary, Hugh Downing, wrote to the Cornwall committee saying that the trouble had been caused because the Camborne players and spectators had resented Roy Jennings being picked to captain Cornwall. He said that, after the game, Jennings had been barracked by the Camborne crowd and it had been necessary for Mr Cock, the Camborne secretary, and a police officer to escort him from the ground.

There was more discussion about relations with Camborne at Redruth's annual meeting in July. The accounts showed that the club had ended the season with a small credit balance of £1 10s, but concern was expressed that the loss of fixtures with Camborne could have a serious financial impact. There was also another lively discussion about Redruth's tradition of playing matches on Good Friday. The club president, Captain Carkeek, was opposed to the practice on the basis that it was 'a day of sorrow', but others were keen to point out that it provided the best gate of the season, outside of the Camborne games. In the end, the matter was not put to a vote.

The meeting was told that the 1925/26 season had been a slightly improved one; the club had finished with fine wins over Exeter and Plymouth Albion, and had won 22 out of 38 games played, losing 14. The reserves had racked up 21 wins from 26 matches, the best result for many seasons.

Redruth's young players were beginning to mature and this showed in improved results in the first half of the 1926/27 season, which included the first-ever game against Exmouth and a Boxing Day fixture with Swansea University. The club committee, concerned at the failure to attract more lucrative county games, decided to improve spectator facilities by building banking around the pitch. This was constructed using the overburden from the council-owned quarry at the North Street corner of the Recreation Ground.

The committee also decided that, given the concerns about loss of income from games against Camborne, it might be advisable to see if peace could be negotiated with their old rivals. However, a letter to the Camborne committee requesting the renewal of fixtures in the 1927/28 season was read and ignored. At the January meeting of the CRFU committee, the Camborne representative, a Mr Couch, stated bluntly that there would be no hope of the two clubs playing each other for at least the next 12 months.

The efforts to have rugby played in schools finally began to pay dividends. A Cornwall schoolboys' side, featuring four players from Trewirgie School, beat Devon 17-0 at the end of January. Two of them, Fred Bone and Gordon Robins, were the only Cornish boys selected for an international trial for England. Bone was picked for the England game against Wales on 19 March.

Both boys would go on to play for Redruth. Bone was a skilful scrum-half who gained caps for Cornwall before going north to join Halifax. Robins, considered by many to be one of the best flankers of his generation, played for the club for many seasons. Other former schoolboys who played a part in Redruth's success during this period included Frank Roberts, Jack Hick and Douglas Roberts. The latter, a pupil at Trewirgie School, won his England Schoolboys cap in a game against Wales at Cardiff in 1932.

A packed Easter weekend saw Redruth host Old Dunstonians on Good Friday and Falmouth the following day. After a break on Easter Sunday, there was a bank holiday game against Midlands club Blackwell and a match the day after when Old Pauline were the visitors. Redruth won all four matches.

It rounded off the club's most successful season for many years. The first XV had won 30 of their 40 matches, the first time they had achieved this total of wins in one season, while the reserve side had won 24 of their 29 games. To mark the success, the Redruth Supporters' Club put on a dinner at the British Legion for both the chiefs and reserve team.

During the numerous toasts, it was reported that, with the work on the banking at the Recreation Ground complete and the provision of a 700-seater grandstand, the club could now offer facilities that would undoubtedly make it the stadium of the county. In a spirit of goodwill, a representative from Camborne, W.H. Jackson, announced that his club had decided to seek a renewal of fixtures with Redruth.

However, it appeared that Mr Jackson was not speaking with the authority of the Camborne committee. At the Redruth AGM in July, the president announced that Redruth had contacted Camborne in light of the remarks but no reply had been received. He also made reference to letters in the local press making negative comments about the Redruth club. It seemed that the rift was still wide open and this, according to Captain Carkeek, had seriously affected Redruth's finances; the club had a debit balance of more than £44. It was a sour note on which to end what had been a successful season on the field.

The secretary, Hugh Downing, announced he had had some success with arranging fixtures after Redruth had defeated all but one of the Devon sides that had visited the town. Sides representing St Mary's and St Bartholomew's hospitals would be coming to Redruth in the new season. The fixture with St Mary's would become a regular part of the club's Easter programme for several decades.

The improvements at the Recreation Ground were not confined to spectator accommodation. In September 1927, the club announced that new dressing rooms and baths had been added at a cost of £50, paid for by a private subscription. Prior to this, players had changed elsewhere, at Tabbs Hotel or the Coffee Tavern, and walked down to the ground for the match.

On 17 September, Roy Jennings was the only Redruth player in a Devon and Cornwall XV which played the New South Wales Waratahs at the Rectory in Devonport. The

Australian team completely outclassed the peninsula side and won 30-3. The following month, Jennings was selected for the first of the season's County Championship matches, which would be against Somerset in October. Three other Redruth players were named in the side – Joseph Hollow, Len Roberts and Jack Andrew. The match was held at Redruth, with the new facilities perhaps helping to persuade the Cornwall Union to award them the game. The CRFU had been sent photographs of the improvements to assist with their decision-making.

The club's performance on the field went from strength to strength in the first half of the 1927/28 season. A 6-0 away win on a snowy Paignton ground on the last day of the year meant Redruth had won 15 out of 17 games. They had scored 216 points while conceding only 33. It was the best performance by the club since the war. Their only defeat had been at St Ives, early in the season, when Redruth had travelled with a much-weakened team. The only other Cornish side which had proved a match for the Reds was Penryn, where an away game had ended in a draw. The Reds kept their momentum going into early 1928, although the programme was disrupted by torrential rain which hit West Cornwall throughout January.

Cornwall won the South Western division of the County Championship for the first time since 1914, having beaten Devon and drawn with Gloucestershire. Roy Jennings, Joseph Hollow, Jack Andrew, Len Roberts and Edgar Brooker were all in the Cornwall side that travelled to Richmond to meet Middlesex in the semi-final in early February. Against all predictions, Cornwall won 5-3 and the difference was a conversion kicked by Jennings. This was the largest contingent of Redruth players in a Cornwall side for many years and equalled the numbers from Camborne. Sadly, an injury sustained during the match by Jack Andrew kept him out of the game for several weeks.

Meanwhile, back in the duchy, it was announced that peace had finally broken out between Redruth and Camborne. It was a mark of the importance of this occasion that what was described as a reconciliation dinner was held at the East Pool Count House. It was attended not just by players and officials from the two clubs but also by the president of the Cornwall Rugby Football Union, Dr R.C. Lawry, who proceeded to pour oil on troubled waters. He told those present that he felt the improving standard of rugby in Cornwall was due, in the main, to the efforts of Redruth and Camborne.

Jack Richards, the Redruth captain, won the toss to decide who would host the first match between the two sides for more than two years, which would be played on 28 April. It was also announced that the traditional Boxing Day game would be reinstated in the 1928/29 season, in addition to three other fixtures between the two clubs.

There was disappointment for the Cornwall contingent who made the long journey north to Bradford for the County Championship final against Yorkshire in March. The game was played in abysmal conditions and Cornwall's chances were undermined when Roy Jennings was injured early in the game. Although he remained on the field, he limped badly throughout the rest of the match and Cornwall lost 12-8. It would be the last time Cornwall reached the final for another three decades.

The arrival of teams from South Wales was usually highly anticipated at Redruth and, in March, the local papers were expecting a display of fine rugby from a Glamorgan Police side featuring eight Welsh internationals. Unfortunately, the match made headlines of a different kind.

The Glamorgan police had something of an unsavoury reputation in Cornwall following their actions against striking china clay workers in the St Austell area in 1913. A detachment from the force, brought in to break the strike, had baton-charged workers, brutally beating anyone who got in the way. The events would have been closely followed by the mining community in Redruth and they would certainly have known of the reputation of the Glamorgan police, even 15 years later.

According to newspaper reports, trouble between the players started almost from the beginning of the game. One local paper was of the opinion that the police had arrived determined to give Redruth a rough time and papers across the country reported that blows had been exchanged. The Redruth captain, Jack Phillips, was advised by his committee to take the team off the field five minutes from time to avoid further violence. Redruth were 5-3 up when the game stopped. The *Western Mail*, which describes itself as the national paper of Wales, reported that matters between the players had remained civil and the problems were all due to the crowd throwing stones at the Glamorgan players.

There is certainly agreement that when the police players emerged from the changing rooms after the match, a large and somewhat hostile crowd was waiting for them. A window of the police bus was broken, but no other damage was caused. The referee's report was considered by the CRFU committee meeting, with William Rich, the Redruth representative, stating that any bad behaviour in the crowd was caused by the conduct of the visiting players. The committee decided to take no action.

The full season was officially over when more than 6,000 people turned up in bright sunshine at the Recreation Ground to see the long-awaited renewal of competition between Redruth and Camborne. A Welsh international referee was brought down to take charge of the game and the ball was kicked off by Dr Lawry, the CRFU president. Those expecting a high-scoring game were to be disappointed. Both sides were evenly matched, but Camborne missed a last-minute penalty and it was Redruth who took the honours 6-3.

Unsurprisingly, the mood at the Redruth AGM on 18 July was buoyant. Having dismissed yet another request to end Good Friday games, this time from the Church of England Men's Society, the secretary, Hugh Downing, stood to make his report of the season to the crowded room. He announced, to cheers, that Redruth had had their best season since the war and one of the best in the club's history. Of the 40 games played, Redruth had won 32 and drawn three. The team had scored 514 points, with just 164 against. The reserves had also had a fine season, winning 20 of their 26 games and drawing three.

The 1928/29 season showed every sign of delivering on this promise. The chiefs were joined by another young player catching the attention of the press in his debut season for the first XV. Fred Rule, still only 17, was already being spoken of as the club's best fly-half since the great Maffer Davey.

As well as having a good run of results against local teams, Redruth continued to have players regularly picked for the county side. Len Roberts, E.I. Andrews and John Uren were picked alongside Jennings for the Cornwall County Championship match against Gloucester in December, which was played at Redruth. However, Cornwall lost 5-6, and it turned out to be a forgettable season in which they lost all three South West Division matches.

This run of losses for Cornwall added fuel to the grievances of clubs who felt they were under-represented in the county side and that it was unfairly dominated by players from Redruth and Camborne. Earlier in the season, there had been complaints from Penryn and Falmouth over the selection of 13 players from the two Mining Division sides for the Cornwall team. Relations with Penryn were further soured when Redruth announced it was cancelling two of the four fixtures against the Borough scheduled for the coming season, citing the refusal of the Redruth players to take part.

For once, Redruth and Camborne were in agreement and when the first Boxing Day fixture between them in three seasons was played at the latter's ground, there appears to have been no ill-feeling between the clubs. The Reds came away 10-0 winners. They were back there again in late February to hammer out a 0-0 draw and, while the game ended in a forward tussle, relations between the players remained cordial. By the end of the 1928/29 season, the chiefs had scored a record 629 points,

200 of them notched up by just one man, the incomparable Roy Jennings. Of the 40 matches they had played, they had won 31. The reserves had won 21 out of 27 played.

Redruth retained all of the previous season's players at the beginning of the 1929/30 campaign, a season that would launch a remarkable seven-year run. A marker of Redruth's intentions was set down in the opening match at home to Plymouth Nomads, which the Reds won 52-3. The players were now wearing badged jerseys, with the letters RRFC embroidered in black silk around the emblem of the lamb and flag on the breast, a design originally used to mark ingots of tin produced in the town. The club still carries this symbol on its shirts today.

Roy Jennings was selected as the only Cornish player in an England international trial at Franklin Gardens, Northampton, at the beginning of December. Lining up for the Colours against the Whites, Jennings played a major part in the match, converting two tries, one of which he had scored himself. He was described in a match report as by far the best of his side's three-quarters. His performance saw him named in the Possibles side for the second England trial on 21 December at Gloucester, where he kicked a conversion. He was then picked for the final England trial to be played in the new year.

Redruth beat Camborne 9-3 in the Boxing Day game, the second win of the season over their close rivals. The final match of 1929, at Penryn, was cancelled because of heavy rain, to the relief of the players, who disliked playing the fixture. The Reds had played 17 matches in the first half of the season, losing just two, a home fixture against Bristol and an away match at Torquay. They had beaten all their Cornish opponents. What would have been even more pleasing was the free-scoring nature of many of the club's performances. Redruth had scored 342 points while conceding just 71. In the national rugby performance table which was published on 1 January 1930, only two other clubs, Neath and Rugby, had scored more points.

Following the final England trial on 4 January, the side which would face Wales was announced; Roy Jennings' name did not appear. However, he was invited to join the British Isles side which would tour New Zealand and Australia, and which was due to leave London on 11 April 1930. This was the first tour in which the team were widely referred to as the Lions and Jennings became the second Redruth player to represent the side, after Maffer Davey in 1908. He also became one of only a handful of players selected for the Lions who had not previously won an international cap. At its annual dinner on 29 March, the Redruth Supporters' Club presented him with a wristwatch to mark his imminent departure for the southern hemisphere.

Less than a week before his departure, he put aside any concerns about picking up an injury which would scupper his chances of travelling and turned out for Redruth in their end-of-season match against Penzance. Redruth won 17-3, with Jennings scoring eight of the points. Within a couple of days, he was on his way to London to join his Lions team-mates.

Jennings played his first Lions game against Taranaki on 24 May, finding himself in the unaccustomed position of full-back when both first-choice players for that position were injured. The Great Britain team won 23-7, but Jennings suffered a shoulder injury that kept him out of contention for the second tour match at Christchurch. He took part in five other matches against New Zealand provincial sides, playing on the wing, rather than his customary place at centre, and scoring a total of four tries. When the Lions reached Australia he was selected for the match against the Queensland Reds in Brisbane, where he scored a try. He then ran in three more in the match against Victoria at Melbourne, which the Lions won 41-26.

Back home, the Redruth club was celebrating the most successful year in its history. The annual meeting heard that the Reds had scored more points and won more games than at any time since they had been founded in 1875. The side had scored 725 points, with just 176 conceded, and won 34 of their 40 matches. They were, as the *Western Morning News* stated, indisputably Cornwall's most successful rugby club. The reserves had also had a good season, having lost just four of their 30 matches. The club's income for the year had topped the £1,000 mark for the first time.

More improvements had been made at the Recreation Ground. The most significant of these was the construction of the entrance directly off North Street. The goalposts were moved nearer to the east side of the pitch to give more room in front of the stand and gas lights were purchased for the pavilion. These improvements, together with the provision of car parking, were necessary modernisations for the new decade.

The 1930s would be a challenging time for Cornwall. The Great Depression had a severe impact on the traditional industries of mining and fishing, and unemployment and emigration continued to rise. However, social change resulted from the emergence of new industries, such as hospitality and entertainment, and the 1930s also saw significant investment in infrastructure and development in Cornwall. Transport links were improved, both within the county and with the rest of the UK. This helped to stimulate economic growth and development.

The 1930/31 season brought new opposition for Redruth, the first of which was Barnstaple in North Devon, to where the Reds travelled in September 1930. They lost by just one point in appalling weather and on a slippery pitch. On 20 September, the Somerset side Taunton made their first visit to the Recreation Ground, where they lost to the home side 32-8. Both Taunton and Barnstaple would become regular opponents in the professional era.

Meanwhile, the British touring side had arrived back home, their ship docking at Plymouth early on the morning of 22 October. As Roy Jennings disembarked, he was met by Percy Holman, the CRFU secretary, who informed him that he had been selected for Cornwall, along with six other Redruth players, for the first County Championship match away to Somerset on 25 October. Jennings also told a reporter that he fully intended to turn out for Redruth the next day, 23 October, when his club would be playing Camborne School of Mines. His appearance in that game saw hundreds of Redruth supporters make the short trip to welcome him back into the side. He did not disappoint them, scoring 13 of Redruth's points in their 32-4 victory.

Bristol were the visitors on Monday, 17 November, arriving at the Recreation Ground with four internationals, a record of 11 games without defeat that season and a reputation of having one of the best back divisions in the game. Bristol came unstuck when the Reds opted to play a forward game, effectively shutting down the visitors' three-quarters before they could get going. Bristol had come to rely on their speedy centre, Don Borland, who would win an England cap the following season, but he was effectively blocked by the rushing tactics of the Redruth forwards. The home side won 6-3. This was an outstanding result for Redruth and the team earned a standing ovation from the 4,000-strong crowd.

The game highlighted the skills of the Redruth half-back pairing of Jack Andrew and Fred Rule, with one report suggesting they were the equal of the famous Maffer Davey and Arthur Thomas partnership of more than 20 years before. Rule scored twice, running a third of the length of the field to score the winning try after a Jennings interception. However, Redruth's tactics were not well received by the correspondent of the Bristol-based *Western Daily Press*, who went by the byline A.G.P. In an article headlined 'Cave Men of the Rugby Game', he launched a broadside at Cornish rugby:

> 'The match resembled one of those grim Cornish League games of the 90s when 30 of the strongest young fellows of Redruth and Penzance were let loose against each other and victory was a matter of the survival of the fittest.'[46]

He went on to say that there was nothing in the rules to stop this sort of play, but neither was there anything to prevent people from saying they did not like this sort of football. He called on the Bristol committee to decide whether it was worth having men injured in the type of dog fighting that passed for rugby in the far South West. No doubt his remarks were read with some astonishment in Cornwall.

As we have seen, the style of rugby played in Cornwall could often be confrontational and it was not unusual for games to break out into violence, usually on the pitch, but sometimes among the crowd. In most cases, this merely involved the settling of old scores, whether real or imagined, and was just seen as part and parcel of the game. It caused little comment when Cornish sides only played each other. But, as rugby advanced into the 20th century, it became more common for sides from up country, unfamiliar with this tradition, to find themselves playing Cornish teams, with this Bristol match a good example.

This more anarchic style of rugby was not confined to Cornwall; it was also part of the game in other working-class areas such as South Wales and the north of England. In the latter case, that style was carried into rugby league. It is no coincidence that Cornish players found little difficulty in transferring to the 13-a-side game. Along with a robust approach on the field, the anti-establishment ethos, particularly when that establishment was the RFU, was very much part of the Cornish psyche. It all came as a bit of a shock to players brought up through the system of public schools and universities, imbued with the idea of the clean-limbed amateur who played for the love of the game, not for the final score.

It would be unwise, however, to believe that this grittier style of rugby was unknown in the higher echelons of the game. When England faced the All Blacks at Twickenham in 1925, the England captain, Wavell Wakefield, had taken the decision that the only way to beat New Zealand was to confront them head-on. From the first scrum, the English forwards had sought to dominate through the use of fists and boots. That match saw the New Zealand flanker, Cyril Brownlie, become the first rugby player ever sent off in an international after the referee saw him stamp on an England forward, quite possibly in retaliation for an earlier incident. Play up, play up and play the game, it certainly was not.

If the *Western Daily Press* article about the Bristol match was circulated in the Redruth changing rooms, it made little difference to the way they played or to their results. A week later, two tries from Roy Jennings gave Redruth a 6-0 victory away to Somerset side Wellington, the first time these two had met for many years. Again, it was Redruth's forward dominance that provided the platform for Jennings's skills and he was also dominant in Redruth's win at Devonport when they beat the Royal Naval Engineering College 16-14. This was their first win for many seasons over the strong services side.

Jennings was now regularly partnered with Harold Curnow in the centre, a combination that would come to be at the heart of the team's success. Curnow, known as 'White Top' because of his pale blonde hair, was one of Redruth's fastest backs. A 6-4 win at Camborne on Boxing Day, the second time the Reds had beaten their nearest rivals that season, rounded off the first half of the campaign, with Redruth having played 18 games and lost just two.

In March, Cardiff arrived at the Recreation Ground, heralding an increase in the number of visits by top Welsh sides to Cornwall. Redruth lost the game 8-0, but they were playing a side with five Welsh internationals. Four thousand people watched what was described as a thrilling game, one of the hardest and fastest imaginable.

There was another cheerful Redruth AGM in July 1931 when the secretary, Hugh Downing, announced the club had won 35 of their 42 games. Over the previous three seasons, the chiefs had played a total of 124 games, winning 100 and drawing six. The reserves had also had a good season, winning

23 of their 29 games. Downing paid tribute to the junior clubs in the area, which had become a nursery for players ambitious to win their caps for the chiefs. Redruth Highway, Lanner and North Country had supplied Redruth with first-team players and the newly formed Redruth Albany had also had a successful season. On a more prosaic level, members present at the meeting also learned that shower baths would be installed in the pavilion.

The fixture list for the 1931/32 season included the club's first away trip to London, where they were scheduled to play St Bart's Hospital in November. There would also be the traditional matches against other Cornish clubs and visits by a number of teams from outside the South West, including Cardiff and Llanelli. It is notable that Bristol did not appear among the sides scheduled to visit Redruth that season. Practice for the new season saw players meeting to train three times a week from the middle of August.

Over the summer, members of the CRFU committee had been ruminating over how best to improve the reputation of the game in Cornwall and mend some fences between the clubs. There had been a great deal of concern over the bad feeling between some Cornish clubs, not least Redruth and Camborne, and the county committee was also worried about comments in the press about rough play. In September, it was decided that one solution might be to establish a Cornish equivalent of the Barbarians, an invitational scratch side made up of players from different clubs. The idea of a Cornish Wanderers team was largely welcomed and Roy Jennings was one of those who took part, but the initiative eventually fizzled out.

Llanelli arrived at Redruth on 14 September with a team which contained six Welsh internationals and four international trial players. Despite lacking three first-choice players due to injury, and playing the second half a man short, Redruth came close to beating their illustrious visitors, finally going down 4-3 in front of a crowd of more than 3,000. The second half was reported to be of a rough and tumble nature, with a steady rush of ambulance men on to the field. Redruth's Albert James collapsed at work the following day as a result of his injuries and was taken to hospital, where he remained unconscious for several hours.

Injuries continued to dog Redruth through the opening months of the season, although the club's strength in depth helped to mitigate the problem. They also had Roy Jennings, who piled on the points in every game he played, not least through his prodigious kicking skills. This was demonstrated in an away game at Newton Abbot at the end of September when Redruth were awarded a penalty in their own half. A group of home spectators began to laugh when Jennings lined up for a kick at goal, but the smiles were wiped from their faces as the ball sailed 60 yards to land squarely between the posts.

Jennings was one of three Redruth players, the others being Harold Curnow and Clifford Triniman, who were selected for the Devon and Cornwall side to face the touring South Africans on 18 November. Jennings was placed at full-back, rather than in the centre, a position he had filled successfully on the recent Lions tour. More than 12,000 people turned up to watch the game at the Rectory Field in Devonport, where outstanding play by the home side contained the Springbok attack, forcing a 3-3 draw. The *Exeter and Plymouth Gazette* singled out Jennings for special praise, his long kicks causing considerable problems for the South African defence. The paper felt sure his performance would have impressed the three members of the England selection committee who were at the game and, indeed, he was selected at full-back for the South side in the first England trial to be held in December.

Just three days later, the Reds made the long trip to London for their match against St Bart's Hospital, the first time they had played in the capital. The team had travelled up by train during the night and, understandably, took time to settle, conceding eight points in the first half. They came back to establish a lead shortly after the break, but eventually succumbed by a single point, 19-18. Before the game, the Redruth team had toured around London and paused by the Cenotaph, where Roy Jennings laid a wreath on behalf of the club.

Having made an impression in the South v North international trial in Coventry on 5 December, Jennings was named at full-back in an England XV to face the Rest at Twickenham two weeks later, the only Cornish player in the side. However, hopes of a first international cap against South Africa in January were dashed when, against all the odds, the Rest beat England 16-6. Jennings had been injured in a tackle early in the game and, although he played on, he could not reproduce his previous form and the place in the England side went to the Leicester full-back Bobby Barr.

Roy Jennings was destined to be one of many fine Cornish players who failed to win the international cap that it was widely felt they deserved. At the annual dinner of the Redruth Supporters' Club in April 1932, the former club captain, Jack Richards, said he had been told by none other than Bert Solomon that many a worse man had been picked for England than Jennings and that he was a victim of bad luck. No doubt some of his audience felt that he was more a victim of the RFU's continuing short-sightedness when it came to players from the far South West. It would be another 15 years, and a different era, before a Redruth player was again selected for England.

It was not just the Cornish who felt Jennings had been overlooked. Several sports reporters in the national press were also asking questions. F.J. Sellicks, a leading reporter on both cricket and rugby, wrote in the *Illustrated Sporting and Dramatic News* about his omission from the England side:

> 'The Cornishman is essentially a spectacular player, which may not count for very much in his favour, but he would certainly have given the Twickenham crowd plenty of thrills. He came close to a cap last season, and

one never felt quite sure that the selectors were right in preferring the Leicester man, R.J. Barr.'[47]

If any single player epitomised Redruth's success between 1925 and 1939, it was Roy Jennings. The legend of Bert Solomon can sometimes overshadow the achievements of later players in the history of the club, but there is a strong case for suggesting that the contribution of Roy Jennings was as great, if not greater, than that of Solomon. Combining electrifying speed with immense strength, he dominated the backs for more than a decade. During the glory years of the 1930s, he would regularly score 100 or more points for Redruth in a season; 200 in one memorable year. Unlike Solomon, he failed to win an England cap, but he took part in a number of trials and it was only circumstances that prevented him being awarded a place in the England side. He was, indeed, one of the greatest players ever to pull on a Redruth shirt.

The end of the 1931/32 season marked the passing of another great Redruth player, one from the club's inception in 1875, the legendary Frank Woolf. He had been an inspiring captain and one of Cornwall's most accomplished forwards. His rugby career had spanned more than three decades and he was still turning out to play when he entered his 50s. He died on 15 May 1932 aged 78. Much of Redruth's success in the latter part of the 19th century had been due to his leadership, so it is strange that there is no mention of his death in the club minutes; nor was he mentioned at the AGM on 27 July.

On the field, it had been another successful year. The chiefs had won 32 of their 41 games, making it the fourth season in succession that Redruth had chalked up more than 30 victories. Some concern was expressed over the failure of the reserves to achieve better gates. They had won 18 of their 26 games, but the Depression was still impacting the local economy and the club had continued a policy of admitting the unemployed at half price, so the revenue from the second XV was affected.

Fortunately, there had been enough funds available to carry out more improvements to the changing facilities, with additional shower baths and a new boiler installed.

The 1932/33 season got under way with Redruth showing no sign of resting on their laurels after several outstanding years. Instead, they laid down a marker by beating Plymouth Albion 17-6 at Beacon Park. It was the first time the two sides had met for several seasons and the Plymouth supporters were no doubt surprised to discover that the Reds were now far superior in all departments. The game was watched by 5,000 spectators, a large number of whom had travelled up from Redruth, and such was the enthusiasm that the railings collapsed and several dozen people were deposited on to the pitch. Fortunately, there were no injuries. The new Redruth captain, Fred Rule, was carried shoulder-high off the ground at the end of the game.

In early October, Bath made their first-ever visit to the Recreation Ground, causing a great deal of excitement in the town. A Roy Jennings try and conversion, in reply to early points from Bath, saw the score even at the break and, with the wind behind the home side, Redruth supporters were hoping for an upset. In the second half, the Reds took the lead through a Jennings penalty but Bath rallied towards the end and ran out 10-8 winners. It was Redruth's first defeat of the season.

A couple of weeks later, another large crowd took to the banks at the Rec, with more than 6,000 spectators turning up for the derby clash between Redruth and Camborne. It was a typically hard-fought game, with numerous penalties on both sides. Camborne became increasingly rattled towards the end and finished with 13 men. Redruth won 8-0.

A week later, Roy Jennings was one of six Redruth players to make the return trip to Bath, this time as part of the Cornwall team playing Somerset in the opening game of the County Championship. He captained the side and was joined by team-mates Harold Curnow, Fred Rule, Gerald Moorhead, Ed Smith and Vivian Richards. Cornwall lost 16-13.

In November, Redruth made their second trip to London to play St Bart's Hospital, this time coming away with a 5-3 win. The rugby club performance table published in the *Daily News* on the eighth of the month announced that Redruth had the distinction of being the first club in the country to score more than 300 points. By the end of the year, the Reds had played 22 games and lost only two, although one of these was a surprising and somewhat galling 8-6 defeat to Camborne away on Boxing Day, their first loss of the season to a Cornish club.

With the new year came some depressing news for people living in and around Redruth. Economic gloom still pervaded the area and, at the beginning of 1933, Josiah Paull, the manager of the South Crofty mine, warned that the outlook for Cornish tin, and the many ancillary businesses that depended on it, was not bright. A fall in demand had depressed world prices to the extent that the mine was only working one shift and it would take a considerable rise in metal prices for any further men to be taken on.

This had a direct impact on those who made their living in the mines, but it also had consequences for all those who supplied goods and services in the town, whose clientele would need to further tighten their belts. Historically, employers in Redruth had been very understanding about giving their workers time off to play rugby, but, in that economic climate, young men with a family might need to think hard about taking an afternoon off unpaid.

It was against this background that Redruth began the second half of the 1932/33 season, although the first match, away to St Ives, had to be called off because of torrential rain. The side made the trip to Bath on 14 January for their return game and the result was closer than many predicted, with Bath winning 8-3 thanks to a last-minute converted try.

The club's recent successful seasons had made the life of the Redruth secretary considerably easier when it came to arranging fixtures with top-flight opposition. In early February, Coventry, one of England's best sides, came to Redruth for the very first time. Having made the unexpectedly long journey down to West Cornwall, the Midlanders took a little while to get going and found themselves 5-0 down at half-time. Redruth went further ahead in the second half in what the *Coventry Evening Telegraph* described as a sensational display of rugby, which included Roy Jennings running the length of the field to send Allen in for a Redruth try. Coventry woke up in the second half and pulled out all the stops in the final minutes, but Redruth tackled hard and hung on for a 13-10 win.

In sporting terms, association football was gaining a much bigger following across the country and was competing with rugby for followers, even in the rugby heartlands. Football had knockout cup competitions and league tables to make the contests more meaningful and the idea of some sort of league system in rugby was revived at the January 1933 meeting of the CRFU. However, after a lively discussion, it was pointed out that the RFU, ever wary of anything that smacked of professionalism, would be unlikely to give permission.

Redruth finished the 1932/33 season in storming style, including a home win over Plymouth Albion, the first time the Reds had done the double against the Devon side. In the middle of March, Redruth became the first club in the *Daily News* rugby performance table to reach 600 points scored. This table featured the top clubs in England and Wales, including sides such as Blackheath, Harlequins, Richmond and Swansea. The table also showed that the club had won 33 of the 36 games they had played so far that season.

On a fine warm day in early April 1933, Cardiff arrived at Redruth with six Welsh internationals in their team. The weather had been so dry that the committee had considered asking the fire brigade to water the pitch in return for free tickets for the rest of the season. Knowing that four of the Welsh internationals were in the pack, Redruth had invited two outside players to join their forwards; Wickett, from the Royal

School of Mines, and Smith, a former student of Camborne School of Mines. In front of a crowd of almost 4,000 people, Redruth made the perfect start, with Jennings landing a goal from a penalty within 30 seconds of kick-off. A second followed not five minutes later. It was a fast and furious game, and the Camborne referee had his hands full, but Cardiff had been rattled by the early penalties and never recovered. The Redruth captain, Fred Rule, landed a drop goal and Robbins scored a try, converted by Jennings, to take Redruth to a 15-3 victory against a Cardiff XV that five short months before had been dubbed 'the Wonder Team'.

Many of those watching were unaware that this was the last time they would see Fred Rule in a Redruth shirt. He had been in negotiations with Halifax rugby league club and, the day after the Cardiff game, it was officially announced that he was turning professional. Several other clubs, including Wigan, had been interested in signing him, but the offer of £300 in advance and £4 a week had secured the deal.

While Rule was negotiating terms with two Halifax officials in an unnamed Redruth hotel, a crowd had assembled outside. The Halifax men, well aware of rugby union's animosity to the 13-man game, were alarmed, thinking that they might be in some danger. However, there was no ill feeling towards Rule and the following season, a huge crowd gathered at Redruth Station to wish him well. The Redruth committee agreed unanimously to heartily thank Rule and to wish him the best in his new career. Even the CRFU thought it right to send a letter to Fred, thanking him for his service to Cornwall. Further tributes were paid at the Redruth AGM when the secretary, Hugh Downing, said no one at the club blamed him for the step he had taken and that he had the best wishes of his fellow players, the club committee and the supporters.

All this goodwill was in stark contrast to the attitude of RFU administrators towards players who deserted the amateur game. Their reaction bordered on sheer vindictiveness, even banning players who went north from entering union clubhouses. The actor and playwright Colin Welland, a staunch league supporter, once said that 'rugby league was forged on the anvil of Victorian snobbery', and that same snobbery remained in place until 1995 when the RFU was dragged kicking and screaming into the professional era. Their blinkered attitude over the years saw hundreds of talented players lost to the game for the crime of earning money from their skills and talent.

Fred lived in Halifax for the rest of his life and died there in 1981 at the age of 69. According to a report in a Halifax paper, he played for Halifax between 1933 and 1947, later taking up a post as a coach at Halifax rugby union club. If this was correct, then it seems that Yorkshire, like Cornwall, had little time for the RFU's lifelong boycott of league players.

Rule could certainly look back on his final season with Redruth with some satisfaction. Under his captaincy, they had scored 696 points, winning 38 of their 45 games, a club record. The supporters' club was delighted when it met in late April, one official boasting that the club had shown in recent years that it could hold its own against any team in the country and that the season's record was the best of any club in Britain.

According to the secretary's report at the AGM in July, the 1932/33 season was, indeed, the best in the club's 68 years. Other than an away defeat at Paignton, Redruth had done the double over every Devon side they had played. The reserves had gone undefeated, winning 21 of their 23 games and drawing two. The club had made a healthy profit of £81 and had welcomed a number of new players during the season, including Les Semmens, who had joined from Redruth Albany and who went on to become Cornwall's first-choice hooker.

The 1930s had brought cultural, as well as economic, change to Cornwall. The county's rich history and heritage were being celebrated and efforts were made to preserve and promote Cornish culture and traditions, such as Cornish wrestling and the Cornish language and folk traditions. The summer of 1933 saw another well-attended Cornish wrestling tournament held at the Recreation Ground, this time under the auspices of the Cornish Wrestling Association. Roy Jennings was named in the catchweight division of the team which would represent Cornwall against Brittany. Lord and Lady St Levan were among those watching the contest, which ended in a draw. Jennings was beaten by his Breton opponent; it was suggested that he had the strength to be a good wrestler, but was still learning the skill.

Redruth started the 1933/34 season having lost a number of key players and there was speculation in the press that they would find it hard to match the success of the previous campaign. Not only had they lost Fred Rule to Halifax, but Moorhead and Binge had left to work in mines abroad, leaving a significant hole in the back division which had been such a part of the team's success. However, the paper suggested that a promising clutch of younger players was coming forward and Francis Gregory, the Cornish wrestler, was reported to have been training with the side. He made his first appearance in a Redruth jersey when the club hosted a Cornwall XV in an early September fundraiser for Hayle rugby club, which had almost gone bust at the end of the previous season.

In the event, the season did see something of a dip in Redruth's performance and it would be the only campaign between 1930 and 1936 when the club failed to record 30 or more victories. Coventry were early visitors to Redruth and reversed the previous season's result by winning 8-3 in front of 3,000 spectators. Redruth's only try came as a result of a fine run by Francis Gregory, who used his considerable strength to get through the Coventry defence and pass to Rogers, who went over. A loss at home to Camborne on Boxing Day was one of three successive defeats over the festive period.

The new year brought further losses, including a 19-3 defeat away to Plymouth Albion, a club Redruth had beaten twice the previous season. The home game against Camborne in February saw Redruth cheer their supporters with a 12-0 win and, on

22 March, a team representing Oxford University arrived at Redruth for the first time and a close match saw the home side win 15-14.

The second game against Plymouth Albion, held at Redruth, saw the Devon men win at the Recreation Ground for the first time in a decade. Redruth's Richards was sent off, for allegedly kicking an opposing player, and the referee reported Roy Jennings, Harold Curnow, Fred Bone and Ken Williams, all of whom, he said, subjected him to insulting remarks in the changing area. The CRFU issued formal cautions to all five players. Redruth ended the season with a 41-0 win over visitors Penzance, a result that brought their tally to 28 wins from 40 and a total of 618 points.

Redruth lost their opening match of the 1934/35 season away at Torquay, who scored a try in the first 30 seconds of the game. Redruth fought back, regaining the lead twice with impressive drop goals from Harold Curnow, but two more tries from Torquay left the Reds trailing 12-8 at the finish. It would be their last loss for some time. Ten days later, Coventry returned to Cornwall for a bruising encounter in front of a crowd of 3,000. This time, the Reds beat the Midlanders 5-3 in a robust game in which two Coventry players left the field with injuries. Roy Jennings was hit in the face, sustaining a broken nose and losing two teeth, but, after a brief time off the field, he carried on playing until the end of the game and was back in the side that defeated Devonport Services at the end of September.

Redruth ran up 11 wins on the trot before a 3-3 draw against St Ives at the end of November. That game saw an incident in which Roy Jennings was kicked in the back by a St Ives player and ordered by doctors to rest for a month. In the run-up to Christmas, Redruth avenged their early season defeat at Torquay, beating the Devon side 12-3 at the Rec, and then won the Boxing Day encounter at Camborne 11-0. The tally at the end of the year was just one defeat and one draw from a total of 19 games.

Jennings was back for the first game of 1935 and scored three tries in Redruth's 41-0 demolition of visitors Teignmouth. A 15-6 win away to Camborne gave Redruth their third victory of the season over their old rivals. Once again, Redruth were full of confidence and, when they hosted Welsh side Neath at the Rec for the very first time in late February, they were determined to send them home empty-handed. The sides were evenly matched until half-time, with both struggling to handle the greasy ball in wet conditions. After the break, the Redruth forwards were able to make better use of the muddy ground and ran in four tries, defeating Neath 14-0.

Easter was late in 1935 – Good Friday fell on 19 April – and it was then that Redruth suffered their first defeat since 10 September 1934 and their first home defeat of the season. They were playing host to Wasps and the encounter was described as one of the hardest-contested games ever seen at the Recreation Ground. Eventually, it was the faster pace of the Wasps' backs that swung the game and the Reds lost 8-6 against one of England's top sides.

Redruth had played 40 games in the season, losing just two of them. This time, they had cleared the 700-point barrier with ease, scoring 718 and conceding 123. Once again, the reserves had not lost a single game, playing 28 and winning 26. They had conceded just 39 points. That year's AGM was chaired by Montagu Jennings in the absence of Captain Martin Taylor, who had served as Redruth's president for a decade. He had been the manager at East Pool mine and was returning to his native Australia. Stanley Wickett was elected to take his place as president and Captain Taylor was sent the gift of a wireless as thanks for his service.

In May 1935, the club minutes record that a Mr Harry Faviell had been interviewed and had agreed to play for Redruth the following season. Faviell had turned out for Harlequins and was an England trialist. He was destined to become one of Redruth's most successful players. Other new players in that era included two Welsh schoolteachers; Dai Jones, who had played for Swansea and captained the Welsh University XV, and H.L. Williams, a powerful forward. They both came to work at Redruth Grammar School.

William (Billy) Phillips joined the club and became one of Cornwall's outstanding scrummagers in a place where strong forward play has always been appreciated. Frank Partridge also rose through the ranks to play first as a wing and later as a full-back. He was renowned for his ability to send opposition players tumbling the wrong way with his sidestep and handling ability. With players of this calibre, it was little wonder that Redruth was almost unstoppable. There was hope for the future as well; two local lads, Jack Hick and Douglas Martin, had won international schoolboy caps. The former was the youngest of four brothers, all of whom played for Redruth.

Harry Faviell made his Redruth debut in the opening match of the 1935/36 season at Torquay. The match, in blazing sunshine, resulted in a 16-13 win for Torquay, with Faviell scoring a try. There was added interest in this game, as the Devon and Cornwall selectors were in the stand and afterwards they named the combined side to face the All Blacks. Frank Roberts was, unfortunately, not in contention, as he had broken his arm in a motorcycle accident at Porthtowan.

Roy Jennings was named captain of the side to play the New Zealanders, in what would be the first game of their tour. Fellow Redruth players Francis Gregory, Dai Jones, Fred Bone and P. Rogers were also named in the peninsula team, which took to the field at Devonport in front of a 20,000 crowd. A New Zealand victory was expected and the All Blacks duly delivered, winning 35-6. Dai Jones came in for some criticism in the press for fumbling passes from Bone, but Roy Jennings was on fine form and kicked a penalty from 60 yards out.

The Feast Monday game between Camborne and Redruth was revived in 1935 after a break of many years. Camborne had little answer to the speedy Redruth backs and the Reds won the game 22-0. The two sides also met the following Saturday, this time at Redruth, where the home side again proved too strong for Camborne, winning 24-3. The highlight of the game was a 40-yard dash by Frank Roberts, back in the side after his injury, to score one of Redruth's six tries. Indeed, Redruth would not only beat Camborne in every game in that magical 1935/36 season, they would achieve a 100 per cent record against all Cornish clubs, scoring 447 points and conceding just 27. During this time, Redruth had 17 players who had been capped for Cornwall.

In the traditional Boxing Day clash with Camborne, Roy Jennings chalked up 500 games for Redruth. At the age of 30 he still retained the strength and the speed that had been such a feature of his many performances. In front of his home crowd, he did not disappoint, scoring the try of the game after a run from inside his own half, and converting a touchdown by Frank Roberts. The 29-0 win was the highest total Redruth had racked up in this fixture. A narrow win away to Plymouth Albion rounded off 1935, with Redruth having lost just one game and become the first club in the national merit table to reach 500 points.

The death of King George V on 20 January 1936 saw the RFU call a halt to all rugby in England until after the funeral. A Redruth committee meeting took place as usual, two days after the death, and it is recorded in the minutes that they stood in silence to remember the late king. They went on to discuss travel arrangements for the County Championship Final, should Cornwall win their semi-final against Hampshire on 1 February.

Cornwall had topped the South West table of the championship in late autumn for the first time since 1928 and won all three group matches for the first time since the four-county group of Devon, Cornwall, Somerset and Gloucestershire had been established after the war. It was a particular source of pride for Redruth that there were 11 Redruth players in the Cornwall side, prompting the *Daily News* to quip that

Hampshire would actually be facing Redruth, rather than Cornwall. Disappointingly, Cornwall fell prey to the superior speed and close marking of the Hampshire backs and once more hopes of a final were dashed.

In February, Redruth lost another player to the professional game when scrum-half Fred Bone went north to join former team-mate Fred Rule. Halifax officials had watched his performance for Cornwall against Hampshire and, despite not being on his best form, he had been signed after the match. Fred had been a schoolboy international and had played for the combined Cornwall and Devon team against the All Blacks back in September. It says something for the status of Redruth at the time that his departure featured prominently in both the national press and regional papers across the country.

On 18 April 1936, Redruth were away to St Ives and their recent free-scoring was held in check by a side determined to rain on their parade. Redruth managed to hold on against a determined pack and eventually won 6-3, maintaining their winning record against Cornish clubs.

Redruth's 1935/6 season saw them unbeaten at home with just three losses from the 40 matches they played. They scored a record 864 points, the highest of any English club that season, and conceded only 101. Harry Faviell scored 53 tries during the campaign. The reserves were in equally good form, losing just two of their 22 games, both times by a single point to Liskeard.

In September 1936, Redruth travelled to Torquay for what had become the traditional opening game of the season. They were without Frank Roberts, Gordon Robins and Harry Faviell, who were all ill. The result, 14-3 in Torquay's favour, mirrored that of the opening day of the previous season. Billy Phillips, who was destined to become one of Redruth's most-capped players, was injured near the end of the match.

The first weekend of October saw a 29-0 home win over Camborne and a narrow 5-3 loss to visitors Bristol on the Monday. Fred Pappin, the veteran Redruth full-back, sustained a fractured jaw during the game and would be out for some considerable time. Fred was in his mid-30s and had played for the Reds for more than 20 years.

By the end of November, Redruth had already lost three games, including a surprise defeat away to Taunton, the first time the Somerset side had beaten the Reds. The home game against Newlyn was abandoned in the second half after some members of the visiting team refused to continue playing following a dispute with the referee. Newlyn complained that Harry Faviell had put a foot in touch before scoring, but the referee had awarded a try. With club officials urging Newlyn to continue, while a section of Redruth supporters shouted that they should all be sent off, the referee called time with Redruth leading 16-0.

The Feast Monday game with Camborne was played for the second year in succession, following the previous hiatus. Camborne had been going through a rough patch at the end of the previous season and had already lost to Redruth in October. They found themselves 13 points adrift in the first quarter of an hour but fought back after the break, eventually losing 18-10.

The annual trip to London to play St Bart's resulted in a one-point win for the Reds in front of a crowd containing several dozen members of the London Cornish Association, all decked out in black and gold. Kneebone and Verran were the scorers for Redruth, but followers from Cornwall who wanted to know more about the game were disappointed, as there was no match report in local papers.

Harry Faviell was named in the Possibles for an England trial match on 19 December at Bristol. He had been away from Redruth playing for the Eastern Counties in the County Championship competition. Faviell, like Roy Jennings, would be yet another Redruth player who failed to make the England side during the inter-war years, despite taking part in a number of trial games. There was a complaint in the *Daily Mirror* that the England selectors continued to favour players from Oxbridge and the London area, ignoring the South West, which the paper said had been steeped in the rugby tradition practically since the inception of the code.

Redruth ended 1936 with a 14-0 defeat of Camborne on Boxing Day. The result meant they had won 15 games out of 21, a creditable record but not up to the previous season's achievement. Home wins over Exeter and Taunton were the highlights of the first two months of 1937 and there was an exciting 19-3 win over visitors Wasps at the end of March. The final victory of the season was a 12-0 win over Camborne in a game held to raise funds for an extension at the Miners' and Women's Hospital in Redruth.

There was concern about the future of Roy Jennings, who had twice had to retire from games with a knee injury and had missed the final four games of the campaign. Later that summer, Jennings travelled to Guy's Hospital in London for treatment on his knee. He spent three weeks in hospital before returning to Redruth and it was hoped that the surgery would enable him to play rugby again.

For several seasons, Redruth had stood head and shoulders above other clubs in Cornwall and had held their own against some of the best teams in the country. It was probably asking too much that they should continue at the level of the 1935/36 season, but they did win 30 of the 42 games they played, drawing seven and losing five. However, games were getting closer and margins of victory were being eroded. In the 1936/37 season, the first XV scored 440 points, only a little over half the total of the previous season, and there was little doubt that Redruth's opponents were getting stronger.

Hugh Downing, the club secretary, told the AGM in July that Redruth had had the best performance of any club west of Bristol, despite the loss of players such as Fred Bone, Francis Gregory and Frank Roberts, and injuries to Fred Pappin and Roy Jennings. The club's strength in depth was underlined by the fact that 49 players had turned out for the chiefs during the season and 12 had been capped for Cornwall. The reserves had won 17 of their 25 games.

Roy Jennings had still not recovered from his knee repair when Redruth travelled to Torquay for the opening match of the season. For three years in a row, Redruth had lost this game and this time was no different. Torquay dominated the match and won 13-5. In mid-September, Exeter travelled to Redruth and the teams were evenly matched until half-time, after which the Reds turned up the pressure. Cliff Howard, at centre, was one of Redruth's bright prospects for the season and he showed his potential by scoring 20 of Redruth's points in their 34-3 victory.

Roy Jennings was back in a red shirt for the first time in more than six months when he turned out for the Redruth reserves against Devonport Services A at the end of October 1937. His kicking seemed as strong as ever, with no weakness in his knee. A week later, he was back with the chiefs and converted two tries in their 42-0 demolition of the Royal Naval Engineering College. Redruth supporters would have been relieved to see their hero back to his old form and in the Feast Monday game at Camborne, he made a fine run to set up Harold Curnow for a try in Redruth's 9-6 win.

Redruth also beat Camborne 8-3 in the Boxing Day encounter in front of a crowd reported to have been well over 4,000. This was the third Redruth win in three years in this annual derby and it brought the total of Redruth wins in the first half of the season to 14. They were one of only four clubs in England and Wales to have scored more than 300 points so far that season.

As the year ended, it was announced that Roy Jennings had been selected for Cornwall in their play-off County Championship match against Devon at Torquay. He joined six other Redruth players in the side, including Harry Faviell, who had previously played county rugby for Eastern Counties. Despite being hit by these county calls and a number of injuries, Redruth continued to sustain their position as the top Cornish club through the second half of the season. Results included a win at Penryn, the first time the Borough had been beaten on their own ground for two years.

A typically robust game against visitors Plymouth Albion, in which fists were thrown in the second half, led to a complaint from the referee that he had been subjected to a continual barrage of abuse from a section of the home crowd. Redruth's representative on the CRFU committee, Will Rich, pointed out that Redruth engaged police officers to patrol the ground and that the committee could not expect people who attended rugby matches to behave like Sunday school children. The CRFU decided to take no action.

The season ended with Redruth having played 38 games, slightly fewer than in the six previous seasons, and won 24 of them, losing nine. It was the tenth year in succession that the club had achieved more than 20 wins in a season and in all but one of those years they had scored more than 500 points. The reserves had lost just three of their 26 games. With a new crop of talented young players, and the expectation of developing more from within the reserves and surrounding junior clubs, the chiefs were optimistic about the season ahead. Redruth showed their intent in the first game of the season when visitors Hayle were defeated 53-3, despite Redruth being without six of their first-choice players. They went on to lose just one match in the opening six weeks of the season.

In October came news of the death of the former Redruth president, Captain Martin Taylor. He had resigned as president in 1935 when he had gone back to Australia, but he had since returned to Cornwall and had been living at Roskear. A minute's silence was observed at Redruth before the start of the county trial on 8 October.

Redruth ended Exeter's unbeaten run when they travelled up to Devon, but the game did little credit to either side. The report claimed Redruth were mainly to blame for what were called 'a number of unpleasant incidents' and two of their players, Robins and Howard, were warned by the referee. There was little open play and the backs failed to shine on either side, but the Reds would have been happy to win 13-0 away.

The Feast Day match at Camborne, now settling back into a regular fixture after the break in the 1920s, saw honours even with an 11-11 draw. That same week, Redruth, somewhat incongruously, featured in *The Tatler* magazine, a publication aimed at high society which included articles on fashion, race meetings and balls of the dancing variety. The article seems to have been copied, pretty much verbatim, from the club's 50th anniversary booklet.

Bad weather marred the Boxing Day match with Camborne. Torrential rain kept spectators away and turned the pitch into a mud bath. Robins' try for Redruth within minutes of the start was the only score of the game. The two clubs decided to meet again the following day at Camborne, where an improvement in the weather saw a better gate and a much higher standard of play. A penalty and a drop goal were enough to give Redruth a 7-3 win.

Redruth were still on track to hold their title of Cornwall's top side after an 8-0 win at Barnstaple on New Year's Eve. Just one game had been lost out of the 19 played in the first half of the season and the club was still one of the top ten points scorers in England and Wales. Their three-month undefeated run came to an end in January when they went down 11-0 at Plymouth Albion.

Their third, and last, defeat of the season came on their annual trip to play St Bart's, this time at the hospital's new ground at Bromley in Kent, where the Reds lost 10-5. Unbeaten at home, the chiefs had won 33 of their 37 games and drawn one, and had once again scored more than 500 points. The club had been able to draw on 40 different players, including Roy Jennings who, at the age of 34, was described at the club AGM as being back to full form.

Fixture lists had been drawn up for the 1939 season, although there was a warning that what was referred to as 'the political situation', might mean players occasionally being unavailable by virtue of being called up for the militia or other military duties. The mood at the meeting was one of cheery optimism. This mirrored what seemed to be the general belief in the country that war with Germany could be avoided. It was clear from reports of the AGM that those present confidently expected that Redruth would kick-off the new season on 2 September with a game at home to Hayle. In the event, it would be six years before the Redruth club took to the field again.

Chapter Eight
Wartime Rugby 1939–1950

FOLLOWING THE declaration of war on 3 September 1939, Redruth were one of the first Cornish clubs to announce the cancellation of all fixtures for the coming season. Two weeks later, the CRFU met and decided that rugby in Cornwall was to be officially abandoned for the duration. The committee, probably worried about any fallout from the RFU, made it clear that any rugby played from that date onwards would be unofficial and not the responsibility of the CRFU, nor under its jurisdiction.

While the season's fixture list had to be abandoned, business at the club did not come to a complete halt. The decision to end all activities, which had been taken at a meeting on 15 September 1939, was rescinded on 2 November. It was agreed that a limited number of fixtures would be set up for the remainder of 1939 and that the club would cover the cost of travel to away games and insurance for the players.

The club was reacting to a general feeling in the community that the sport should continue in some form. This was expressed in a letter in the *West Briton* of 28 September from a correspondent signing himself 'Cambornian'. He felt that closing the game down would not help public morale and that representatives from clubs in the Mining Division, the parliamentary constituency that encompassed Redruth and Camborne, should get together to arrange for some games to take place.

The first such match took place on 14 October 1939 when a Redruth XV defeated a side representing Redruth County

School and pupils from Marylebone Grammar School, the latter having been evacuated to Cornwall. The club had already agreed to let the ground to the London school for a rent of £12 10s, provided the club could use it on Saturdays and bank holidays. The Redruth side was comprised almost solely of Redruth RFC first XV players.

It is likely that this game resulted in the meeting of the Redruth committee at which it was decided that they would keep playing against other Cornish clubs, but on an ad hoc basis and outside of the auspices of the CRFU. The players were warned that the club would have to consider economies, which included limiting expenses for away matches. The committee also stopped the practice of hiring police officers for home games and of paying men to guard the hedges.

With no fixture list, and often little advance notice of games, the club agreed to have 100 posters printed for each home match, to be displayed around the town. They also arranged to have a slide advertising match details displayed during performances at the Regal Cinema at a cost of 2s/6d a week.

The Feast Monday game with Camborne had been cancelled but Haydn Williams, the Welsh schoolteacher who had joined Redruth a few years previously, took a team to Camborne to play a side representing Camborne and the Camborne School of Mines. Redruth fielded a good clutch of their first-choice players. As with many matches of this period, money raised was passed to war charities or the Red Cross. There was one notable absentee from the Redruth side. Roy Jennings had moved to live in Weymouth, where he had involved himself with a new side, Weymouth Wanderers, which had been created for the duration of the war.

The decision to keep the game alive in the town through the war years would prove to be invaluable for Redruth in the late 1940s and early 1950s. Some of the older players would not be in a position to return to the game after the conflict but many of the younger men who had played in the late 1930s, and then through the 1939–45 period, kept their fitness and skills alive and formed the core of the team when the club started playing again. Some representative games were arranged and two Redruth players, Les Semmens and Harry Faviell, appeared in a Devon and Cornwall XV which took on a Royal Navy side at Devonport on 2 December 1939.

Old traditions die hard and a match between Redruth and Camborne was played on Boxing Day 1939 in front of a crowd of around 2,000 people. Roy Jennings returned briefly to Redruth and turned out for his old side, scoring a try and helping them to a 15-0 home win. He would make other appearances in a Redruth XV during the course of the war when visiting family in the town.

In May 1940, William Willimott, one of Redruth's co-founders, died at the Taunton home of his son, with whom he had lived since the death of his wife, Frances. Together with Henry Grylls, he had been the driving force behind the establishment of Redruth Rugby Club and had continued to take an interest in the side.

His legacy was a club and a rugby tradition in Redruth which was so deeply engrained that it would continue throughout the war. Although the last Redruth committee meeting for five years was held in April 1940, there was never any serious prospect of the game falling into abeyance. Just as during the First World War years, many of Redruth's men worked in reserved occupations. These included railway workers, miners, farmers and agricultural workers, engineering workers, schoolteachers and doctors. These men often served in the Home Guard and they made up the teams which played during the war years. Among them were former members of the Redruth first XV. Albert James, who had played at fly-half, pulled together a series of teams from members of the local Home Guard and was given permission to play at the Recreation Ground.

Bert Solomon, now in his late 50s, appeared again on a rugby ground on Boxing Day 1942, albeit with a linesman's flag.

Two invitation sides comprising many former county players contested a game at Camborne in aid of the Red Cross. His fellow linesman was Redruth's former captain and Cornwall player Jack Richards. Redruth's Harold Curnow and six former team-mates were in one team, while Roy Jennings featured in the opposing side. The game was played at a furious pace, with no quarter given.

Over the war years, Redruth averaged 28 matches a season. As well as games with local rivals, there were matches against sides representing the various military services stationed in Cornwall. Later, as the build-up to D-Day began, sides from overseas services came to play at Redruth. One memorable game in 1944 was against a Royal Australian Air Force XV, captained by a noted rugby league star, G.H. Beverley.

While the needs of the mines, factories and farms of Redruth prevented many men from serving, other Redruth players did join the forces and a number of them failed to return. John 'Jackie' Maynard, who had played at scrum-half in the seasons leading up to the war, was the first player reported to be killed in action. He died in north Africa in July 1941 at the age of 24. Maynard had returned home from working in west Africa to join the Devon and Cornwall Light Infantry before being seconded to what was referred to in the *West Briton* as a special service of a particularly dangerous nature. He was, in fact, serving with No. 8 (Guards) Commando and died from wounds received while taking part in what is known as the 'Twin Pimples' raid on Italian lines during the siege of Tobruk.

Len Goldsworthy, who was a member of the Royal Air Force Volunteer Reserves, was reported killed on 26 January 1942 during the Japanese invasion of Malaya. A former pupil of Trewirgie School, he had completed an apprenticeship as an electrician before volunteering for the RAF. As well as playing for the chiefs, he had also turned out for Redruth Albany RFC and the Redruth Cricket Club. His former teacher at Trewirgie, Hugh Downing, the Redruth club secretary, described him as a boy of the highest integrity and a sportsman in the truest sense of the word.

Eddie Bawden had been a prominent Redruth player and had worked for Camborne-Redruth Urban Council's water department before joining the RAF and qualifying as a pilot. He was killed while piloting a Halifax bomber over Germany on 24 May 1943, although he was posted at the time as missing and his death was not confirmed until after the war.

William Henry John 'Jack' Martin, who served as a signaller in the Royal Corps of Signals, died in hospital on 22 September 1944 as a result of being wounded on active service. He had worked in his parents' grocery business before joining up and had been in the retreat from Dunkirk and served in Sicily and Italy. He left a widow and a six-year-old daughter. He is buried at the Redruth Cemetery in St Day Road.

At the beginning of February 1945 came the first intimations that rugby might soon be restored to a more normal state of affairs. Germany's surrender was still three months away when Redruth and Camborne announced plans to revive their traditional Feast Day and Boxing Day fixtures in the 1945/46 season. The first post-war committee meeting, on 20 June 1945, agreed to restart the club and a month later it was confirmed that fixtures would begin again in September 1945. It was also announced that St Mary's Hospital would be bringing a side to Redruth on Good Friday, 1946, the first such fixture since 1939. Practice sessions began on 25 August 1945 and, because rationing was still in force, players were asked to bring their own soap and towels.

The committee also decided that playing members, ex-officials and committee members of the Redruth Home Guard XV should automatically become members of Redruth RFC with an entitlement to vote. It was a gesture of thanks to the Home Guard for keeping rugby alive in Redruth throughout the war. It was also agreed that fixtures already arranged by the Home Guard side would pass to Redruth. This meant that the Reds would start the season with games against Falmouth, Penryn, Camborne School of Mines and, a new name on the fixture list, Penzance-Newlyn. Against all the odds, the two far west sides had finally decided to settle their long-held differences and merge. Aware that the new name was rather a mouthful, the committee had urged followers to use the cry 'Up the Pirates!' All those in the area were pirates at heart, they reasoned.

Some of Redruth's first-choice players remained on military service and it was decided that, for the time being, there would be just one first XV team. Five players remained from the pre-war era; Billy Phillips, Cliff Howard, Tony Bidgood, Les Semmens and Frank Partridge. A number of younger men had come into the side, some of them with familiar names. Among them was Doug Smith, son of Bernard, who had played between the wars, and Willie Pappin, whose father, Fred, had been a full-back for both Redruth and Cornwall. They had also been joined by Martin Tobin, a former Kent county three-quarter, who scored two tries in Redruth's 17-0 win over Falmouth on the first day of the season.

Redruth had not lost a game by the time they entertained Camborne on 13 October, the first club derby between the two sides since the war. There was an enthusiastic welcome from the Redruth supporters for James O'Shea, a pre-war player who had just returned home after having been held as a prisoner of war for more than three years. Around 1,500 spectators saw two evenly matched sides battle it out in a scoreless draw. However, a week later, when the two sides met on Feast Monday, it was Camborne who came out on top, 6-5. The Boxing Day fixture, played in heavy rain and in front of a large crowd, ended in a 6-6 draw. After three matches, the two clubs were only separated by a single point.

Plymouth Albion arrived at Redruth in March 1946. Plymouth had been badly bombed during the war and the Devon side had struggled to get going again in the immediate aftermath. Redruth had offered to give the visitors the gate receipts for the game, which ended in a 3-3 draw. There was a close relationship between the two clubs in the post-war period, with a number of Redruth players, including Billy Philips, John Gribble, Frank Partridge and Tony Bidgood, occasionally playing games for Albion, while Les Semmens joined them for several seasons.

Eight Welsh internationals were in the Cardiff side which arrived to play Redruth on 2 April. Redruth were determined to shut down the speedy visiting three-quarters and managed it well, although at the cost of scoring chances of their own. Neither side crossed the line for a try, but Cardiff snatched a 6-3 win after being awarded a second penalty right in front of the posts, a decision that was hotly disputed by the home crowd.

Trevor Harvey from Lanner recalled being taken to this game as a boy by his great uncle, Morcom Richards. It was the first Redruth game Trevor had ever seen:

> 'At the end of the match, as the players were leaving the field, Morcom ducked under the barrier and ran across the field, with me in hot pursuit. He shouted at each Cardiff player in his broad Cornish accent: "You never crossed the line didee! You never crossed the line!" I had no idea what he meant in those days and I suspect, with his accent, neither did the Welshmen.'

In Redruth's first post-war season, they won 22 of their 37 matches and lost eight, the best record of any Cornish club. At the club's annual meeting, Roy Jennings was elected a life member in recognition of his outstanding contribution to Redruth's success in the previous decade. This was an honour usually reserved for past presidents of the club.

The highlight of the 1946/47 season was the first visit to Redruth of Swansea, one of the top clubs in Wales. A large crowd saw the Reds defeated 7-0, but they could once again console themselves with the fact that the Welsh side had not crossed the home line. Much of the credit went to the Redruth full-back, Frank Partridge, whose last-ditch tackles kept out the speedy Swansea three-quarters. The following week, Newbridge, another successful Welsh side, were the visitors, but this time it was Redruth who took the honours, 9-8. Bath arrived in October, fielding Scottish international Ian Lumsden and would have considered themselves lucky to leave with a 5-3 win.

There was a great deal of roughness and ill feeling when Redruth travelled to Penzance at the beginning of November to face the newly created Penzance-Newlyn. The first half saw a good, open game with little to choose between the two sides, although the Redruth scrum and line-out were just a little better at getting the ball to their backs. The second half was a different matter. One Pirates player had to be taken to hospital with a gash over his eye, while another was carried off with an injured leg. The Reds won the encounter 9-0.

The following week, Redruth met Camborne for the first time that season in the annual Feast Monday encounter. More than 4,000 people watched a distinctly off-form Redruth lose 13-0 to a Camborne side featuring three players borrowed from the Camborne School of Mines. There was a shock just before Christmas when Redruth lost 13-0 away to Falmouth, the first time in 18 years they had been beaten on the Falmouth pitch. The Boxing Day match against Camborne ended in a draw.

January saw the Reds make the trip to London to play St Mary's Hospital. Their opponents had been regular Easter visitors to the Recreation Ground since 1928, but this was the first time Redruth had faced the medics on their own turf. Despite taking a large number of enthusiastic supporters, some of whom had been offered accommodation by members of the London Cornish Association, Redruth lost 20-11. Only good anticipation and accurate kicking from Frank Partridge at full-back prevented the gap from being wider.

One of the speedy backs on the hospital side was Edward Keith Scott, who had just been selected for his first England cap. A Truro man by birth, he had also captained the Cornwall side and been a regular in the Oxford University rugby and cricket teams. Scott was shortly to return to Cornwall to practise as a doctor and, once there, he would join Redruth, giving the club their first England international since Bert Solomon, 39 years previously.

Rugby was badly disrupted by the arctic weather conditions that hit the whole of the UK at the end of January 1947, with many games cancelled as a result. With a foot of snow on the ground, milk was delivered in Redruth by tractor and a student from Camborne School of Mines was seen going down Beacon Hill on skis. With no rugby on which to report, 'Full-back', the sports correspondent of the *West Briton*, amused himself by picking what he felt could have been the best Cornish team from the inter-war years. Given Redruth's stunning performance throughout the 1930s, it is perhaps surprising that only six of the club's players – Harry Ham, Roy Jennings, Harry Faviell, Fred Rule, Les Semmens and Tommy Harris – made his final selection.

Redruth were under way again at the beginning of March when they hosted a side from the Royal Navy Artificer Training Establishment, which had been commissioned at HMS *Fisgard*, a shore establishment near Torpoint in East Cornwall. The Reds proved too much for the young naval trainees who, despite being full of enthusiasm, were heavily outgunned and lost 40-6. Meanwhile, a future Redruth star was about to make his international debut. Roy Harris, a pupil at Redruth County Grammar School, was selected as scrum-half in the English Schools side to face Wales on 22 March. Harris would play a pivotal role in the success of Redruth in the mid-1950s.

Later that month, rugby and other spectator sports were hit by a government decision to ban weekday matches, confining play to Saturdays and bank holidays. Ministers felt that removing the distraction of midweek sport would improve productivity, encouraging people to stay at work, and would help the country to recover from the Second World War.

Rugby union, still an amateur game, was less affected than professional sport, but Redruth and other Cornish clubs had been playing top touring sides like Wasps and Swansea on weekdays. These matches brought in large crowds, which helped bolster club finances. The RFU extended the season to 3 May so clubs could finish their programmes, but the ban turned out to be short-lived and the restrictions were lifted at the beginning of the 1947/48 season.

Easter Saturday brought Wasps to the Rec, but driving wind and heavy rain had turned the Redruth pitch into a lake. Just five minutes into the game, it was impossible to identify the colour of the players' shirts. Only 20 minutes were played each way and it was no great surprise that the game ended without score. Wins over Exeter, Penzance-Newlyn and Paignton rounded off a season which saw Redruth finish, once again, as Cornwall's most successful club.

Henry Grylls, the remaining co-founder of the club, died at his home in Redruth on 4 May 1947 at the age of 90. Apart from his time at Clifton College, and a spell training as a solicitor, he had lived his whole life in the town. As well as running his own law practice, he had represented Redruth on Cornwall County Council, serving as chairman before the war. He was probably the last survivor of the original group of men who had come together to form the club in 1875, when Grylls was only 18.

The club's AGM heard plans to improve the facilities at the Recreation Ground, with a proper clubhouse being added to the changing rooms already in place. This would need a programme of fundraising and the supporters' club was revived in the hope that Redruth's passionate fans would help. Gwen Semmens, wife of the club's hooker, Leslie, was appointed as the organiser and was encouraged to get more women interested in the game.

It had perhaps not escaped their notice that the Pirates had a woman president, Mrs R.C. Lawry, wife of the recently retired president of the CRFU, and it was also hoped that increasing the number of ladies present might inspire more courteous behaviour in the crowd.

Les Semmens was selected to captain the combined Devon and Cornwall team that faced the Australian touring side at Camborne on 13 September. Billy Phillips was the other Redruth player in the team. The Wallabies won 17-7, with both Semmens and Phillips singled out for their performances. On the same day, Redruth opened their season with what, before the war, had become the traditional first match, an away game at Torquay Athletic. It resulted in what had also become the traditional result in this particular fixture, a Redruth defeat. It must have been the sea air.

The programme for this game indicates that the Reds were continuing to play with letters on their jerseys, rather than numbers, something they had adopted in 1919. While numbering systems of various kinds had been in use since the 1890s, there was nothing in the game's laws to determine how individual players should be identified. Clubs could pick whatever system they liked, so it was not unusual for one side to number one to 15 upwards, from the loosehead prop to the full-back, while the other side went the opposite way. Other clubs chose to use letters but, again, not necessarily in the same order as each other.

Keith Scott appeared in a Redruth jersey for the first time when Penryn, now one of Cornwall's leading clubs, visited the Recreation Ground on 20 September. A crowd of well over 2,000 spectators turned up, keen to see the England international in his first Redruth game and hoping for plenty of tries. Sadly, Redruth's two penalty goals by Carpenter were the only points scored. Carpenter also kicked Redruth's only points in their 14-3 defeat by Aberavon on 30 September, the first time the Welsh club had visited the Rec. After the game, both teams were entertained at a social and dance organised by the newly re-formed supporters' club.

Redruth forward power proved too much for Exeter in an away game at the County Ground where the Reds came back from a 3-0 deficit at half-time to win 14-3. It was a good result against one of the South West's top sides. On 14 October, Abertillery became another Welsh side making their first visit to the Recreation Ground, the visitors winning 11-5. The same week, Keith Scott was named captain of the Cornwall side for the first County Championship game against Devon, where he was joined by fellow Redruth players Frank Partridge, Les Semmens and Tony Bidgood.

A feature of the Redruth game of this era was a return to a more compact game relying on forward play, to the exclusion of a more open approach. Before the war, the Redruth pack had been one of the lighter ones in English rugby, but they now had a much heavier scrum. It had been used to good effect against Exeter and it turned the tables at Penryn where, in a return game, the Reds won 3-0. The *Western Morning News* described the Redruth performance as disappointing because their backs were underused. For Redruth, the result was more important than the manner in which it was achieved and criticism from the press was a price worth paying to grind out a win. This philosophy would prove useful in the league era.

The Boxing Day match against Camborne resulted in a 6-3 win for Redruth. A guest player on the Camborne side that day was a 20-year-old wing named Robert Shaw, a former Truro School pupil, who scored Camborne's try. He would later make a name as an actor, appearing in a number of films including *From Russia With Love* and *Jaws*.

Devonport Services were the visitors on 2 February 1948 – Redruth Feast – winning 6-0 and avenging their defeat by the chiefs in early December. Rugby in Redruth on this day never seems to have become as established as the Camborne Feast games. The match coincided with the death of the Redruth chairman, Ernie Pearce, who had played for the club between 1894 and 1909 and had served as player and committee member for more than 50 years.

A week later, it was announced that Keith Scott, Redruth's star centre, would become the first Cornishman to captain an England side when they took on Ireland at Twickenham on 14 February. He had already played for England against Wales back in January. England narrowly lost the Ireland game, 11-10. There were more honours in March when Les Semmens was selected to play for the Barbarians. He was the third club player to turn out for the famous nomads, emulating Howard Faviell in 1935 and Keith Scott in 1946. Semmens was yet another player many thought should have been selected for international honours; the standard of his hooking was admired throughout the game.

One encouraging feature of Cornish rugby at this time was the number of spectators coming to watch games. An article in the *West Briton* in March 1948 reported that more than 2,000 people had watched Redruth beat Camborne School of Mines 9-3. Redruth was certainly providing value for money in terms of results, as the club began to regain some of its pre-war prestige. With players of the calibre of Scott, Semmens and Phillips, there was an unrivalled pool of talent within the club.

Then came a blow for both Redruth and England when Scott's jaw was broken while he captained his country against Scotland at Murrayfield. The severity of the injury was not apparent to him until after the game, when he discovered he had difficulty eating and drinking. It ruled him out of the England side to play France in the final round of that year's Five Nations and left Redruth without him for the rest of the season.

Scott's injury was just one of many that plagued Redruth during the final quarter of the 1947/48 season. Billy Phillips broke an arm, as did Gordon Robins. This was the second time Robins had sustained the same injury and he took the decision to hang up his boots. A former schoolboy international and one of the best forwards the club had ever fielded, he would be a great loss. In the latter part of the season, Redruth found themselves fielding up to eight reserve team members, so it was a much-weakened side that lost 6-3 to Exeter in one of the final matches of the season.

The following week, players from Redruth joined those from Camborne and Camborne School of Mines to play as the Mining Division against a combined Falmouth and Penryn team. It was a benefit match for the family of the former Redruth player, Aubrey Craze, who had died in December 1947 at the age of just 27 and only six months after getting married. More than 4,000 spectators attended the match, which the Mining Division narrowly won 19-16. By all accounts, it was one of the best games seen in Cornwall for many years and a fine display of running rugby. Aubrey's widow, Gwendoline, was at the game.

A second benefit game was held later in April when a team made up of pre-war Redruth players faced the current Redruth side. The former players, dubbed the 'Old Crocks', included Roy Jennings, Howard Curnow, Fred Pappin, Ken Williams and Dai Jones and they also borrowed the services of Les Semmens. The veterans more than held their own until the last quarter, when the superior speed and fitness of the younger Redruth XV proved too much for them and they lost 29-3.

At the AGM, the secretary attributed the club's mediocre season largely to the wave of injuries which had plagued them in the previous few months. Only 20 of the 45 games played by the chiefs had been won, although there was brighter news from the reserve side, which had lost just two of their 28 matches. The plans to build a clubhouse with a licensed bar were being delayed by a post-war shortage of materials.

There was a turn for the better in the 1948/49 season, which would see the Reds rack up their best performance since the war. An early 25-3 defeat of visitors Plymouth Albion was followed up by a stunning 14-3 win against visitors Llanelli, summed up in the *Western Morning News* headline 'Irresistible Redruth pack outplays Llanelli'. Billy Phillips led what was considered one of the best displays of forward play seen in Cornwall for a long time. However, no matter how well they played, they seemed to be unable to end a run of away defeats against Torquay, who were rapidly becoming their bogey team. This time, they went down 17-3. There were better results to follow; an away win at Penryn was followed by a thrilling 13-3 victory over visitors Bath at the end of September.

A last-minute try on a rain-soaked Beacon Park gave Redruth a double over Plymouth Albion. Freddie Bray went over virtually unopposed while the Albion players stood waiting in vain for the referee to blow up for offside. Redruth's former hooker, Les Semmens, who had turned out occasionally in the past for Albion, was now playing for them regularly, while his brother, Len, was now a regular for the Reds. However, Les did play for his former club in a very wet Boxing Day clash when the strength of the Redruth forwards was instrumental in a 9-0 win over Camborne, in spite of them having recruited three players from Camborne School of Mines for the game. The next encounter between the two sides saw the Redruth backs play a major role in Camborne's 8-3 defeat, meaning the Reds had won all four matches that season against their closest rivals.

The end of March brought one of the hardest games seen at the Recreation Ground for some time. When Welsh visitors Cross Keys came to play on a rock-solid pitch, the crashing encounters had several players seeing stars. Their defence held firm until the last five minutes when Gribble jinked through a sea of players to score a try, which Phillips converted to give the Reds an 8-3 victory.

As the season drew to a close, Redruth ended Penryn's unbeaten home record against any Cornish club that season by beating the Borough 8-6 and they forced a 6-6 draw against Wasps on Easter Monday, despite having to field a weaker side than normal. The Reds ended the season having won 31 of their 43 games, losing nine, with only one club, Exeter, managing to do the double over them.

During the close season, the supporters' club had, at its own expense, erected toilets on the ground, the first time such facilities had been provided. Previously, the sole sanitary structure was a rather decrepit urinal which constantly suffered from a blocked drain. One imagines female spectators were required to have strong bladders. The supporters had taken on the task of ground maintenance alongside their core function of raising funds for the club. This community spirit, which prompted members to volunteer their time and skills for a host of tasks, has been and remains the bedrock of the club to the present day.

In the late summer of 1949, Redruth was entering its 75th anniversary season and there was a mood of optimism that the recent results would lead to another successful spell. While they could perhaps only dream of reaching the heights of the 1930s, the club would certainly recreate some of the magic from that golden era and continue to produce players who would become household names in Cornish rugby and beyond. Redruth began the season with nearly all the players from the previous year and young players from the reserves, and from the junior clubs around Redruth, continued to harbour the ambition of moving up to the chiefs.

The strength of on-field opposition from other Cornish clubs was growing. Truro started the season as a senior club for the first time, while further east at Launceston, Liskeard and St Austell, rugby was now being played at a competitive standard. Hayle, Penryn and Falmouth had all considerably strengthened their sides. However, Redruth's first match was against another visiting Welsh side, Pontypridd, who were making their first trip to the Rec. The Welsh international Glyn Davis was the star of the evening, his kicking often causing problems for the Redruth defence. The game hung in the balance until a last-minute try for the visitors allowed them to snatch victory, 8-6.

Redruth finally managed to notch up an away win at Torquay, their first victory at the Devon club since 1910. In the second half, Billy Phillips scored a drop goal which, added to a converted try just before the interval, gave the Reds an 8-0 win. In the next match against Truro, which both sets of supporters assumed the Reds would win easily, the new senior club turned in a fine performance before eventually succumbing 24-10.

Camborne, who were having a poor season, were confidently expected to be well beaten at the Boxing Day fixture at Redruth. However, the Cherry and Whites silenced the home supporters with a storming display in the first half, which saw them turn around 11-3 up. Order was restored in the second half when Redruth scored 16 unanswered points to win 19-11.

Redruth's last game of 1949 was away to Plymouth Albion, where they arrived without the services of Phillips or Scott. Albion were determined to prevent a repeat of the previous year's double defeat and won 6-0. Once again, Les Semmens, playing for Albion, faced his brother, Len, in the scrum, both playing hooker. The defeat left the Reds having won only 13 of their 21 games so far that season, although, more encouragingly, they had lost to just one Cornish side, an away defeat at St Ives.

The hitherto good relationships with Welsh touring sides were put to the test when Maesteg arrived at Redruth in late March, brandishing an unbeaten record that season. Redruth mounted a fierce battle against their opponents. Tempers became frayed and fists started flying. It was only in the dying minutes of the game that the visitors dropped a goal to win by the narrowest of margins. It was all too much for Maesteg, who subsequently decided to remove Redruth from their fixture list. According to their fixture secretary, a Mr Prosser, this was because of the spirit shown in the games between the clubs that season and the previous year. To add insult to injury, he went on to praise the other Cornish clubs his side had played on the tour.

Redruth's response was swift. In a press statement, the club said that requests for games between the two sides had always come from Maesteg, whose decision not to visit Redruth simply saved the Redruth club the necessity of declining the fixture should they have been approached. The statement went on to say that the club had many letters from touring sides praising the fine spirit shown in games and the hospitality extended after them.

The highlights of Redruth's away game at Teignmouth in April were broadcast on BBC Radio, in a programme called *Sport In The West*, a regional opt-out of the Home Service, which would later become Radio 4. It was the beginning of the broadcast media's engagement with sport, a liaison which, by the 1960s, would increasingly see people choose to stay at home in comfort rather than stand on a cold touchline in winter. A radio transmitter had opened at Redruth in 1943, but it would not be until 1956 that television would arrive and then only the BBC. Westward Television, the first commercial station in the South West, would not go on air until five years later. Television would, over the decades, fundamentally change the way rugby supporters followed the game and fund the eventual move to professionalism.

At the end of April, a match was held against Swansea as part of the commemoration of Redruth's 75th anniversary. The Welsh club had been regular visitors to Redruth and were celebrating their own 70th anniversary at the same time. Four thousand supporters turned up at the Recreation Ground to see Swansea win 6-0. After the match, a dinner was held at the Clinton Café and the Redruth Supporters' Club organised a dance.

Jack Richards, the Redruth chairman and soon-to-be president, told the club's AGM in July that Redruth had played some of the best games in its 75-year history that season. The club had won 30 of its 45 games and drawn two. The reserve side was unbeaten at home and had won 25 of its 33 matches. He also took the opportunity to reiterate Redruth's opposition to any sort of so-called 'competitive rugby', whether it be league or cup competitions, claiming that the standard of Cornish rugby made such things unnecessary. He then went on to praise a number of younger players, mostly present in the room, who were beginning to make their mark at the club, including a young hooker, who had joined from Redruth Albany, named William J. Bishop.

It is interesting to wonder whether, in future years, Bill Bishop ever thought back to that evening in 1950 when his club chairman spoke so forcefully against competition in the game. After a distinguished playing career, Bishop would go on to serve as CRFU secretary and then to hold elected office with the RFU. In the 1980s, he would chair the Bishop Commission which oversaw the introduction of the competitive league system in English rugby. A decade later, as only the third Cornish president of the Rugby Football Union, he would take the game into the professional era. Quite what Jack Richards would have made of that, we shall never know.

Chapter Nine
A Return to Form 1950–1961

AT THE dawn of the 1950s, Redruth was still struggling to recover from the effects of the war and the continuing decline of the mining industry. There had been high unemployment in the town before the 1939-45 conflict and it had returned when the demand for Cornish metals fell when the conflict ended. The wages men had been able to earn in the mines and associated engineering works could not be matched in the alternative jobs available, many of which were in the service sector. There were plans to develop Redruth as the main shopping centre for West Cornwall, but they would never come to fruition and could not have replaced the type of jobs which had been lost.

The new decade would bring some improvements. The price of tin on the world markets began to rise, and would continue to do so for a decade. This encouraged mine owners to invest in modernisation, enabling the exploitation of ground previously thought uneconomical. Many more men were employed at good rates of pay and this fed into the local economy.

It was against this background that Redruth launched into the 1950/51 season, temporarily without the services of Keith Scott who, as a cricketer of considerable talent, was unavailable until the summer game had finished. Billy Phillips was still recovering from an injury sustained towards the end of the previous season and would be out for another month. National Service meant players were regularly called up for the military, which in those days paid little heed to sporting commitments. The club secretary, Hugh Downing, told *The Cornishman* that there was a good number of young players coming through and he expected that the large gates which Redruth had always attracted would continue.

Redruth went to Torquay hoping to repeat the success of the previous season, when they had broken their 39-year duck. It took Torquay three-quarters of the game to get the measure of their visitors, but they eventually won 14-6 and the Reds left disappointed. In mid-September, Halifax RFC made their first visit to Cornwall, losing to Redruth 8-5 in a close contest.

Another team making their first visit to Redruth was Rosslyn Park, who arrived with two Irish internationals in their line-up. Redruth almost pulled off a surprise win against their illustrious visitors, finally losing 5-3. The Rosslyn Park secretary sent Redruth a letter praising the club for the hospitality they had received, paying tribute to the enthusiasm of the supporters and complimenting the club on the playing surface.

Improvements continued to be made to the ground and its facilities. The club received permission from Camborne-Redruth Council to sell food at matches, although alcohol still did not feature. In November, the Redruth Supporters' Club paid to improve the lighting on part of the path at the rear of the stand, where the current clubhouse now stands, and a tender was accepted from the Electricity Board.

To the surprise of almost everyone, Redruth lost the opening fixture of the season against Camborne, but they got their revenge on a gale-swept Camborne Feast Day, winning 3-0. The two results showed that Town were starting to recover their form after a couple of poor seasons. November rain and gale force winds caused many matches to be cancelled and it was a dull run-in to the end of the year.

Just before Christmas, a milestone in the club's player development was announced when it was decided to form an Old Boys' side. Frank Roberts agreed to set up the new team with financial aid from the club. It would, in time, form the basis for the colts section, vital in bringing in young players and developing them until they were ready to be considered for the senior teams. Many of Redruth's best players have followed this path into the chiefs.

Plummeting temperatures on the approach to Christmas saw Redruth's match at Plymouth Albion fall victim to a frozen pitch. However, the annual Boxing Day clash with Camborne did go ahead and turned out to be one of the best games between the two sides for a long time. Camborne shocked the home crowd by running in two tries close to the final whistle, taking the match 14-9, the first time they had won the Boxing Day game since 1933. The match seems to have been played in good spirit, with both sets of players singing carols on the pitch at the interval, conducted by the referee.

Alfred Thomas, the former Redruth and Cornwall scrum-half, died at the end of December 1950. His partnership with James Davey in the early 1900s had provided one of the greatest half-back combinations ever seen by club or county. Thomas had been injured while in South Africa and had been unable to lace up his boots again when he returned to Cornwall. His funeral was well attended and among those paying their respects was his old team-mate Maffer. Davey himself lived on for less than a year, dying in October 1951.

The season as a whole was nothing more than average for Redruth, with the club still looking to hit its stride in the post-war era. The chiefs won 28 of their 48 games and lost 12, with Billy Phillips once again scoring more than 100 points in the season. The reserves lost just one game, against Redruth Highway on Easter Monday, despite players having to move up to cover injuries in the first XV. The club's finances were in good health, with a surplus of more than £800.

The growing popularity of soccer in Cornwall remained a cause for concern among adherents of the handling code. Rugby clubs feared that it might prove an irresistible attraction to players and supporters. At a meeting of the supporters' club in August, the Redruth chairman, Jack Richards, encouraged those present to keep faith with rugby in Cornwall. He told the gathering that, while the round ball game had not, until then, had much impact in the Mining Division, it was increasingly strong in east Cornwall and making inroads in the west. The supporters' club, which had now swelled to more than 500 members, continued to be an important ally to the club and its stalwart members underpinned the playing side's success.

A vociferous group of Redruth supporters made their presence felt when they cheered their team to a rare 14-11 win at Torquay at the start of the 1951/2 season. The *Torquay Times and South Devon Advertiser*, by no means a neutral voice, felt that the home side had played the better rugby, while the Cornishmen had relied on kick-and-rush attacks. Quick thinking by Caddy and Rhys had delivered two tries to secure the win for the Reds.

Back in Cornwall, momentum in the rivalry between Redruth and Camborne was swinging towards Town. According to the *West Briton*, Redruth had been given little chance of beating their rivals when they met at Redruth on 15 September, but for a while an upset looked to be on the cards. As the game entered the final five minutes, Redruth were 11-9 up. A late rally by Camborne saw the visitors snatch a converted try to take the honours.

Tragedy struck at Redruth's away match at Penryn on 6 October. Out on the wing was a promising young player called Lewis Collins, a 21-year-old farm worker who had joined Redruth from Stithians. Collins had the ball and was heading towards the line when, three yards out, he was tackled by two Penryn players. One of them, Ronald Edney, heard a bone snap as Collins went down and immediately pulled back his team-mate and called the referee.

Collins was taken to the Royal Cornwall Infirmary in Truro, but died the following morning following surgery on his leg. An inquest heard that he had suffered an embolism following the operation, a rare event after such a fracture. The Redruth captain, Billy Phillips, told the coroner that the game had been played in good spirit and that the tackle had been perfectly fair. Stanley Collins, the young man's father, had been at the game and also said he had no complaint about the way it was played. The coroner held that no blame could be attached to anyone for the incident. The Redruth club later presented the player's parents with a framed blazer badge inscribed 'In memory of Lewis Collins, 1951–52'.

Redruth lost the Feast Monday game against Camborne 14-6, largely because their backs completely failed to take advantage of the superiority of their pack. It was perhaps a sign of Redruth's inability to fire on all cylinders that only three of their players – Thurston Thomas, Tony Bidgood and Billy Phillips – were in the Cornwall side that lost to Somerset in the County Championship in December. It would have been only two, but Penzance's rising star, John Kendall-Carpenter, missed his train connection and Bill Phillips was drafted in at the last minute.

Bill Bishop, now a regular in the Redruth side, scored a vital try in the Boxing Day game against Camborne, described by the *West Briton* as one of the most competitive matches between the two clubs for years. For sheer toughness and undiminished ferocity, the struggle between the two packs was one of the hardest within memory. Bishop's score almost won it for Redruth, but a late try from Camborne saw the sides finish on equal terms.

Another young Redruth player was singled out for praise after the match; C.R. Johns, better known as "Bonzo'. Like Bishop he stood on the threshold of an illustrious rugby career and his name would soon appear on the roll of honour alongside other club legends. At the time, however, Redruth were plagued with injuries and struggling for form and Camborne had the best of the games between the two clubs for the first time since the 1925/26 season.

Redruth were again having something of a mediocre season by their standards, having won ten and lost eight of the 20 games played up until the turn of the year. Injuries continued to plague the side. The former Fylde player and Lancashire trialist, John Stopforth, who had recently joined the club, broke a leg in the game against the Royal Naval Engineering College. He was one of eight first-choice players who were out of action. Redruth had also lost the services of Keith Scott, the former England captain, who had decided to retire from the game to concentrate on his job as a GP.

The second half of the season failed to show any improvement. Redruth went down 16-8 to Penzance-Newlyn and Hayle did the double over them for the first time in many years. At the AGM, the chairman, Jack Richards, admitted it had been a lean season but said there were a lot of young players coming through. The Redruth Old Boys, founded just a year before, had won 17 of their 29 games and Richards hoped that many of them would eventually play for the chiefs.

The AGM came just before the announcement of the death of John Charles 'Barney' Solomon at the age of 69. Bert's older brother had played at full-back and centre for both Redruth and Cornwall, and without his encouragement and support, it is doubtful that Bert would have overcome his natural reserve and pulled on a Redruth jersey. The example of the two older Solomon brothers, who played side-by-side at centre for several years, in turn inspired their two younger brothers, James and William (Dickus and 'Jocky') and then the generation which followed.

The traditional away game at Torquay started the 1952/53 season and this time it ended in a pointless draw. Judging by the match report, Redruth were full of fight but failed to come together as a unit behind the pack. Their next game was a home defeat against St Ives, but there was some joy in the Redruth camp when they defeated Camborne 6-5 in the first game that season between the two neighbours.

Before the game, a new scoreboard was unveiled at the Recreation Ground. It had been donated by Mr and Mrs

William Martin in memory of their son, Henry John Martin, the former Redruth player who had died in the war while serving with the Royal Corps of Signals. Several thousand spectators stood bareheaded as the memorial was unveiled in front of the two teams by the president of the CRFU, W.J. Robbins. Mr Martin told the crowd that they had been privileged to have the memorial accepted on the field on which their son had played for a club with such a great reputation and tradition. The scoreboard still stands at the corner of the ground.

Results were mixed in the early part of the 1952/53 season. Hopes that Redruth were beginning to improve were dashed by a 22-8 home defeat by Penzance-Newlyn, although the Reds did win 8-3 away at Plymouth Albion. However, a good win away at Hayle and a 6-6 draw against Camborne in the Feast Monday match suggested things were beginning to improve. Had it not been for a knock-on in the dying minutes, Redruth might well have secured a win over Camborne.

Redruth Reserve side were having a much better season. They had lost just one of the nine games they had played and scored 200 points, conceding only 25 in reply. Fifty of those points had been scored in a single match against the Camborne School of Mines reserves, in which the opposition failed to score. They had also, to their great satisfaction, beaten their counterparts at Camborne twice.

The first XVs of the two clubs were due to meet, as usual, on Boxing Day, and the encounter was previewed in a *London Daily News* round-up of festive fixtures: 'Whatever the weather I predict a really warm time at Redruth. They entertain, if that is quite the word, their near neighbours and rivals, Camborne.' Redruth forward Billy Phillips was rather more succinct: 'We'll wish each other the compliments of the season, then get stuck in.' Get stuck in they did, as Redruth won the match 11-6.

The game of the season came on 24 January when Penzance-Newlyn arrived at the Recreation Ground with an unbeaten record of 23 games, just three short of a rugby union club record.

The Reds had not lost at home since 9 October and the match attracted one of the largest crowds ever to watch such a game at Redruth, bringing in £200 on the gate. The Pirates fielded their England international, John Kendall-Carpenter, as well as three other exiles, Luke, Jennie and Nicholas. The two teams battled it out, with the Reds having a stronger pack, but the Pirates' backs showing a greater turn of speed. Five minutes from time, Redruth were ahead, but then Penzance scored an equalising try to take the score to 6-6 and preserve their unbeaten record. The report suggested a draw was a fair result, with both sides being able to claim something from the game.

By the end of March, Redruth had put together a five-month run of being unbeaten at home. It was finally ended by visitors London Hospital, who beat them by a single point, 9-8. There was some consolation in having ended their run against out-of-county opposition and by such a narrow margin.

The final game of the season, away to Camborne, saw the Reds lose 8-0 in an unusually boring match for a local derby between the two sides. However, the season's honours went to Redruth with two earlier wins over their arch-rivals and one game drawn. At the same time, Redruth Reserves hammered their Camborne counterparts 47-0, which made them the only Cornish rugby team to have been unbeaten all season. They had scored a total of 707 points, conceding 73, and won 31 of their 34 games without a single loss.

Overall, it had been a better season for Redruth. They had finished fourth in the merit table behind Penzance-Newlyn, St Ives and Penryn, but ahead of Camborne. However, in the table that just featured games against other Cornish sides, they took second place, beaten to the top by the Pirates, who had played three fewer games. At the annual dinner at the end of May, the club celebrated the progress being made. The former Redruth international, William Grylls, was a guest of honour.

A few days later, the Recreation Ground became a centre of festivities to celebrate the coronation of Queen Elizabeth

II. The Redruth silver band played there at a large open air church service on the last Sunday in May and two days later, the band led schoolchildren in a procession from Penventon to the ground, where they were given saffron tea-treat buns and soft drinks, and then took part in sports, dancing and a pony gymkhana. What Arthur Faull, the club groundsman and caretaker, thought about having ponies trotting about on the pitch is not recorded.

The beginning of the Elizabethan age ushered in a sense of change across Britain and the arrival of the modern world had an impact at the rugby club, too. The 1950s brought a rise in car ownership and the committee found itself having to grapple with the problems of parking and traffic control, particularly at well-attended games. From time to time, the AA and RAC were approached to provide assistance; on other occasions, additional police were hired to direct traffic and to assist on the gates. The presence of one or more constables at a game, a sight rarely seen in modern times, was still common in the decades after the war.

The police were certainly required when the Surrey side Esher came to the Recreation Ground on the evening of Friday, 11 September 1953. The referee, a Mr Knox from Penzance, was the subject of barracking from the home crowd, many of whom felt his decisions were favouring the visitors. Feelings were running so high that police officers had to escort the unfortunate official from the ground. Esher won 15-9.

The following day, Redruth made the trip up to Devon to face Torquay Athletic, an early season fixture that usually went the way of the home side. However, for only the third time since the 1920s, the Reds recorded an 11-0 victory. This was followed by a 6-0 win over Rosslyn Park, with Bill Bishop applauded for some brilliant hooking which denied the opposition forwards the ball.

The team had been joined at the start of the 1953/54 season by Harold Stevens, a Cornwall county player and formerly the St Ives captain. He was teaching at Trewirgie School and decided it was more convenient to transfer his allegiance to Redruth. Stevens was destined to be another of the club's more memorable players. Like Roy Jennings and Bert Solomon before him, he was a centre of great skill and he would eventually collect 60 caps for Cornwall, have an England trial and play for the Barbarians.

In late October, Stevens was man of the match at what was claimed to be the first floodlit rugby match to be played in Cornwall. He was selected as part of a Cornwall XV to play a Presidents XV at the Cornwall Stadium, a speedway track at St Austell. Only 1,000 people were present, but the white ball was clearly visible. It seems the hosts and the newspaper reporters were unaware that rugby had been played under lights at the Redruth Recreation Ground 74 years earlier.

Stevens and Tony Bidgood were the only Redruth players selected for Cornwall in the autumn County Championship matches. Les Semmens was called up, but was still playing for Plymouth Albion. However, a number of the club's younger players were now being spoken of as potential county players, including the forwards Bill Bishop and Alan Mitchell. Other players, such as Paddy Bradley, Fred Bray and Keith Eddy, were beginning to make their mark.

Redruth Reserves continued their winning ways, including an amazing 80-0 defeat of the reserve team from Camborne School of Mines. As the *West Briton* helpfully pointed out to the mathematically challenged, this averaged one point for each minute of the match. Redruth's scrum-half, Roy Harris, had a personal total of 32.

By mid-October, the Redruth senior side had already played 13 games, more than any other Cornish club. On Boxing Day, Redruth made up for their defeat at Camborne on Feast Monday by beating the Cherry and Whites 6-0 in atrocious weather conditions. With the ground a quagmire, the play was mainly confined to the two packs and Redruth were fielding their strongest forward line-up that season, led by Billy Phillips. This was to be the veteran's last season; he had first played for the

Reds before the war and many felt that, had the conflict not intervened, he might well have been in line for an England cap.

The second half of the season brought continuing improvement in Redruth's performance and, by the end, they had won 29 of the 48 games they played, losing 12. The reserves were unbeaten in their 1953/54 campaign, winning all of their 22 games and amassing a total of 754 points, conceding only 22. The season had also seen work on new banking for the Recreation Ground, providing a much better facility for spectators.

The 1954/55 campaign started with the visit of the first Scottish side to play at Redruth, Jedforest, from the Scottish Borders. The visitors scraped a 9-8 win, with the help of forward Charlie Renilson, who would later turn professional and play rugby league for Great Britain during the 1960s. The following week saw a 20-0 win away at Torquay, the best result Redruth had ever achieved on the South Devon ground.

In early October, an article in the *London Daily News* drew attention to a 6ft tall 16-year-old whose 14st frame had already secured him a place as Redruth's first XV lock forward. John Phillips, son of the legendary Billy, had been named in the side to play against RNAS *Culdrose*. Had his father continued playing for just a few more months, they would have lined up together.

There followed a hard-fought game against a touring side under the banner of the John Williams XV, which included no fewer than eight internationals and two Barbarians. Penzance-born Williams had won two caps for England in 1951 and had skippered Richmond RFC. The tourists pulled ahead 14-11 in the last few minutes, but Redruth could hold their heads high after a match that had swept from one end of the ground to the other and was declared to have had everything from hard forward play to brilliant passing and running.

A 12-0 win at Camborne in the annual Feast Monday fixture promoted Redruth to the top of the rugby performance table published in the *London Daily News*, pushing Harlequins off first place. At that time, tables were usually based on winning percentage, which evened out discrepancies in the number of games each side had played. This system would continue to be the most popular way of determining performance until the advent of the league system three decades later.

In November 1954, it was announced that Bonzo Johns had been selected for an England trial game. It would be the first of many such selections over the years, but he was to join the long list of talented Cornish players who were passed over for a full England cap.

In a mid-season round-up of rugby in Cornwall, the correspondent of the *West Briton*, who wrote under the name 'Full Back', noted that Redruth had not lost a game since the tussle with the John Williams touring XV back in September. His opinion was that the club's success was due to sound teamwork under the excellent leadership of Harold Stevens and to having available some first-class reserves. Redruth added to their tally of victories with a 6-3 win over Camborne on Boxing Day. The *West Briton* reporter was not impressed with the match, calling it a bit of a bore, although he admitted that it was unlikely that it had been seen the same way by the partisan crowd, the biggest gate in Cornwall that day.

Hugh Downing, who had been Redruth's long-serving club secretary, collapsed and died in the street on 29 January 1954. His death brought to an end a remarkable term of service stretching back to 1901 when his father, Henry Downing, had been appointed secretary. Henry had held the office until 1914 and Hugh had taken on his father's old position when the club had restarted after the First World War. He had served as secretary from then until 1950 when ill health had forced him to stand down. However, he had immediately taken on the post of treasurer, which he had been holding at the time of his death.

Redruth continued in winning form for the rest of the season, rounding off their run of good results with an 8-0 win over Camborne. The victory sealed an unbeaten record against Cornish sides, against whom they had won 20 of the 22 games played. It was the fourth time Redruth had beaten Camborne that season – a clean sweep. In total, Redruth had won 35 of their 44 games, losing just four. The reserve side had lost only three of their 27 games. The success was reflected in the club's finances which, according to a report given to the Redruth AGM in July, saw gate money rise by more than £200, contributing to an annual surplus of more than £1,300.

Boots on the ground, and in the stands, were the club's main source of revenue, so whispers about the possibility of people being able to watch rugby on television were beginning to cause concern. The first live televised rugby match had been in March 1938 when the BBC had covered the Calcutta Cup match between England and Scotland, although, at the time, only a small number of people owned TV sets, nearly all in the London area. The war had temporarily ended transmission and it had been late into the 1940s before the BBC had begun covering rugby regularly again.

Until the mid-1950s, regular media coverage of Cornish rugby was limited to the newspapers, although summaries of games involving Redruth had appeared sporadically on BBC radio. The BBC had begun construction of a new television transmitter on Dartmoor, designed to serve most of Cornwall, which would begin service in 1956. The club's secretary, Ken Williams, was quick to see the threat posed by the new medium. He warned members that it was absolutely necessary for all teams to play open and attractive rugby if they were to maintain their power to attract the crowds.

Williams was also the driving force behind improvements to the Recreation Ground, which he said would make it one of the finest rugby facilities in the country. The redevelopment included enlarging the stand, the addition of a new clubroom, improved dressing rooms for the players, a changing area for referees and the addition of a treatment room. A programme of fundraising had already raised enough money to begin work, with a large donation coming from the Redruth Supporters' Club.

The beginning of the 1955/56 season saw the John Williams XV return to the Recreation Ground. The Reds held their own up front but lacked the pace in the backs shown by the tourists, who could once again boast a sprinkling of internationals. The watching crowd was rewarded with a close match, with the visitors held to an 8-6 win. The annual early season trip to the seaside at Torquay saw Redruth produce a tearaway brand of rugby that had Torquay rocking on their heels. Having established that losing was not a foregone conclusion, the Reds notched up a 19-6 win. The following week, they entertained Surrey side Esher, beating the visitors 14-8. One Redruth player singled out in the press was the speedy winger, Eddie McCloughlin, one of the most naturally talented players to come out of Cornish rugby.

Touring sides tended to favour the early part of the season and the resulting congestion in the fixture list put immense pressure on the players. In one six-day spell, in the middle of September 1955, Redruth travelled to St Ives on the Thursday for a scoreless draw, beat Penryn 14-0 on the Saturday and then faced Rosslyn Park on the Monday, losing 15-3. Evening games, while the light allowed, were very much part of the rugby calendar, leaving little time for recovery.

Fortunately, younger players were coming into contention, several having moved up from the reserves side which had been so successful in the previous two seasons. Their resilience contributed to the overall strength of the side. Among them were Raymond Peters, Paddy McGovan and Ken Abrahams. Sadly, Redruth's dominance in Cornish rugby at the time was not reflected in the county side, with Bonzo Johns their only player selected to face Somerset in the opening round of the County Championship, although Harold Stevens was drafted in as a late replacement before the game.

Having beaten Camborne 11-6 on Feast Monday, the Reds were again victorious on Boxing Day, 11-0. On the following day, a combined Redruth and Camborne side took on a team representing Falmouth and Penryn. The fixture brought speculation that this type of inter-regional game could take the place of the traditional county trials. There had been some discussion between club secretaries about matches of this nature which might put a bit more money into the game, as well as showcasing talent for the Cornwall selectors. One thing is certain, the idea of a joint side featuring Redruth and Camborne players in the same team would have been unthinkable in the days when the teams often refused to face each other, never mind play shoulder-to-shoulder.

In January 1956, a quarter of a century after Redruth had been labelled 'the cavemen of rugby' by the Bristol press, they made their first visit to the city, facing what had become one of the best rugby sides in the country. Bristol won 11-5, but the Reds were applauded off the field for their strong performance. The *Bristol Evening Post* said there was determination written over every move the visitors made. It bemoaned the fact that the crowd might well have been bigger had many home supporters not felt that Bristol would thrash Redruth in the same manner they had routed Camborne in a previous fixture.

Redruth's hopes of retaining the unofficial Cornish championship were dashed when, having been beaten at home by St Ives, they lost their final match of the season to Falmouth, 6-3. It was the first time in 35 years that Falmouth had done the double over the Reds.

For the very first time, the club AGM at the end of June was held at the Recreation Ground, thanks to the completion of the new clubroom. The secretary told those present that it had been a fairly successful season under the captaincy of Harold Stevens. They had played 50 games, of which they won 27 and lost 19, scoring 440 points against 295. Not only had they played an unusually high number of games, but bad weather in February and March had caused rugby to be cancelled for five weeks, making the remaining weeks even busier. It was explained that this long break and a lot of injuries had led to a decline in the club's record.

One bright spot was the formation of a colts side out of the former Redruth Old Boys XV, which had folded two years previously. Harold Stevens had stepped in and revived the side, with the aid of a new committee. Colts rugby had been inhibited in the past because of having to share the club's main pitch. Now a new colts pitch had been constructed just above the main ground, with new posts provided by the kind gift of one Brigadier Williams. This level of the game was now firmly established in Cornwall and played under the supervision of the CRFU.

The new Redruth clubhouse was officially opened on 3 September 1956 ahead of a match against the visiting John Williams XV. Roy Jennings came to do the honours, recalling that when he had first played in the early 1930s, players had changed in the town and walked down Green Lane to the Recreation Ground for the game. The addition of a licensed bar would provide a new source of income. More than half the £5,000 cost of the building work was raised locally, with the balance coming from the RFU. Work on a new grandstand would start once more money had been raised.

The match that followed the grand opening saw 11 internationals, including five British Lions, take the field against Redruth. The home side managed to stay in touch throughout the first half but found themselves down to 14 men shortly after the break when skipper and full-back Fred Bray went off with what turned out to be a broken arm. The visitors turned up the heat and won 30-12.

On Feast Monday in Camborne, Redruth ran up their biggest winning margin over their neighbouring rivals, romping home 41-3, with 23 of the points scored by Harold Stevens. The *West Briton* reported that it was a fantastically easy victory and that the only interest for non-partisan spectators was how many points Redruth would actually score. On Boxing Day, the Reds clocked up their third win of the season over Camborne, 13-0.

Redruth's momentum continued through early 1957, giving them one of their best seasons since the glory days of the 1930s. At the Recreation Ground in late March, a punishing defeat of Newton Abbot by some 30 points resulted in the away team applauding the Redruth players off the field. This sporting gesture from Newton Abbot after they had suffered such a heavy defeat was appreciated by the home crowd. The *Torbay Express* said Redruth had deserved the tribute, for they had played dazzling rugby and been on top throughout.

Easter came in late April and it was a particularly memorable one for one young player, who was home from school in Devon for the holidays and playing regularly in a Redruth jersey alongside his older brother, Nigel, for the first time. He was Richard Sharp, the son of Freddie, a mining engineer who had played for Camborne School of Mines and Wasps, and had put his son's name down for membership of the latter as soon as he was born.

His mother, Kathleen, née Chandler, was from Redruth, but Sharp had been born and spent his early years in India and was eight years old when he saw his first Redruth game. He later reminisced in his autobiography that he could not remember who the opposition were, but he remembers being awestruck at the sight of Billy Phillips and collecting his autograph on every possible occasion thereafter: 'He seemed to me to bestride the field like a giant; there seemed to be nothing that he could not do.'[48]

That Easter of 1957, Sharp was a member of the team that played against St Mary's Hospital on Good Friday, Lloyds Bank on Saturday afternoon and a touring Wasps side on the Monday, winning all three games. Wasps had been hard hit by injuries and Sharp and his brother also played for them against Penzance-Newlyn on the Saturday evening, managing two matches in one day. In his book, Sharp recalls the Redruth team that played Wasps on that Easter Monday and it stands as one of the most memorable XVs ever to pull on the Redruth shirt.

B.H. Seabourne was at full-back; Eddie Mcloughlin, Harold Stevens, Nigel Sharp and Michael Richards made up the three-quarters line; Richard Sharp and Ken James were the half-backs; and the pack was made up of Tony Bidgood, Ken Abrahams, Alan Mitchell, Bonzo Johns, John Phillips, Raymond Peters, J. Westwood and Paddy Bradley. Small wonder that of the 51 games played that season, the side lost just six.

Sharp discovered that rugby at Redruth was great fun, but far removed from the style of game he was playing at school. He recalled that in club rugby: 'One is knocked down rather than tackled. […] One must learn to avoid a short arm tackle, flying fists and boots and the other coarser elements in the game if one is to be successful and survive.' [49]

However, Sharp was not put off: 'I have nothing but gratitude to Redruth, my home club, for providing me with such happy experiences in those early days.' [50]

There was much to celebrate at the 1957 summer AGM. The secretary, Ken Williams, told the room that the team had played football of a very high standard and that their style of play had compared most favourably with the best Redruth teams in living memory. The reserves, now known as the Redruth A team, had also had a successful season, winning 32 of their 36 matches.

The 1957/58 season started well, a 5-0 win over Rosslyn Park was the highlight of the early weeks. Gerard Walter of the *London Daily News* reported that:

> 'A drizzle of rain, a greasy playing surface and a treacherous ball could not dampen the enthusiasm of the terrific Redruth pack. It was a pleasure to watch a pack which obviously trains properly for their job and plays as a unit.'[51]

News of the match evidently reached the ears of the England selectors, as Harold Stevens was picked at full-back for the first England trial, playing for the Possibles. His performance was not up to his usual standard and he was dropped for the second trial and, like so many Cornishmen before him, not selected again. If he was disappointed, it only served to redouble his efforts on the pitch and there were points galore for the taking over the Christmas and New Year period. In the Boxing Day derby against Camborne, the Reds beat their old rivals 38-5 and in a match against Hayle early in the new year, they won 58-0.

Stevens and Bonzo Johns were the two Redruth players selected for a combined Devon and Cornwall side which held the touring Wallabies to a 3-3 draw and almost snatched victory at Plymouth's Home Park in late January.

The following month, Redruth was chosen as the venue for the County Championship semi-final against Lancashire, a game that Cornish supporters had been anticipating for decades. The club built additional temporary stands for the occasion, which saw 20,000 people pack the Recreation Ground, with many others who could not get in perched precariously in trees and on hedges. Harold Stevens captained the Cornwall team, playing alongside fellow Redruth players Ken Abrahams, Alan Mitchell, Bonzo Johns and John Phillips. Stevens was the hero of the hour, scoring eight points in a 14-8 victory that put Cornwall into the County Championship Final for the first time since 1928. Unfortunately, Cornwall lost 16-8 to Warwickshire in the final at Coventry.

Jack Richards described 1957/58 as an up and down season which had started brilliantly, but in which play had not maintained the previously high standard. Nevertheless, the club had done enough to keep their position as the most successful Cornish club. Of the 45 games played, the chiefs won 32 and drew six while the A team had won 27 of the 31 games played.

Redruth's momentum continued into the 1958/59 season, although they lost an early game against first-time visitors

Cambridge University, the students having far too much pace on the outsides. By the end of the year, Redruth had won 19 of their 25 games, including a 14-6 win over Camborne on Boxing Day in which Richard Sharp made his derby debut. The year ended with a win over a combined Falmouth-Penryn side played, according to newspaper reports, in a sea of mud.

Redruth went to Falmouth on 18 February, defeating their hosts 34-3 in the first match in the town played under floodlights. This game saw Redruth maintain an unbeaten record against Cornish clubs which stretched back nearly two seasons, but within a fortnight it had come to an end. A weakened Redruth side lost 6-0 away to Penzance-Newlyn, the only slight consolation being that the Pirates had failed to cross the Redruth line.

A scoreless draw against Camborne and a surprise defeat by Camborne School of Mines knocked Redruth off the top of the merit table. It was the first time they had lost to the students since 1948. A win at Penryn in the final match of the season would have allowed the Reds to reclaim the title of Cornish champions, but the Borough ran out 11-3 winners. One notable statistic for the season was provided by the Redruth winger, Gordon Osborne, who broke the club's try-scoring record, having crossed the line 28 times.

Terry Mankee, an 18-year-old who played for the Redruth colts team, was selected to captain the England Schoolboys' side to face Wales at Bridgend on 18 April 1959. Another graduate of the Trewirgie School rugby nursery, he was making his second appearance in an England shirt and had already made his first XV debut for Redruth.

September 1959 saw something of a revival. Harold Stevens, still playing at the top of his game, moved from centre to stand-off. The change clearly suited him and he scored 15 of Redruth's points in a 21-12 defeat of visitors London Scottish. Two days later, Redruth delivered another storming performance, coming back from 9-0 down to beat Esher 20-9, the first time they had beaten the strong Surrey side. Once again, Stevens was the top scorer with 11 of Redruth's points. Esher claimed in the programme notes for their subsequent match against Exeter that the sloping pitch at Redruth was worth ten points to the home team.

A Penryn supporter took this up and declared that it was little wonder that his club had not won at Redruth for 30 years. He argued that Redruth's home record could not be compared with those clubs which did not have the benefit of such an incline on their pitch. This sparked the inevitable riposte from a Redruth supporter that the teams changed ends at half-time, so any advantage from the slope would be shared equally.

The first of the season's games against Camborne ended with a 36-3 win for the Reds, with the *West Briton* complaining that: 'Much of the glamour of the derby matches between Redruth and Camborne has been worn off simply because, in recent seasons, it becomes less a question of who will win than by how many points Camborne will be beaten.'[52]

That same week, the Cornwall side to face Devon in the County Championship was announced, with Harold Stevens, Ken Abrahams, Bonzo Johns, Richard Sharp and Paddy McGovan the five Redruth players on the starting sheet. Cornwall would, once again, progress to the semi-final, but they would fall in the final furlong, losing 14-11 to Surrey at Twickenham with 5,000 loyal supporters cheering them on. Harold Stevens was lauded as the hero of Cornwall's run, emulating the performances of Roy Jennings and Bert Solomon from previous eras.

The *West Briton's* harsh words about Camborne's lack of success against Redruth must have had an effect. The Cherry and Whites held them to a 3-3 draw on Feast Monday, a game in which the backs from both teams seem to have played a minor role. Boxing Day allowed Redruth to continue their winning record in this fixture, but by a narrower 6-0 margin. Camborne had only won the festive encounter once since 1933. Redruth ended the decade having won 18 of the 26 games they had played so far that season, putting them top of the merit table, with just one loss to another Cornish side.

In the mid and late 1950s, Redruth had again achieved the sort of success that mirrored the magic of their 1930s triumphs. They had won the unofficial championship of Cornwall four times in six years and it would have been five had it not been for a stumble in the last months of the 1958/59 season. The name of Redruth was again linked inextricably with rugby wherever the game was played and individual players had taken part in semi-finals and finals of the County Championship, international trial matches and schoolboy internationals.

The new decade was to signal something of a plateau as far as Redruth's performance was concerned, although individual players continued to raise the club's profile outside Cornwall. Not least of these was Richard Sharp. He was selected in January 1960, in his first year at Oxford, as a late replacement at fly-half for England against Wales in the opening game of the Five Nations. Sharp recalls being particularly moved by the support he had from Cornwall; among 80 telegrams waiting for him in the changing room were messages from Roy Jennings, Harold Stevens, and, of course, the Redruth rugby club. Their common theme was the instruction to do a 'proper job!'

By the beginning of March 1960, Redruth were being touted as favourites to win the unofficial Cornish championship, having gained a convincing 14-3 win at Penzance-Newlyn. A week later and the bookmakers would have been hastily revising their calculations, as Penryn defeated the Reds 17-8 at the Recreation Ground, the first time they had won a game at Redruth in 36 years. To add to Redruth's woes, their hooker, Ken Abrahams, was sent off following what was described as an unsavoury incident, a catch-all phrase much used by the press of the day.

The arrival of a speedy new player in the ranks boosted morale. Derek Prout joined from Launceston after moving to study at Cornwall Technical College. He would go on to play for Northampton and win two England caps in the 1968 Five Nations. During his time at Redruth he was a prolific try scorer and he helped Redruth nail down their place at the top of the Cornwall table when he scored twice in a 13-10 defeat of visitors Stroud. The final game of the season was against Bridgwater and Harold Stevens scored 11 points, helping his club to victory and taking him over the 200 points mark, making him the most prolific scorer in Cornwall. Since coming to Redruth from St Ives in the 1953/54 season, Stevens had scored a remarkable 1,128 points for his club.

The 1960 AGM shone light on the wider changes happening as the world entered a new decade. The president, Jack Richards, said it had been a disastrous season from a financial point of view due to the counter-attraction of the *Grandstand* BBC television programme. He said the standard of play could be improved if the players of all teams made open and attractive play their paramount aim. He was, however, prepared to give competition rugby a trial to see if interest could be stimulated after a difficult season for the club.

The secretary, Ken Williams, also referred to the comparative decline in interest in club football [rugby], but said Redruth's suggestion that a form of competitive rugby be tried in the county as an experiment for one season had not met with sufficient approval. The treasurer's report from Alan Todd underlined the severity of the problem. Decreased gates, the cancellation of a game against St Luke's College and poor weather for the Good Friday game against St Mary's Hospital had resulted in a deficit in the general account of £430. Fortunately, the social club and the supporters' club had both made generous contributions which had restored the club's liquidity.

The start of the 1960/61 season saw changes in the opposition, too. Among the touring sides making their first appearance at the Recreation Ground were the Metropolitan Police, who arrived in September. They proved a handful for the Reds, who lost the match 19-3. This followed a loss to Cambridge University. Redruth were still struggling to find their form ahead of the first meeting of the season with Camborne on 1 October, but they were good enough to beat their old rivals 9-3.

Performances began to improve as the season unfolded. Redruth won the Feast Monday game at Camborne 14-0, although Camborne played most of the game with 14 men following an injury to Heard. They followed this up with a 38-0 home win against Newton Abbot, their biggest win over the visitors for ten seasons, with the Redruth skipper, Roy Harris, kicking seven conversions out of the eight he attempted.

Redruth remained unbeaten against other Cornish clubs until 11 December at Penzance when the Pirates pushed through to a 10-5 win, leaving the race for the unofficial Cornish championship wide open. The Boxing Day derby against Camborne ended in a 14-14 draw, the first time Camborne had shared the honours for a decade. There was a good result at Plymouth Albion in February. The home side had not lost to a Cornish side that season but were defeated 14-11 after a rampant Redruth performance.

Redruth's unbeaten home record ended with an 11-9 defeat by Penzance-Newlyn, who were making their return trip to the Rec, although the Reds did manage to fight back from an 11-0 deficit at half-time. There was a much improved performance in mid-March when St Luke's College arrived with a team containing five county players and a Welsh international. The Redruth pack, led by Ken Abrahams, managed to shut down the speedy college backs and Redruth romped home 35-6. St Luke's was a noted nursery of rugby talent and fixtures with Redruth would resume in the league era, with the college rebranded as part of Exeter University.

Redruth lost their hold on the Cornish championship and had to be content with second place behind Penzance-Newlyn, a club which would flourish in the 1960s. On a brighter note, it was reported that the club's colts side had won 13 of their 25 games, with four of its members selected to play for the Cornwall Colts XV. From a shaky start in the 1950s, the colts would grow into one of the main sources of players for the chiefs in the ensuing decades.

The club continued to find it a challenge to retain paying spectators. The BBC's *Grandstand* television show was drawing large audiences on a Saturday afternoon and, in a few years, ITV would provide the additional attraction of *World Of Sport*. The age of the armchair sports fan was dawning and the effect on gates, particularly if there was a Five Nations match on the television, was noticeable. The 1961 Redruth AGM was told that gate receipts had fallen again that season, resulting in another financial loss.

However, pleas that the RFU should follow the example of The Football Association and ban the broadcasting of live rugby matches would fall on deaf ears. The RFU, while continuing to champion the principles of amateurism, was quite fond of the new money that television was bringing into the game. For the first time, the rugby authorities were happy to sacrifice the interests of individual clubs to swell the coffers at Twickenham. It would not be the last.

Chapter Ten

A Time of Ups and Downs
1961–1987

THE LEGENDARY Redruth player, Bert Solomon, died at Tehidy Chest Hospital on 30 June 1961, aged 76. Whatever had taken him to Guy's Hospital 50 years earlier had not prevented him from enjoying a long life. Since his sudden withdrawal from rugby in 1910, he had lived quietly in his house at Close Hill, next door to the Recreation Ground. He continued to work in the local bacon factory until his retirement and in his spare time had tended to his racing pigeons and his allotment. He still regularly watched Redruth play, but always tucked himself away behind a hedge at the Camborne end of the ground to avoid any attention.

It is a measure of his status in the game that, just a few years before he died, the former RFU president and Harlequins fly-half, Adrian Stoop, came to visit him. He had played alongside Bert in that 1910 England victory over Wales and he spent some time chatting with Bert in his kitchen while a chauffeur guarded his car from the attentions of local lads. Stoop, like many others of his era, had never forgotten the mercurial Cornishman. The headline on the *West Briton* obituary summed up his contribution to the game: 'Bert Solomon – Gleaming Jewel in a Golden Age of Cornish Rugby'.

The 1961/62 season opened with the visit of Bordeaux to the Recreation Ground. The match was widely advertised in the weeks leading up to the game, but turned out to be disappointing for the spectators. The visitors arrived without a number of their internationals and were obviously tired from a 36-hour journey from the south west of France. Redruth won the game 18-3 and, according to reports, could well have increased the scoreline.

Redruth lock Fernley Furze found himself much in demand in late September, playing for both Devon and Cornwall in friendlies against Surrey. Ken Abrahams, Bonzo Johns, Paddy McGovan and Derek Lawrence were the other Redruth players in the Cornwall side. Three days later, Cornwall played a second friendly, against Lancashire at Redruth, with Abrahams, Johns and McGovan selected. The matches were effectively trials for the coming County Championship matches and most of them would make it through to the final sides, along with Derek Prout.

A few days later, Richard Sharp was the outstanding player for the Reds when they inflicted a 25-6 midweek defeat on Penzance-Newlyn, the worst defeat the Pirates had suffered for over a decade. Sharp, at fly-half, scored 16 of the Redruth points, including a try in the final minutes. It was a different tale the following Saturday. With Sharp unavailable, Redruth lost 5-0 to Falmouth thanks to a storming performance from Ray George, the Falmouth flanker, who would later transfer his allegiance to Redruth. Sharp found himself playing against his home club when he appeared in a visiting Oxford University team that beat Redruth 21-9 at the beginning of October.

There was a shock for Redruth in the annual Feast Day match against Camborne, when they lost 11-9, the first time the Cherry and Whites had beaten them since 1956. The game was in the balance until near the final whistle when the Reds conceded a penalty try, the referee having judged that Camborne's John Rocket had been obstructed while chasing an attempted clearance kick. Under the rules at the time, a successful kick was still required to secure the points for a conversion after a penalty try and Camborne's Sweeney did the honours.

Penzance-Newlyn gained revenge for their heavy defeat earlier in the season by beating the Reds 20-3. The press were beginning to notice, and emphasise, the disparity between Redruth's storming performances when Richard Sharp was playing and the more lacklustre occasions, as in this game, when he was not. Sharp's commitments to his Oxford University studies, and his international career, meant he often missed games for his home club.

Sharp was not the only Redruth player to be considered for international honours. That year, Paddy McGovan, Ken Abrahams and Bonzo Johns would all take part in international trials, but McGovan and Abrahams were destined to join Johns on the list of Cornwall players who would be considered by the selectors but never wear an England shirt.

Redruth had a good Christmas in 1961, recording their first win over visitors Taunton in four games, while winning the Boxing Day derby against Camborne 14-0. However, results in the new year were patchy, even when Maurice Sloggett, Brian Stephens and Bill Orkney joined from Penryn. An 8-0 defeat at Hayle, a club that Redruth had regularly defeated over many decades, seemed to sum up the mood of the season. Redruth dropped to fourth place in the Cornwall championship behind Penzance-Newlyn, Falmouth and Penryn. The merit table system skewed the results somewhat, as Redruth had played only 19 games against other Cornish opposition, compared with 23 each for Falmouth and Penryn. Nevertheless, it highlighted Redruth's drop in form.

One name missing from the side was that of Harold Stevens. He had contributed handsomely to Redruth's success over the years, but had failed to be selected for several key Redruth games the previous season and had decided to return home to play for St Ives. While he had undeniably lost some of the speed that had made him so deadly behind the scrum, his tactical brain remained sound and it was no coincidence that the St Ives club were playing better rugby since his return. It was suggested in the local press that Redruth had been foolish to let him go.

The following few seasons continued to mark a distinct swing of the rugby pendulum away from the Mining Division, for so long the heart of Cornish rugby. Penzance-Newlyn had topped the table and Penryn, Falmouth and Hayle all presented much stronger opposition than in the past. In September 1962, Truro inflicted an 11-3 defeat on Redruth, the first time the city club had beaten the Reds since it had moved up to the senior level after the war. It was little consolation that Camborne were going through a similar poor patch.

Redruth did beat their old rivals 15-3 in the first derby game of the 1962/63 season, aided by 12 points from the new half-back pairing of Mike Sweeney and Dieter Whear, who had both joined from Camborne that season. Whether it was their perceived treachery which caused ill feeling is not clear, but the game was marred by scuffles between players and the referee had to call together the two captains on more than one occasion. Camborne gained their revenge on Feast Monday, beating Redruth 11-9, a carbon copy of the previous year's result.

Redruth came back at their old enemy in the Boxing Day derby, helped by what was now a rare appearance for his home club by Richard Sharp. He was playing in the unaccustomed position of full-back, from where his darting runs through the Camborne defence were instrumental in Redruth's 11-5 victory. After Christmas, it was announced that Sharp would become only the second Redruth player and the third Cornishman to captain England, following in the footsteps of Keith Scott and Penzance's John Kendall-Carpenter.

He would quickly become, at the time, Redruth's most successful player at international level, both in number of caps and in performances, playing 14 times for England and leading the side to a Five Nations championship in 1963. In the summer of 1962, he had been on the Lions tour to South Africa, although he had missed six weeks of it with a broken cheekbone after a much-criticised tackle by Springboks winger Mannetjies Roux during a match against Northern Transvaal. On his return home, he presented his collection of international rugby shirts to the Redruth club.

Whether playing for club, county or country, Sharp was one of the most admired players of his generation, his ability to seemingly glide past opponents with effortless grace making him a favourite with the crowds. His best game for England was probably the 16-0 defeat of Ireland in 1962. *The Times* almost broke into poetry over his performance.

'There is a languid grace about this modest young man which is fascinatingly deceptive. Opponents realise this only after he has passed them, lissom and beautifully balanced, he glides like a silent wraith through gaps nobody else has spotted.'[53]

Sharp quit rugby in 1965 to concentrate on a teaching career before working in the china clay industry for 30 years. He was not someone who could give less than his best and he believed strongly in the need to be at peak fitness in order to play the game. His four years of top-level rugby had coincided with his time as a student at Oxford and he explained in his autobiography that the time and energy required by the serious business of international rugby were simply not compatible with the need to earn a living.

While he was at the very top of his game, Sharp was one of the most recognised and talked about figures in the sport. His name would, in time, become familiar to a new generation, but for quite a different reason. The author Bernard Cornwell was an admirer and, when he began writing his novels about a soldier in a rifle regiment during the Napoleonic Wars, he took Richard Sharp's name for his hero, adding a final 'e'.

In the middle of the 1962/63 season, Sharp had been shuttling around the country for England trials, wondering how fellow players who were working could possibly meet all the commitments, when rugby came to an abrupt halt. The whole country was hit by a big freeze which made most pitches unplayable. The final England trial was transferred from a frozen Twickenham to Torquay in the hope that the pitch there would be playable. Four hours before kick-off, the town's parks department was baling the five tons of straw which had been covering the pitch for the previous 48 hours in an attempt to stop it freezing. The England v the Rest match went ahead, with England winning 6-0, and Sharp was duly chosen for the upcoming match against Wales. Redruth's Paddy McGovan was also there, playing for the Rest, but he did not make the England team.

Cornwall had also been badly hit by the big freeze. Redruth were out of action for nearly the whole of January and when they did take to the field, on 9 February at Camborne School of Mines, the game was called off after 50 minutes due to driving rain, gale force winds and a pitch that had become unplayable. The refusal of the RFU to extend the season meant Redruth, like other clubs, were struggling to fit in rearranged fixtures, although the coming of lighter evenings allowed some midweek games.

The season ended with a visit by Gloucester to the Recreation Ground, the visitors eventually winning 15-9. Gloucester had raced to a 15-0 lead at half-time but Redruth rallied after the break. That game summed up the Reds' performance in a disappointing season. A strong pack, led by Bonzo Johns, more than held its own up front, but weaknesses in the three-quarters were exploited by speedier opponents. It was but small consolation that Camborne had been defeated in all four games played.

John Phillips followed in the footsteps of his father, Billy, when he was elected Redruth's captain for the 1963/64 season. Phillips had made a huge impression when he arrived at the club as a teenager, but a spell of ill health had threatened his rugby career. However, he had recovered to be a powerful presence in the Redruth pack. His captaincy kicked off with the usual early season matches against touring sides, including a John Williams XV, now dubbed 'the Tankards', which boasted a number of international players. Redruth delivered a superb performance to win 12-11 and managed to put on a good show against a visiting London Scottish side that fielded six internationals, eventually losing 11-6.

It is difficult to overemphasise the importance these touring sides had in helping to hone the standard of Cornish rugby. The duchy remained remote from the centre of the rugby world, but many well-known clubs were keen to have a few days in Cornwall as a build-up to their own seasons. These early season tours also maintained the profile of Cornish rugby across the country.

The traditional match on Camborne Feast Day went ahead for the last time in November, with Redruth winning 8-0. The writing had been on the wall since the previous year, when the workers at Holman, Camborne's biggest employer, had voted to go to work on Feast Monday in return for having Christmas Eve as a holiday. Not only did this have an effect on player availability, it also resulted in a lower gate.

The race for the Cornish championship was won by Penryn, whose star newcomer that season was a 16-year-old winger named Kenny Plummer. Redruth were second in the table of games against other Cornish clubs, but well down the table that covered all matches played. The end of the season saw the departure of two of Redruth's best players – flanker Raymond Peters, who had played for the club for 12 years, and the skilled hooker, Ken Abrahams, who had won 39 caps for Cornwall. The club had been boosted by the return of Kingsley Thomas, who had been playing fly-half for Taunton and Somerset, but had returned to his home town. He was elected captain for the 1964/65 season.

The continuing fall in form resulted in both Penryn and Truro doing the double over Redruth. This was the first time since 1921 for Penryn and the first time ever for Truro. Penryn continued to set the pace in Cornish rugby, with Camborne suffering from the same lean spell as Redruth. Richard Sharp made one of his increasingly rare appearances for his home club in the 1964 Boxing Day game, in which Redruth snatched a draw against their old rivals with two late tries.

Redruth's home tie with Plymouth Albion, which ended in a 3-3 draw, saw the final regular appearance in a red shirt of flanker Paddy McGovan. He had quit his job with the South Western Electricity Board to join the Metropolitan Police. McGovan had been capped 29 times for Cornwall and been an England trialist on three occasions. His strength and experience would be a serious loss to the club.

In an acknowledgement of the effect of televised rugby internationals on home gates, Redruth took the decision to delay kick-offs against Penryn, on 13 March, and Penzance-Newlyn, on 20 March, to after 5pm. They hoped armchair supporters might be encouraged to come down to the Recreation Ground for a breath of fresh air. Not everyone was happy with evening games. Redruth's agreement to play Penzance-Newlyn in their final game of the season on a Friday evening caused one supporter to vent his displeasure. In a letter to the *West Briton*, C. Goldsworthy beseeched the Redruth committee to consider 'the few supporters who were left', and complained he had never had a hope of having tea and getting to Penzance to see the game. If he had gone, he would have seen his side go down to a 9-0 defeat.

The end-of-season merit tables for 1964/65 told a sad story for the Reds. Their record in all games played was just 18 wins out of 45, putting them third from bottom. In matches against other Cornish clubs, Redruth did finish a little higher, but trailed behind Penryn, Truro, Hayle and Penzance-Newlyn. Even allowing for the fact these tables were based entirely on winning percentage, ignoring the number of games played, they were seen as an indication of who was up and who was down in Cornwall.

In September 1965, Redruth pulled off a major surprise when they beat visitors London Scottish 5-0. The victory was built on the strength of the Redruth pack, with Bonzo Johns, Rex Buckingham and Derek Collins to the fore. Victory against St Ives, added to a close win at Truro and a surprise 19-8 win at Hayle, gave the Reds a better start to the season than they had experienced for some time. One of the tries at Hayle was scored by Trevor Wherry, a scrum-half who was beginning to make his name in a red shirt.

The following month, Redruth travelled to Launceston for the very first time. The East Cornwall side was in its second season at senior level and still trying to find its feet against more experienced teams, and Redruth won the game 27-5. In later years, the two clubs would find themselves at the same level in the national league system and, with Camborne languishing in a lower division, games with Launceston would become some of the most closely contested matches between Cornish clubs.

Optimism generated by a better performance in the first half of the season quickly evaporated and results went downhill from January. Having already lost a number of key players, Redruth entered a two-month stretch without the services of Bonzo Johns, due to injury. While he was out, the club failed to win a single game. In mid-March, there was another blow when an injury to John Phillips put him out for the rest of the season. Altogether, Redruth won 23 of their 46 games, well below their success rate in the past. The club's president, Gordon Beckerleg, summed up the season by saying that Redruth had managed to beat the best but had themselves been beaten by the not-so-good.

The 1966/67 season saw little improvement and the Cornish rugby landscape was once again dominated by Penryn. Redruth found themselves in eighth place in the unofficial merit table, with even Newquay Hornets and RNAS *Culdrose* having better playing records. With Camborne one place below them, it had become abundantly clear that the heart of Cornish rugby was no longer in the old mining towns which had dominated the sport for decades. Redruth's record 59-6 loss at home to Exeter went down in the records at the time as the worst defeat in their history, a reflection of the dire straits in which the club found itself.

The *West Briton* headline 'Rugby at Redruth in the Doldrums' summed up the 1967/68 season. The defence was leaking badly, with an average of 14 points conceded by Redruth in each of their 53 games. It had become impossible to muster a reliable and consistent first XV and 70 different players had run out on to the pitch. Redruth had reached the final of the newly introduced Cornwall Knockout Cup, the first structured competition to be introduced in Cornish rugby since the abortive attempt by the CRFU to introduce a cup back in 1897. Unfortunately, the Reds lost 5-0 to Penryn in a lacklustre game played at Falmouth.

The Redruth legend Roy Jennings died on 5 October 1968 at a pub he had been running for many years at Ham Green, near Bristol. One of the outstanding goal kickers of his generation, he had played more than 650 games for Redruth and been capped 61 times for Cornwall in a career that had lasted from 1922 to 1938. He was one of a handful of players who had been invited to play for the British Lions without ever having been selected for his country and he had been part of the squad which had toured Australia and New Zealand in 1930.

Redruth RFC organised a memorial service at the town's St Andrew's Church, which was attended by 200 people, some of whom had played with Jennings and many more who had watched him in action. Paying tribute to his impact in the community, the rector explained how, in the 1920s and 30s, when work had been hard to find and food scarce, something was needed to take people out of their difficult life. 'Roy Jennings, the footballer, had done just that.'

In 1969, Redruth hosted all but one of Cornwall's home games as the black and golds fought their way to the County

Championship final, in which they faced Lancashire at Redruth. Cornwall had always been well supported, but the club faced the prospect of accommodating the biggest crowd ever to watch a game there. In preparation for the event, the club demolished the old changing rooms, which had stood in the north eastern corner of the ground and had been the background for many photographs of Redruth teams of the past. This provided more standing room on the bank and, added to a temporary stand which had been built for the semi-final, meant that an estimated 23,000 people packed into the Recreation Ground. Derek Prout, Bonzo Johns and Ray George were the three Redruth players in the Cornwall side. They were 9-0 up at half-time but failed to score in the second half and eventually lost the match 11-9.

There was a slight improvement in Redruth's performance in the 1968/69 season, resulting in a fourth-place finish in the merit table. Penryn remained at the top of the table of matches between Cornish clubs, just ahead of Hayle. In the table of all matches played, Redruth were fifth but, after several years of disappointing results, it was a small step in the right direction and their best season since 1963/64. A young prop forward named Terry Pryor was beginning to make his mark and he would continue to help drive improvements in the strength of the pack.

Ken Williams, the long-serving secretary, told the Redruth AGM in July 1969 that the lack of good coaching was to blame for the club's sub-standard performances. He said that players and selectors must adopt a 'professional approach', a phrase that would have had RFU officials clutching at their pearls, but it summed up the determination of the club to raise standards. He said that the same tactical errors were being repeated match after match and that this would continue unless the players were prepared to get together and discuss these problems.

In modern times, it may seem astounding that, after a century, the RFU was still trying to maintain the Corinthian spirit of the game's founders and believed that formal coaching was a step in the direction of professionalism. Rugby had always relied on younger players learning skills from their more senior team-mates and this approach extended all the way up to international level.

In *Slammed*, a 2023 BBC documentary, John Taylor, one of the heroes of the all-conquering 1970s Welsh side, recalled that, until the end of the 1960s, the Welsh team were not permitted to come together until the Thursday afternoon before a Saturday game. They had one run-out on the Friday and warmed up before kick-off on matchday by doing press-ups in the car park.

Pressure to change this amateur approach was eventually driven by encounters with southern hemisphere teams who, sensibly, ignored many of the RFU's diktats and were consistently arriving on tours with a higher degree of fitness and superior skills due to quality coaching and fitness training. Even so, Wales did not appoint a full-time coach until 1967 and England waited until the end of 1969.

Once Redruth's annual meeting had moved on from the thorny topic of coaching, there was some positive news about plans to cater for the increasing success of the colts side, which had won 24 of its 31 games that season. Extra changing facilities were to be added and a new full-size colts pitch would be installed. There were also plans to extend the clubhouse. Congratulations were extended to Arthur Faull, the club groundsman and caretaker, who had completed 50 seasons in the role, which was described as an amazing record of devotion and loyalty to the club.

Ray George, who had transferred to Redruth from Falmouth, was appointed captain at the beginning of the 1969/70 season, a position he would hold until 1972. He led his side to one of the best early season spells for years, with high-scoring wins over the Royal Naval Engineering College and a hard-fought 17-10 defeat of visitors Exeter. Penryn had dominated the last few years of Cornish rugby, so there was much excitement when Redruth entertained the Borough on 1 November 1969, with both sides having been unbeaten by any other Cornish club. The match officially resulted in a 19-19 draw. In fairness to Penryn, it should be recorded that the Hampshire referee had signalled 'goal' for a Redruth penalty kick, despite his two touch judges signalling 'no goal', as it had sailed a foot wide of the posts.

Bonzo Johns played his final game for Redruth when they hosted Coventry on 1 May 1970. Although the Midlands side ran out easy winners, 19-6, Bonzo had the satisfaction of scoring Redruth's only try of the game. The referee, Vic Martin, made himself the most unpopular man on the field when he disallowed a second Bonzo try. At the end of the match, Bonzo was carried from the ground by his team-mates.

He had made more than 600 appearances for his club over a 21-year period and had been capped 88 times for Cornwall, a record he held until overtaken by fellow Redruth player Tony Cook two decades later. His character, strength and natural humility made him popular with supporters and players alike. Although he had been invited by the Barbarians to play in their prestigious Easter tour of Wales in 1962 and had been an England trialist multiple times, many in Cornwall felt he had, like many Cornish players before him, been unjustly overlooked by the England selectors.

His skills as a power scrummager would be sadly missed at Redruth and the secretary Ken Williams told the club AGM in July 1970 that it was vital to build up the forwards in order to provide a platform for a new generation of backs who were coming into the club. Graham May and Keith Gilbert were two new recruits to the back division and would join more established players such as Mike Downing, Doug Yelland, John Mills and Mike Sweeney. Williams announced that Sweeney had scored 292 points in the previous season, which he said was probably a club record. The meeting also heard that the colts had won the Cornwall Sevens tournament for the first time. Such was the influx of young players that a colts second XV had been formed.

The 1970/71 season saw a continued improvement in Redruth's performance. A *West Briton* article in November 1970 advised readers that Redruth was a club to watch over the coming months. The first XV now had a squad of 20 players, the newest member being Max Aitken, who had come to Cornwall from Waterloo, then one of the most successful clubs in the game. He made his mark immediately, scoring a try in his debut game, against Falmouth, which the Reds won 16-6. Terry Pryor, at prop, was also proving to be a huge asset to the club. He had been capped by England Schools while still a pupil at Cornwall Technical College and had now settled back in Cornwall after qualifying as a teacher at Loughborough College.

Redruth finished the season in third place in the inter-Cornwall clubs table, behind Penryn and St Ives, and fifth in the table of all games played. Full-back Mike 'Mighty Mouse' Downing became the first recipient of the Roy Jennings Cup, donated to the club in memory of the great Redruth star by his sister, Florence Bartecki. It was presented to the player judged by the selectors to have made the greatest contribution on the field that season.

Debate in the press about the overall quality of Cornish rugby when compared with clubs further up country rumbled on. Redruth's 43-13 home loss to Exeter in October 1971 was cited as evidence that clubs to the west of the Tamar were falling behind the rest of the country. The only bright spot was the performance of a 17-year-old fly-half, Nigel Eslick, who kicked nine of Redruth's points and was tagged in the match report as a star of the future.

Redruth's progress began to stutter in November when they suffered a crushing 43-0 defeat in a home match against Penryn, their second loss to the Cornish champions that season. There was some small consolation in January 1972 when the news came through that the following year's game between Devon and Cornwall and the touring All Blacks would be played at Redruth. Anticipation of such a prestigious event gave a real boost to the club and its supporters, but the news was not well received down the road in Camborne. Their club chairman, Richard Evans, said that he was absolutely shattered, that it was the first time Camborne had not been chosen to host an international touring side and that it was an 'utterly incredible' decision.

The former London Welsh player, Andy Morgan, moved to Redruth in early 1971 to take up a position with the Cornwall county education committee in Truro. He was announced as the club's new coach at the end of the 1971/72 season. A former Wales B player, he had turned out for the Reds on a few occasions, but a recurring knee injury had made it impossible for him to continue playing. However, to Redruth's delight, he was still eager to be involved in the game. Derek Collins, who had won the Roy Jennings Cup at the end of the previous season, was elected captain for the following campaign.

In October 1972, a visit by the Romanian national side provided a superb exhibition of running rugby, which saw them beat Cornwall 18-3. The *West Briton* rugby correspondent, Gerald Phillips, grumbled that Cornwall scarcely deserved to share the same pitch as the super-fit Romanians. Terry Pryor and Steven Tiddy were the only Redruth players selected for the match.

Redruth had an indifferent start to 1972/73 season, but their 14-3 defeat of Camborne on Boxing Day lifted the young side. By the end, they had worked hard enough to win 25 of their 45 games, scoring 860 points, including 140 tries. John Harvey alone, playing at centre three-quarter, had scored 34 tries.

Sadly, the improvements on the pitch had not persuaded more people to attend matches and income had fallen by almost half compared with the previous season, largely due to the continuing appeal of television. This prompted a suggestion at the AGM that Redruth home games should be played on Sunday when an international match was on television on a Saturday afternoon.

The return of John Harvey from a long injury lay-off injected some much-needed strength into the backs early in the 1973/74 season. He celebrated by having a hand in all three tries scored in Redruth's 23-10 win over Camborne in late October. In early December, a 40-year-old Bonzo Johns returned to action to play against Devonport Services. While he had lost some of his mobility, he was as strong as ever and still possessed the vital know-how to control a game. It was Bonzo who made possible the game's only try when he charged down a clearance kick and the ball went straight to Tim Penna, who touched down.

Keith Martin, who later served for a time as the club's solicitor, remembers coming back home to Redruth with the University College of London team in the early 1970s to play the reserves on a Sunday morning. The Johns-Penna combination was still a formidable force:

> 'The Redruth side included Bonzo Johns, some time after he had finished playing seriously, with Tim Penna at scrum-half, and Peter Toy on the wing marking me. Tommy Buzza played in the second row and I remember bending down to collect a loose ball which, had I done so cleanly, would have given me a clear run from our 25-yard line. However, I caught sight of Tommy bearing down on me and knocked the ball on – an appropriate reflection on my rugby career.'

Martin also remembers that when he began watching Redruth games as a boy in the late 1950s, the 1956 hit, 'Zambezi', by Lou Busch and his Orchestra, was played over the public address system at every home game. 'Perhaps,' he says, 'it was the only record the club owned'.

As Christmas 1973 approached, the Reds prepared to host Penryn, who had all but set up camp at the top of the Cornwall table during the late 1960s. This time, the Borough came off worse and a 10-0 win allowed the Reds to celebrate a double over their visitors. There was little seasonal goodwill, with Redruth hooker Trevor Tonkin sent off after swinging a fist, while John Harvey had to leave the field for 20 minutes with an injury. The Boxing Day derby was also expected to go Redruth's way, as they had already beaten Camborne twice that season, but it ended in a 3-3 draw.

Redruth's hopes of winning the Cornwall Knockout Cup were dashed when they fell to a 10-6 defeat by eventual winners Falmouth in the semi-final at the beginning of March. Since the cup had been revived in 1967, after a 71-year hiatus, Redruth had been runners-up twice, losing to Penryn and St Ives, but they had failed to lift the trophy.

Three weeks later, news came of the death of William 'Billy' Phillips, one of the giants of Redruth rugby. A farmer of considerable strength, he had proved one of the best scrummagers in Cornish rugby, usually playing in the second row. He had made his debut for Redruth at the age of 16 in 1933 and later captained the side for six seasons, having returned to the club after the war. He had played his first game for Cornwall in 1935 and won 29 county caps. Only a knee injury had stopped him playing and that was not until 1954. He had later served the club as chairman and had sat on the selection committees for Redruth and Cornwall.

He had immense presence on the field and had been the childhood idol of many young rugby fans, including an eight-year-old Richard Sharp, who later wrote of him:

> 'It was he who provided the shove in the scrums; he who caught the ball in the line-out, scored the tries, kicked the penalties, punched the opposing forwards and made the tackles. Through my young eyes there might just as well have been no one else on the field.'[54]

In the summer of 1974, Redruth could look back on an improved season, in which they had won 24 games out of 46. Although

Falmouth had been champions of Cornwall, Redruth had beaten them in two of the three matches they had played. The reserve side had won 27 of their 40 games. So many players had been ready to turn out for the club that an unprecedented third XV, known as the Extra A, had been assembled, giving players who would otherwise struggle for selection the opportunity to enjoy themselves playing the sport. However, the real success for Redruth had come from the colts, who had lifted the Cornwall Colts Knockout Cup and won the Colts Sevens tournament. In one game, the Colts had scored over 100 points, a Redruth club record. They had been excellently coached by the first XV prop forward Terry Pryor, who was not only a superb sportsman but a brilliant teacher who would devote much of his life to young people.

At the end of August 1974, Redruth celebrated the start of their centenary season with the opening of an extension to the clubhouse. The work doubled the size of the bar area and provided a new kitchen, toilet facilities and a physiotherapy room. Bonzo Johns performed the opening ceremony and George Pappin, the former Redruth full-back, regaled the crowd with stories from his playing days, which had begun in 1919.

A month later, the centenary celebrations continued when Redruth entertained a Cornwall XV. The performance saw them run rings around the Cornwall side, beating them 16-0, and five Redruth players were subsequently added to the county team for their final warm-up fixture against South Wales Police the following week. The game also saw the publication of a special booklet to mark the first 100 years of the club. The cover illustration was drawn by Redruth member Ernie Loze, a noted caricaturist. Inside was the account of the foundation of the club which had appeared in the 50th anniversary booklet in 1925, with added details from the next half century.

Despite having five players on duty for Cornwall, Redruth defeated Camborne 15-6 the following week. It was sweet revenge, as Town had knocked them out of the Cornwall Cup some weeks previous. They also had five players selected for the Cornwall Colts team to face Somerset; Nick Brokenshire, Brett Pedley, John Kitto, Graham Still and John Peters. Pedley kicked two penalties in Cornwall's 14-3 win.

A muddy encounter at Penryn, won 12-10 by the home side, saw the debut for Redruth of the former Wasps player, Dave Parsons. At 6ft 4in he dominated the line-outs, after one of which he crashed over for the only try of the game.

Five days later, visitors Camborne rained on Redruth's centenary parade at the annual Boxing Day derby when they took the honours 14-6. A game against a Ken Williams XV on New Year's Day, as part of the club's anniversary celebrations, turned into something of a damp squib due to the number of players withdrawing from the president's invitational side. Redruth ran out comfortable 44-14 winners.

In January, Redruth recorded a double over the reigning Cornish champions, Falmouth. The following month, they beat Plymouth Albion 22-12, their tenth win in succession, bringing their season's tally to 15 wins from 17 games. However, despite doing the double over both Taunton and Torquay, Redruth failed to top the merit table, and Penryn took the honours.

St Mary's Hospital arrived for their traditional Easter weekend fixture, having selected the great Welsh international, and former St Mary's student, J.P.R. Williams, at full-back in commemoration of Redruth's centenary year. Those who were there remember the star arriving in a Rolls-Royce driven by his GP father. The weather was most unseasonal for Easter in Cornwall and heavy snow meant that the game had to be abandoned with Redruth 10-0 down. One player recalled that conditions were so bad that when the white ball was kicked into the air, it seemed to disappear completely. Wayne Gunn, who was doing duty on the scoreboard, remembered he could only see as far as the halfway line. J.P.R. seemed to shrug off the cold weather, playing, as usual, with his socks rolled down to his ankles.

At the end of the season, Redruth had won 27 of their 44 games, while the Colts side had again lifted the Cornwall Cup. Graham Still, the Colts skipper, had been selected for the England Colts.

Some of the club members showed their depth of rugby knowledge when a team representing the club won the Rothmans rugby quiz, which earned them a cheque for £500. John May, Eddie Bawden, Roger Pryor and David Penberthy made up the winning Redruth A team in the final at Bridgwater. The club also entered a B team, captained by Terry Pryor and also featuring David May, Roy Thomas and Graham Parkyn.

The 1975/76 season saw Redruth still playing catch-up in the Cornwall Merit Table, finishing in third place after winning 25 of their 39 games, with Falmouth in top position. In the final of the Cornwall Knockout Cup, Redruth lost a dull game 4-3 to Penzance-Newlyn. The visit of Ebbw Vale in early April brought little cheer, as the Welsh side were in a different class and won convincingly by 39-9, all Redruth's points coming from fly-half Neil Williams.

Cornish rugby took a faltering step forward at the beginning of the 1976/77 season when the CRFU formally adopted an official merit table to measure the success of clubs over the season. Like the previous unofficial one, it counted only the first home and away games between each of the 12 participating senior Cornish sides. There was no longer a separate table to take account of games played against clubs from outside Cornwall. The Alan Barbary Memorial Trophy was to be presented to the most successful club, which would also have the opportunity to compete in the RFU's South West Merit Table. Redruth were in fourth place at the end of the Cornwall Merit Table's first official season, although they had achieved their best playing record since the 1959/60 season, having won 29 of their 47 games.

It was their merit table position that led Ken Williams to tell the AGM in July 1977 that it had been the second disappointing season in a row. The secretary, John Penberthy, told the meeting that the club was looking to set up a coaching committee in an effort to improve standards. He also encouraged players to strive for cup success, as winning the Cornwall Knockout Cup would qualify them for the RFU National Knockout Cup and bring the wider recognition the club had enjoyed in the past.

The remainder of the 1970s saw Redruth still failing to recapture the position they had once held as the most successful Cornish club. There were hopes of a revival in the first half of the 1977/78 season, when they scored 134 points in the first four games and entered the new year in second place in the merit table after a Boxing Day win over Camborne. However, they were unable to sustain their performance in the second half of the season.

In April, Redruth's Terry Pryor was announced as captain of the England B team which was scheduled to play two games in Romania the following month. Pryor was captain of Cornwall that season, he had been on the England senior bench twice for internationals against Ireland and Scotland, and he had also appeared for the Barbarians against Northampton in the Mobbs memorial match and against Swansea on their Easter tour.

In August 1978, the death was announced of Arthur Faull at the age of 86. He had been the groundsman at Redruth for 52 years, having finally retired from that position in 1975. At his funeral at the town's Wesley Chapel were representatives of the club and the CRFU and the notice in the *West Briton* referred to him as one of Cornish rugby's best-known groundsmen.

The following season brought no respite and was marked by the fact that, for the first time in decades, no Redruth players were selected for the Cornwall county side. While the Colts were still dominating their age group, the senior side lacked consistency and, by the end of the 1978/79 season, the club had won just 23 of their 48 games. They had also lost John Harvey, one of their most successful players. Despite the fact he had only played for half of the season, he had still been the club's top points scorer. Terry Pryor had been injured for a large part of the season, which was a serious setback for Redruth and which probably prevented him from gaining the England cap to which he had come so close the season before.

As Cornish rugby entered the 1980s, there was a general mood of pessimism and this was reflected in press reports of meetings at club and CRFU level. The frequency of tours by top sides from England and Wales was declining, partly due to the increased cost of travel and accommodation. Redruth, like other Cornish clubs, had seen a general fall in attendances, which had limited the amount of money they could afford to pay visiting sides to help defray expenses.

Even clubs in Devon, such as Exeter, Torquay and Plymouth Albion, now only wanted to play one match each season rather than the home and away combination that had regularly been part of the fixture list. In the past, Redruth had also enjoyed regular fixtures with the likes of Bristol, Gloucester, Esher and Exeter, as well as Welsh clubs such as Newport, Neath and Ebbw Vale. These sides often brought with them international players whose presence would encourage supporters to come and watch the games.

In addition, County Championship matches were becoming less important to the England selectors as a place to view talent. Instead, they focused on watching players when they wore their club jerseys. This made it even harder for players in Devon and Cornwall to catch the eye of selectors whose stamping ground was the Home Counties. Winning a cap for Cornwall was no longer a guaranteed way to play in front of the men from the RFU, who might be sufficiently impressed to invite a talented player to an England trial.

However, optimism returned to Redruth as the club recorded a fine 1979/80 season. They finished fourth in the table, but lifted the Cornwall Knockout Cup for the first time, thrashing Penryn 29-0 in the final. It gained them automatic entry into the National Knockout Cup. Two Redruth players,

Mike Downing and Brett Pedley, were selected for Cornwall. Three Redruth Colts – Adrian Curtis, Mark Rogers and Kevin Lane played in the senior Cornwall Cup triumph against Penryn and the Colts continued to be successful at their own level, winning the Cornwall Cup and the sevens tournament.

Redruth's first match in the 1980/81 National Knockout Cup involved a trip to Abbey RFC in Reading, which they won 9-6. Disappointingly, any hopes of retaining the Cornwall title which had opened the door to the national competition ended in October when, to the surprise of almost everyone, they lost a home tie against Launceston 9-0. Their National Cup second round clash was away to Guildford and Godalming. Redruth had never been strangers to a long road trip and they showed once again that they travelled well, returning home as 9-3 winners. Boxing Day provided a further boost when Camborne arrived for the traditional fixture sitting at the top of the Cornwall Merit Table, but Redruth took the game 9-6.

The rugby big guns entered the John Player Cup in the third round, with Redruth hosting London Irish. The exiles fielded one of the most powerful packs ever seen at Redruth, regularly destroying home possession and making things difficult for the half-backs, John Simmons and Nigel Eslick. Redruth eventually went down 12-4 but the 3,000-strong crowd made no secret of their delight in watching Clive Meanwell, the Irish kicker, miss seven attempts at goal.

Redruth would take part in the National Knockout Cup in a further 20 seasons, playing a total of 38 matches. Their best performance was in 1992/93 when they reached the fourth round, having disposed of Camborne, Bridgwater and London Welsh before losing 8-3 at home to Exeter. The competition ended in 2005 and was replaced by the Anglo-Welsh Cup, which was limited to English Premiership sides and the four Welsh regions.

The Reds would go on to lift the Cornwall Knockout Cup a further nine times after their success in 1979/80. They were prevented from playing in the competition following their 45-7 victory over Mounts Bay in 2006/07, when it was decided that Cornish clubs playing at National League level should be ineligible to take part.

The battle for the Cornish Championship had become a three-way race by February 1981, with Redruth, Camborne and Penzance-Newlyn battling it out for the trophy. However, later that month, Redruth suspended 20 of its players, including most of the first XV squad, after what were referred to as 'incidents' at a hotel in Gloucester following a 48-6 defeat by Cheltenham. The hotel manager alleged that some players had been excessively drunk, had caused damage to the hotel and had prevented other guests from sleeping, so they had been asked to leave.

The suspensions meant that Redruth fielded a reserve side for their away match at Launceston the following week and their 11-6 defeat, their first Cornwall Merit Table loss of the season, meant Camborne went back to the top. They remained there until the end of the season and won their fourth consecutive title. Redruth came second, a surprise defeat at St Austell the final embarrassment in a disappointing end to the season. There was success for the Colts, however; they won the Cornwall Cup for the sixth time in eight years.

Ken Williams retired as Redruth president at the end of the 1980/81 season. He had served the club for 55 years as a player and an official, and a presentation was made to him by Richard Sharp at the club's annual dinner. Eric Edmunds, another former player, was elected president at the club AGM in June. The meeting heard that it was a spate of injuries which had been responsible for the club's late-season fall in performance.

Redruth had applied to join the 16-team Bass South Western Merit Table for the following season, hoping to replace Taunton, who were due to be dropped after a disastrous campaign. They were refused on the grounds that they had failed to meet the requirement of having at least ten fixtures against other sides in the table. They were, agonisingly, just one short.

The merit table system was a frustratingly loose way to calculate the best-performing teams each year. While some, like the RFU South West Merit Table, were official, others were simply based on results, with no clear rules about the number of fixtures or who could take part. These were often run either by newspapers, mainly the *Sunday Telegraph* and *Daily Mail*, or by sponsors, such as breweries like Bass or Whitbread. In the South West, after 1979, clubs could find themselves in their county, RFU, *Sunday Telegraph* or Bass merit tables.

After what had been, overall, an encouraging performance the previous season, 1981/82 was a disaster for the club. The lowest point was a 30-6 defeat at Camborne on Boxing Day, the heaviest loss Redruth had suffered against their old rivals in the long-running fixture. It was described at the AGM as the worst post-war performance and the number of points scored was the lowest for 18 years.

In order to address the problems, the club formed a rugby committee and Terry Pryor was appointed as the club coach with Bonzo Johns as chairman of selectors. There was some suggestion at the AGM that players were not fit enough and that some of them were missing training sessions. Once again, the Colts side were the success story of the season, losing just three of their 36 games and lifting the County Cup for the seventh time.

Redruth members had been told at the meeting to look to the future and the rugby world was about to undergo a dramatic transformation. With increased financial pressures and the need for more structured and marketable competitions, there was growing momentum to introduce a formal league system to rugby. In April 1980, the RFU, which had spent 110 years fighting competition, announced that it was working on an alternative to the haphazard merit table system. However, it would be another five years, featuring a lot of wrangling, before the league system proper would get under way.

One of the highlights of the early part of the 1982/83 season was the arrival at Redruth of a Fijian touring side to take on the South and South West Counties. In their wisdom, the selectors had decided not to include any Cornish players in the Counties side so, naturally, the 3,000-strong crowd cheered loudly in support of Fiji. This turned to jeers when, at 21-6 ahead, Counties captain Phil Blakeway signalled full-back Stuart Barnes to kick a penalty, which the crowd felt was a poor choice given their lead at the time. Counties eventually won 36-6.

Results began to improve as Christmas approached and in the Boxing Day match it was only a last-minute penalty from Camborne's Chris Durant that levelled the scores and saved the Cherry and Whites from their first Cornwall Merit Table defeat of the season. As 1983 began, it was Launceston who were setting the pace, with Redruth in fourth place. However, the Reds, now playing in the Bass Merit Table, were more successful against non-Cornish sides, with heavy defeats of Brixham, Newton Abbot and Torquay, followed up by a 7-6 win at Cheltenham in February.

Full-back Mike Downing took the field against Devonport Services in March 1983, making his 765th appearance in a Redruth shirt and overtaking the previous record set by Bonzo Johns. Unfortunately, there was to be no celebratory victory and Redruth went down 25-7 in their first Bass Merit Table defeat of the season.

Wasps arrived on tour at Redruth on Easter Monday, having already beaten Camborne 26-10 and hammered Penzance-Newlyn 59-6. However, the Reds were more of a match for their famous visitors. A penalty from Nigel Eslick gave them an early lead and it was only a try by the former Falmouth player, Roger Pellow, that gave the London club a 4-3 victory. An improved performance throughout the season saw the Reds finish third in both the Cornwall Merit Table and the 16-team Bass South Western Merit Table, while Launceston were crowned Cornish champions for the first time in their history.

The following season brought even more improvement and Redruth began 1984 in second place in the Cornwall Merit Table and with a place in the semi-finals of the Cornwall Knockout Cup. The Reds cruised to the cup final with a 22-9 win over Falmouth. One of the try scorers was tight-head prop Richard Keast who had joined the Reds from Newquay Hornets. Keast, who had played for England Colts, was a 6ft, 17st farmer's son from Indian Queens who was to become a vital part of the Redruth side. Like Billy Phillips before him, he would become an inspiration for another Cornish player, a youngster called Phil Vickery, who would later play for Redruth before going on to a distinguished international career. Vickery once described Keast as his absolute Cornwall hero.

Redruth's 58-0 defeat of Bridgwater on 14 April saw Nigel Eslick kick two penalties and six conversions to give him a club record of 324 points for the season so far. He added nine more points in Redruth's 27-12 win at Hayle in the Cornwall Cup Final, played at Penryn. Redruth secured the Cornish double when, in their final merit table game of the season, they defeated struggling St Austell 44-3. To round off the 1983/84 campaign, they had the satisfaction of defeating visitors Ebbw Vale 17-4 to record their first-ever victory against the Welsh side. Nigel Eslick's final tally for the season was an astounding 373 points, which set a new Cornish club record.

In total, Redruth had scored 994 points, their highest season total for more than four decades, and winger Mark Stevens had scored 24 tries. While there was, naturally, immense satisfaction at the season's performance, the club's AGM was warned by the president, Eric Edmunds, that there would be new, and greater, challenges ahead. Their Cornwall Cup win had granted them a place in the following season's John Player Cup, while becoming Cornish champions would see them in the RFU South West Merit Table, facing games against Plymouth Albion, Bath and Bristol. There was concern about the pressure on finances of the additional games, particularly as gates were down despite

Redruth's successful season. This prompted an advert in the *West Briton* at the end of August inviting applications from all rugby enthusiasts in the duchy to apply for season tickets.

Redruth laid down a marker in the first week of the 1984/85 season by crushing visitors Newton Abbot, with whom they had resumed fixtures, by 72-0, the biggest defeat they had ever inflicted on the Devon side. Redruth had pulled out of the Bass South Western Merit Table after they had been advised that, as members of both the Cornwall and the RFU South West Merit Table, they were not permitted to be in a third competition. This highlighted the shortcomings of the merit table system, which was over-complicated and in need of a drastic overhaul.

In the John Player Cup, a 26-9 home win over Bletchley put Redruth through to the second round, where they faced visitors Crawley. The long trip was too much for the Sussex team and they lost 14-4. Redruth's cup run ended in round three when the Forest of Dean side Lydney defeated them 29-11 and denied them a lucrative fourth-round home game against Sale. Their bid to retain the Cornish championship took a knock over the Christmas period with a 9-3 defeat at St Ives and, on Boxing Day, a 12-9 loss against Camborne after conceding a penalty try for collapsing the scrum.

Redruth's RFU South West Merit Table campaign was also derailed when Bath arrived at the Recreation Ground on 2 March and delivered a 67-0 pasting to the home side. Most of the damage was done by exiled Cornishmen in the Bath side, with full-back Chris Martin scoring 17 points and Barry Trevaskis scoring five tries. The result, Redruth's heaviest defeat, illustrated the huge gap that had opened up between Cornish sides and the leading clubs from over the border. This was underlined when Bristol arrived two weeks later and scored 66 points, with just an Alan Buzza drop goal in reply. Redruth finished bottom of the RFU South West Merit Table and reapplied to join the Bass Merit Table, where at least they stood more chance of punching against their own weight.

Redruth wanted the opportunity to play games against opposition from across the country and at the highest level, as they had done throughout their history. Being in the John Player Cup had enabled them to play clubs they had not faced before and their season in the RFU South West Merit Table had provided fixtures against top sides like Bath and Bristol, but there was a cost to taking a team on the road. Travel and accommodation ate into the budget and gates no longer provided the income they had in the past. The committee decided to invest in improvements which it hoped would put the club in a stronger financial position. A £20,000 extension to the clubhouse was built, which would allow the club to raise additional income from catering for outside functions. The bar area was doubled in size and the kitchen facilities were extended and refurbished. There was also a drive to increase club membership.

The club was determined to look forward and make plans for the future. However, a 1985 article in a Midlands newspaper reminded them once again of the era in which they had forged their reputation. The Coventry club fixture secretary, Harry Walker, recalled a visit in the 1930s:

> 'In those days it was a feared place. The signpost on the road said "To Redruth and the graveyard" and that was enough to strike fear into you. Their players were a nasty bunch and they had a big rugged bloke in the centre who was built like a brick out-house, with cauliflower ears. We had a winger called John Wormell and he was ever so nippy. I remember him dashing over for a try but I swear he ran back to us twice as fast. He ran back for protection from Redruth's players. Hellfire Corner's the right name for that place I can tell you.'[55]

It is possible that the 'big rugged bloke' might well have been Roy Jennings. The name Hellfire Corner had been used for years to describe the corner of the ground into which the infamous sloping pitch ran down, a favourite haunt of the most vociferous fans for both Redruth and Cornwall. Indeed, it was said by some that the name had originated from those occasions when Redruth had hosted Cornwall County Championship games, which would draw many thousands of devotees of the gold and black through the gates. It was in the 1980s that the expression was seized upon by the press and became synonymous with Redruth rugby.

Having failed to retain the Cornish championship and the County Knockout Cup, both of which had gone to Camborne, Redruth faced a difficult start to the 1985/86 season. While Richard Keast, Tony Cowling and Kenny Curtis were back in the side after recovering from injuries, a number of players were leaving for college and university, including Alan Buzza, Colin Laity and Stewart Whitworth. The coach, Terry Pryor, said that he placed more importance on winning the Knockout Cup than the Merit Table as the former provided entry to the National Cup competition. Winning the Cornwall Merit Table did gain promotion to the South West table, but that meant playing the likes of Bath and Bristol.

The success of the Colts over the previous seasons had begun to feed through to the first XV, with teenagers Stuart Hood, Andy Knowles and Paul Gillow playing a full part in Redruth's 48-0 away win at Newton Abbot. Such victories were rare, however, and performances tailed off as the season progressed. Christmas proved disappointing, with Camborne winning the Boxing Day clash 33-3, their biggest victory margin to date in the derby game. Redruth had been holding their own in the first 40 minutes but after hooker Ralph Tregoning was sent off, the Cherry and Whites ran in seven tries. An 8-7 home defeat by Launceston left Redruth in second place in the Cornwall Merit Table, but chasing Camborne, who had a 100 per cent record and were favourites to repeat their league and cup double.

Camborne were confirmed as Cornish champions in February 1986 after defeating Penzance-Newlyn 60-0, thereby putting themselves out of reach at the top of the table. Redruth managed late-season wins over Penryn and the Pirates, which secured them second place, but they failed to get past the quarter-final stage of the Cornwall Knockout Cup and so lost any chance of qualification for the John Player Cup.

Overall, it was a relatively successful season, but questions were asked at the club's AGM about the standard of discipline on the field. For three seasons, not a single player had been dismissed but in 1985/86, nine were sent off, all for what the retiring president referred to as 'spontaneous punching'. There was better news about club funds; the money invested in the extension of the clubhouse was paying dividends, with an overall profit for the year of £16,000. John Penberthy was elected as the new club president.

Across Cornwall, there remained concern that rugby in the duchy was falling behind the rest of the country and was in danger of withering on the vine. Redruth's Easter programme had highlighted the problems. Whereas in the past they might have been facing the likes of Wasps, Bristol or Ebbw Vale, they now had to be content with their usual Good Friday match against St Mary's Hospital and a 35-0 win on Easter Monday over Crawley. The other visitors to Redruth were the West Midlands side, Walsall, who were defeated 18-8 in a dour game.

After much prevaricating, the RFU had finally announced that a national league would be set up for the 1987/88 season. They had to fight off opposition from county unions who feared, with some justification, that the new set-up would devalue the County Championship. Ironically, among the fiercest critics was the CRFU. Cornwall had a strong following at county games and the committee felt their first responsibility was to them and not to the individual clubs who could benefit from having a wider variety of opponents. Redruth's former hooker, Bill Bishop, was chairman of the RFU competitions subcommittee and it was he who took the lead in steering the game into the new era.

There was one more season to be played under the existing system. Redruth were determined to go one better and clinch the final Cornwall Merit Table under their new captain, Royal Navy lock Phil Elliott. The pack was a formidable one, with the likes of John May, Richard Keast and Adrian Curtis joining Elliott up front. The success of the Colts side, which had won ten of the previous 13 Colts' Cornwall Championships, was feeding the development of a new generation of players for the first XV.

A touring rugby side from Japan faced a Cornwall XV at Redruth on 4 October in a match that had been brokered by Bill Bishop. Alan Buzza, John May, Richard Keast and Phil Elliott were the Redruth players in the starting line-up, with Adrian Curtis and John Simmons on the bench. Although Japan were not then the rugby power they have since become, their speed and handling ability was too much for Cornwall, who lost 36-15. More than 5,000 people were at the Recreation Ground to witness a fine display of running rugby.

Redruth reached Christmas 1986 in third place in the Cornwall Merit Table and had the satisfaction of beating Camborne 9-6 in the Boxing Day clash, their first win in the fixture since 1980. Two penalties by Simon Blake and a drop goal from Jerry Penna sealed victory. The end of March saw another huge game played at Redruth when Cornwall took on the New Zealand Barbarians. The Kiwis arrived with no fewer than 12 All Blacks in their side and proved far too much for Cornwall, running in 11 tries and winning 63-9.

Redruth finished the 1986/87 season with a decisive 48-4 win over Weston-super-Mare in the Bass Merit Table, but they failed to improve on their second-place ranking against Cornish clubs, finishing behind Newquay Hornets. They were also runners-up in the Cornwall Knockout Cup, losing 18-3 to Camborne in the final. However, a change to the qualifying criteria meant that both Redruth and Camborne would be in the John Player Cup the following season.

In May 1987, 35 Redruth players left Cornwall for Spain for the first overseas tour in the club's history. The £7,500 needed to cover the costs had been raised by the players themselves. They beat Villagosa 55-7 and scored 35 points without reply at Calpe Benidorm. On their return to Redruth they would begin preparations for their first season in the new league structure. It was an opportunity the club would seize with relish and heralded yet another successful era in Redruth's history.

Chapter Eleven

The Coming of the Leagues
1987–2000

NINETY-NINE YEARS after the foundation of the
association football leagues in England, the RFU introduced a
similar system to rugby union. Until then, anything that smacked
of professionalism or competition was steadfastly rejected by the
suits at Twickenham. A hundred and two years before, in 1895,
the attitude of these defenders of the Corinthian spirit had led
to a schism in the game and, ultimately, the game of rugby
league. Now it was feared that, without structural change in
rugby union, the game would not have enough strength in depth
to sustain it at the elite level and England would fall behind on
the world stage.

The merit tables had established a clear need for more
regular and competitive fixtures for clubs across different levels.
The cup competitions that had long been a staple of the game
were in decline and there were concerns about their sustainability
and ability to attract consistent sponsorship and broadcasting
revenue. It is hard to retain interest when half of your potential
audience is no longer invested in the competition after the first
round and another 50 per cent is lost with each subsequent
round. With increased financial pressures and the need for more
structured and marketable competitions, the clubs looked at
the success of leagues in sports such as association football and
rugby league, and found that their popularity and commercial
success provided a compelling argument for adopting a similar

format in rugby union. In the late 1970s and early 1980s, several pilot programmes and trials had been conducted to assess the feasibility and viability of league structures in the game.

It was by no means an inevitable transition. Many of the fiercest defenders of the amateur status over the years held the belief that clubs should be able to choose their opponents and not be forced to play them by the diktats of a league. This was probably driven by concerns from the predominantly white collar, middle and upper-class men who ran rugby that they might not see eye-to-eye with the uncouth, working-class players who turned out in some parts of the country. Worse, the sons of those establishment figures might find themselves facing kicks and punches from the louts it was feared would mow down their opponents on the pitch.

The County Championship, which had first been established in 1889, had remained the only national competition in England for the following 82 years. Even during the era of county cups and merit tables, the fiction remained that clubs only played each other by invitation and mutual agreement.

The new pyramid-style league system got under way at the beginning of the 1987/88 season, with sponsorship from the brewers, Courage. Redruth were placed in South West One, with plenty of incentive to chase promotion because Camborne had been allocated a place one level higher, in Area League South. The Reds would face familiar opposition in Taunton, Bridgwater and Weston-super-Mare, but would also play sides from more distant Berkshire and Buckinghamshire.

What was lost, with a league system, was the traditional rivalry between Cornish clubs that had been part of the game since the 1870s. Redruth was now committed to playing sides from further up the country and there was no space in the calendar for fixtures with local teams, which would only serve to widen the gap between clubs in Cornwall. When the CRFU later decided that the Cornwall Knockout Cup should exclude National League sides, it brought to an end decades of history between Redruth and sides such as Penryn, Falmouth, Truro and St Austell. These would now be games for the club's reserve side, rather than the first XV.

Before the leagues got under way there was another landmark event in rugby history, the first Rugby World Cup, co-hosted by New Zealand and Australia. Sixteen nations took part and New Zealand beat France in the final, with Wales beating fellow semi-finalists Australia to take third place.

When the domestic season got under way, after the excitement of the summer spectacle, there was press speculation that Redruth was on the verge of signing two Fijian stars. Kaiava Salusalu, who played at centre, and lock John Sanday had both played in Fiji's World Cup side. Unfortunately, both men had joined a so-called rebel tour to South Africa, in breach of the anti-apartheid sports boycott, and faced a lifetime ban from playing rugby on their return.

Having been runners-up in the Cornwall Knockout Cup the previous season, Redruth started 1987/88 with a place in the John Player Cup, as well as the new leagues. They faced the holders of the Somerset County Cup, Old Culverhaysians, in the first round, winning at home, 26-9. Round two of the cup brought Blackheath to Redruth, but a 13-9 defeat meant the end of their cup hopes that season.

However, the club was doing well in its first season in the new league structure. At the turn of the year, a 21-13 win over Clifton saw the Reds in third place in the table, just two points away from the top spot. That was held by High Wycombe, to where Redruth travelled the following week, and an 18-6 win moved them up to second place behind Clifton on points difference. The new league structure required only one game to be played between any two sides, leaving time for other matches. Redruth's strong pack powered them through a Cornwall Cup quarter-final at Penzance, where they won 13-9.

An away win against Maidenhead saw them go top of South West Division One with just one game to play, away at Oxford. This was duly won 13-3 and Redruth went top on points difference, gaining promotion in their first season of the new leagues, having lost just two of their ten games. The next tier up, Area League South, was then the fourth highest in the game and Redruth would not drop below that level over the next three decades.

As well as their league success, Redruth added the Cornwall Knockout Cup to their trophy cabinet, beating Launceston 9-7 in the final. It was the sixth time in its 20-year history that Redruth had reached the final of the competition, but only the second time they had lifted the trophy.

Redruth finished fourth in their first season in Area League South, frustratingly denied third place on points difference by Camborne, although they had the satisfaction of beating their near neighbours 12-3 to win the Cornwall Knockout Cup for the second season in a row. In the National Knockout Cup, now sponsored by Pilkington, they saw off Worthing in round one but succumbed 18-3 away to Exeter in round two.

Redruth's Kevin Thomas, John May, Adam Ellery, Paul Thomason and Glyn Williams were all in the Cornwall team that faced a USSR touring side at Redruth on 9 December 1989. Only a last-minute missed penalty denied Cornwall a win, with the game finishing level at 12-12. Hopes were expressed that Cornwall might make the trip to Russia the following year, but the USSR fell apart before arrangements could be made.

Redruth improved their league performance in 1989/90 by finishing in third place in the table, just above Camborne, but three points adrift of the play-off place, which went to Clifton. This was the last season of Area League South, which the RFU renamed National Four South. It was the first of many attempts to rebalance the leagues to ensure well-matched opposition, practical travel distances and good supporter and sponsor interest, and the union would continue to tinker with the league structure over the following decades.

Trewirgie School was a nursery for aspiring players and many of their pupils went on to play for Redruth, including 'Maffer' Davey, Bert Solomon and Gordon Robins. Kresen Kernow collection

The all-conquering 1934/35 side, (l-r) back row: F.Hitchens, Francis Gregory, F.Roberts, Billy Phillips, Gordon Robins, D.E.Smith, Les Semmens; middle row: Len Roberts, Fred Pappin, Roy Jennings, P.Rogers, Harold Curnow, Ken Williams, J.Knowles. Front: D.T.Jones, Fred Bone. Kresen Kernow collection

Harold Curnow outpaces the Plymouth Albion chasers on 12 January 1935. Redruth won 16-9.
Kresen Kernow collection

Harry Faviel on his way to a try in the 29-0 defeat of Camborne on 3 October 1936.
T.P Roscrow

Gordon Robins kicks on against Camborne on 3 October 1936.

Roy Jennings is upended by two Camborne players on 3 October 1936. He kicked four conversions in the 29-0 victory.

The 1941/42 Redruth XV. Players from the Home Guard helped keep rugby alive during the war, (l-r) back: W.Knuckey, V.Roberts, Sgt Evans, Capt. Hughes, T.John, T.Bidgood, A.Eley, W.Pryor, H.Ham (referee); front: S.Selwood, W.Sweet, D.Gribble, W.Phillips, K.Williams, A.James, Capt. B.Lock, Lieut. H.Hall, D.Scoble.

St Luke's College Exeter proved too much for Redruth in March 1954, winning 13-9. Raymond Peters (l) and Bill Bishop are centre stage for the Reds.

Redruth Colts in 1959. Back (l-r): J.Instance, R.McGovern, A.Roberts, K.Hick, P.Instance, B.Trevena, D.Instance, D.Thomas, T.Speed, B.Stephens (touch judge); front: L.Oliver, N.Tallack, T.Hattam, A.Thomas, M.Foster, R.Hole, P.Tonkin, R.James, T.Mankee, I.Peters, T.Pryor.

Redruth Legends. From left: Richard Sharp, Kenny Abrahams, Paddy McGovan and Bonzo Johns.

1974/75 Cup-winning Redruth Colts, (l-r) back row: T.Pryor (coach), G.Still, P.Etherington, M.Greenslade, B.Pedley (capt), D.Tresidder, F.Down, J.Kitto, S.Wetherelt, N.Brokenshire; front row: P.Angove, J.Peter, P.Tiddy, N.Parkyn, I.Johns, D.Penberthy.

Cornwall Club and Cup champions, 1983/84, (l-r) back row: S.Whitworth, M.Stevens, I.Eslick, J.Simmons, J.May, M.Eddy; middle row: W.R.Peters, J.Kitto, P.Thomason, P.Elliott, K.Curtis, B.Pedley, M.Greenslade, P.Andrew, T.Penna; front row: C.R.Johns, T.A.Pryor, R.Tregoning, N.Eslick, A.Curtis, N.Brokenshire, R.Keast, N.Craze, N.Hosking.

Scrum-half Chris Whitworth in full cry against Cross Keys, 7 September 1991.

A victorious Redruth team celebrate winning promotion to National Two after beating Macclesfield in the play-off, 30 April 2005.

Redruth pack down against Taunton on a muddy ground 5 October 2013.
Dan Barbary

Redruth RFC season 2023/24.
Roland Woods

In August 1990, Redruth announced a new five-year sponsorship deal with the Cornish Brewery Company. The agreement saw the appearance on players' shirts of a logo advertising Newquay Steam beer, probably the company's best-known product. The company was a successor to the brewery which had provided Redruth with their first playing field when the club launched in 1875.

It was during this period that Redruth launched a mini-junior section. This level of rugby had started in England in the early 1970s and was designed to introduce youngsters to the game. Children begin to take part from the age of five in a non-contact version of the sport before moving up through the age bands. They finally reach the 15-a-side game at the age of 13.

Hundreds of youngsters, both boys and girls, have taken part. Players such as Luke Collins, Nathan Pedley, Ashley Hocking, Aaron Penberthy and Dean Bonds are just some of the many former mini-juniors who eventually turned out for the club's first XV. Thanks to the enthusiasm of the participants, and their parents, this has been a huge success at Redruth, with sides consistently winning trophies at all age levels.

The 1990/91 season was the most successful in the club's recent history. They were unbeaten in National Four South, winning all of their 12 games. The match that paved the way to promotion was won by the tightest of margins. Hundreds of Redruth supporters had made the journey to fellow promotion-chasers Basingstoke in mid-January. The only score of the game came when scrum-half Chris Whitworth chipped a kick forward, which was gathered by winger Andy Knowles, who slid into the corner for a try, worth four points at the time. The second half was a dull affair for anyone who was not a committed fan, as Redruth shut down the match to keep them on course to become the first Cornish club to reach National Division Three.

It was a season in which almost every match seemed to turn in Redruth's favour and they also won the Cornwall Cup with a 6-4 win over Camborne. Redruth's promotion marked the end, for some considerable time, of league games against Camborne, the last such match being played on Easter Monday 1991. Redruth won 24-6, with winger Marcel Gomez scoring what would be Redruth's last league try against the Cherry and Whites until the clubs were reunited in National Two West more than three decades later.

The annual Boxing Day encounter with Camborne continued, but it had become a shadow of its former self. Redruth's league commitments meant that, from the mid-1990s, only a reserve side would fulfil the fixture. There was some understandable grumbling from Camborne supporters but, in the days before there was any break from the league campaign over the Christmas period, Redruth were not going to risk first-team players for the sake of nostalgia.

When Redruth did field their first team in 2001, for the first time in seven seasons, they resoundingly defeated Camborne 48-7. Ambitious players wanted to play at the highest level possible and, with Camborne beginning the new century at level seven, three tiers below the Reds, a number of their players – including Richard Carroll, Mark Richards and Joel Matavesi – would all make their way to Redruth.

The success of Redruth in 1990/91 was mirrored by that of the county team. For the first time since the famous victory over Durham 83 years earlier, in 1908, Cornwall won the County Championship. Redruth had been the venue for the semi-final against Warwickshire, which Cornwall had won 14-6. The final at Twickenham against Yorkshire has passed into rugby legend. A crowd of 57,000 descended on the great stadium and it was estimated that at least 40,000 of these spectators had made the trip from the duchy. The exodus from Cornwall was memorably captured by Redruth rugby legend Bill Bishop, the previous CRFU president, who asked of the supporters on the eve of the match: 'Would the last one leaving Cornwall kindly turn the lights out?'

Five Redruth players were in the squad; John May, Richard Keast and Glyn Williams were in the Cornwall starting line-up, with Stewart Whitworth and Paul Thomason on the bench. Kevin Thomas, a former Redruth player, and Tony Mead were, at the time, with Plymouth Albion, but both would play for the Reds in the future. With 20 minutes left on the clock, Yorkshire were 16-3 ahead and all looked lost for Cornwall. Somehow, the team lifted themselves to greater effort and, after 80 minutes, the scores were level at 16-16. Ten minutes of extra time was played and Cornwall ran riot, winning the match 29-20 to the delight of an ecstatic crowd and many thousands more following the game at home in Cornwall.

It had been an exciting and exhilarating season for fans of rugby in Redruth, but it ended with a worrying piece of news about the club's biggest sponsor. Sponsorship was now bringing in between £15,000 and £20,000 a year in much-needed support. Much of this came from a variety of local businesses, but a large chunk came from the deal with The Cornish Brewery, which was only at the end of its first year. Devenish, the brewery's parent company, had been the subject of a takeover bid and it was feared this could jeopardise the remaining four years of the agreement.

This threatened loss of income came as promotion to National Division Three brought its own issues in terms of the expense and time of travelling to away matches. Of the 13 sides Redruth faced in 1991/92, seven were based in Lancashire or Yorkshire. The league was still structured on just a single game between any two sides, but it did mean that Redruth players often found themselves leaving home on a Friday afternoon and travelling half the distance to the opposition club before completing the journey the next morning. They would then face the long trip back to Cornwall after the match. An away game at the time could cost the club more than £3,000 in travel and accommodation costs. The club also relied heavily on understanding employers being prepared to release players for these marathon journeys.

It proved impossible to revive the promotional deal with the brewery but, happily, the club was not without major sponsorship for long. Success on the field, coupled with the fact that the club was selling an estimated 100,000 pints of beer a year, prompted bids from three different firms. A new deal was signed with Treliske Cellar Suppliers in Truro. The arrangement would allow the club to add a third bar and improve the changing facilities, as well as to help cover the costs of away games.

The playing side had been strengthened with the signing of four members of the County Championship-winning Cornwall team, who had all played for Plymouth Albion the previous season. Kevin Thomas returned to Redruth and he was joined by Mark Wesson, Tony Mead and Adrian Bick. Prop Adam Ellery had also signed from Albion.

Glyn Williams, who had played a key role in Cornwall's win, became Redruth captain for the 1991/92 season and led them in a successful campaign at their new level, winning six of their 12 games and finishing in fifth place in the league table, just below Exeter. The 1992/93 season saw them go one better and finish in fourth place, thus avoiding the relegation of every club below them when the RFU carried out yet another league restructure.

The third tier of the English league system was to be the highest level the club would reach. The following season saw the introduction of home and away games for the first time and the Reds found themselves facing sides of the calibre of Bedford, Blackheath and Rosslyn Park. These were well-resourced clubs which did not have to bear the huge travelling costs of a side from the far west of Cornwall, for whom every away game was something of a marathon.

October 1993 saw the arrival of the touring All Blacks at Redruth to play a side representing the South West Division of the RFU. The agreement to play the match at Redruth had been made at a meeting of the body representing the South West counties and was in line with a long tradition of Cornwall's top clubs hosting touring sides when they played against a regional team. However, it did not find favour with everyone.

John Reason, the rugby correspondent of the *Sunday Telegraph*, launched an astonishing attack on the decision, claiming that the South West players were 'spitting blood' at having to make the trip west. Bath player Stuart Barnes was mentioned as one of the more vocal critics. In what was still typical of the mindset of the London-based media, Reason claimed that supporters would 'need a couple of native guides and two days off work' to get to the game and so no one would bother to go. He claimed that the Redruth stand was too small and would be 'packed with local dignitaries and their wives'. He also confidently asserted that the club would never sell the 15,000 tickets available.[56]

Of course, in a rugby-mad place like Cornwall, the match sold out in days. As it happened, the author was at the time responsible for liaising between the Redruth club, the South West Division and the All Blacks and on matchday was delighted to see John Reason enter the press area and sit in the next seat. The author was unable to resist the temptation to pick up the microphone and tell the packed crowd how delighted everyone was that Mr Reason had managed to secure the services of some native guides and that everyone hoped he would manage to find his way safely back to London.

The spectators were treated to an outstanding, if somewhat brutal, game, with the added bonus that the South West side featured two players with Cornish connections, hooker Graham Dawe, another alumnus of the County Championship-winning side, and prop Victor Ubogu. Had it not been for an off-day from Bath's Jon Callard, who missed four kicks at goal, the South West might well have pulled off an historic win. They eventually lost 19-15 after a game in which the injury toll was high and no pity nor mercy was shown.

Redruth won just two of their 18 games in the 1993/94 season and finished bottom of the table, dropping, along with

Hampshire side Havant, to National Division Four. One casualty of the club's poor performance was the coach, Terry Pryor, who resigned in February 1994, claiming he had been made a scapegoat for the lack of success. A much-respected local teacher, he had been associated with Redruth for three decades, won 55 caps for Cornwall and had captained England B. He had been coaching the first XV for 12 seasons and had taken them successfully into the league era.

Despite the season's poor results on the field, the club had made a profit of more than £43,000, helped by additional sponsorship and the proceeds from the All Blacks game. As a sign of the growing financial burden of league rugby, the club had spent more than £30,000 on travelling to away matches. Even in National Division Four, the club would face long away trips. These included a 900-mile round trip to Aspatria in Cumbria, a journey which was, at the time, the longest in English league rugby. The fixture list would also require two trips to Yorkshire and two to Lancashire.

In June 1994, Redruth announced the appointment of Peter Johnson, the first salaried, full-time director of rugby. A qualified senior RFU coach, he had gained three schoolboy international caps for England and had played his club rugby at Bristol and Clifton, captaining the latter side. As well as coaching the first XV, he would take responsibility for building a coaching structure through all levels of the club.

Redruth's 1994/95 season started with a 40-25 loss at Exeter in a game which was not a league fixture. Exeter was beginning its climb up the league system, which would end in promotion to the Premiership in 2010. Redruth had lost some key players, including veteran prop John May, who had returned to Wadebridge, Adam Ellery, who had moved to Penzance-Newlyn, and second-row Mark Wesson, who had joined Exeter. The club did gain Nick Yelland from Wadebridge, while Peter Congo was recruited from Saltash. The club was also running an under-21 side on a more regular basis.

The league season started badly with an away defeat at Havant and then the surrender of a 23-12 half-time lead at home to Reading, allowing the Berkshire side to win 28-23. The game had been delayed for seven minutes while fly-half Simon Blake was stretchered off with a neck injury. Performance failed to improve, with a 31-17 defeat up at Rotherham leaving the Reds in seventh place. It was in that match that Redruth winger Marcel Gomez was sent off for making an obscene gesture to a touch judge and subsequently received a year's ban from a CRFU disciplinary committee.

A home draw against an unbeaten Liverpool St Helens on 1 October shone a chink of light into the gloom and this was followed up by a win at Kent side Askeans, which took Redruth into the third round of the Pilkington Cup. Lock Simon O'Sullivan, who had been drafted in because first choice Tony Cook was unavailable, scored Redruth's winning try in extra time.

The Reds had to make the trip to Askeans again a week later in the league fixture, which they won, and they followed that up with a 25-14 win over Plymouth Albion, which moved them up a place in the table.

The Pilkington Cup draw was not kind to Redruth and they had to travel to Division Three side Blackheath in the third round. The hosts were too much and the Reds lost 31-0, missing out on the chance of a lucrative fourth-round match against one of the top sides, who entered the competition at that stage.

A three-hour RFU disciplinary hearing into an appeal by Marcel Gomez against the severity of his one-year ban ended with it being reduced by just three weeks. It would rule him out for the rest of the season. The hearing was told that he had claimed to have been racially abused by a Rotherham supporter something which had not been raised before the original panel. Redruth director of rugby, Peter Johnson, claimed that the appeal chairman had told the player he would just have to put up with it.

Redruth's Tony Cook won a record 89th Cornwall cap when he captained them in their County Championship game against Dorset and Wiltshire at Camborne on 26 November. The record had been held for 26 years by fellow Redruth player, Bonzo Johns, who had made 88 Cornwall appearances between 1954 and 1969. Redruth marked the achievement with a celebration dinner at the Penventon Park Hotel. Cook would go on to make a total of 102 appearances for Cornwall.

Boxing Day brought more gloom for Redruth when they lost 16-13 at home to Camborne. The scores had been tied at 13-13, with just five minutes to play, when referee David May awarded a penalty against Redruth for dissent. Mr May's decision found little favour with the Redruth crowd, who made their feelings known in no uncertain terms as Camborne's Darren Chapman slotted the penalty through the posts.

Redruth's run of indifferent performances led some supporters to start barracking the team at home games. This was condemned by Peter Johnson, who referred to them as 'boo boys'. He claimed he was having difficulty attracting players to the club because of the attitude of a minority of fans and said the team was not always comfortable playing at home because of the taunts. His comments came as Redruth struggled to avoid relegation for the second season in succession.

Redruth lost 23-15 at home to Aspatria in their first match of the new year, leaving them fourth from bottom in National Division Four. The Cumbrian side had snatched a last-minute try, despite being down to 14 men. One of their props had earlier been sent off for clashing with Redruth hooker Jonathan Clifton-Griffiths, who had himself received a yellow card.

A home draw against Havant steadied the ship, with 17 of Redruth's points coming from Simon Blake, but defeats away to Reading and at home to Rotherham left the Reds seriously close to the relegation zone. As the end of the 1994/95 season approached, the team rallied to finish in seventh place, just above Plymouth Albion. A 32-19 defeat against Aspatria brought their league season to a close, but the club did have the consolation of lifting the Cornwall Knockout Cup. Having just squeezed past Camborne 15-13 in the semi-finals, they were back at their old rivals' ground to take on Launceston in the final, which they won 26-20.

The balance sheet for the 1994/95 season brought home the increasing costs of competing at the level of National Division Four rugby. The handsome profit made in the previous season had plunged to a £39,000 loss. A large part of this was the £28,000 salary paid to the director of rugby, but there had also been increases in travel and hotel costs. Fortunately, the club still had substantial cash reserves. One casualty of Redruth's financial problems was the club's commercial manager, Bryan Prouse. He had been the unpaid club treasurer for more than a decade before taking on the newly created paid role. The club reluctantly made his position redundant.

In May 1995, rugby changed forever when the game finally went professional. On the eve of the World Cup Final in South Africa, World Rugby announced that the game would become open and players could be paid. The decision came almost precisely precisely 100 years after the Northern Union had broken away from the RFU over exactly that issue.

The main impetus had come from the growth of satellite television, not least Sky, whose boss, Rupert Murdoch, knew he could grow his audience if he could acquire the rights to broadcast the most popular sporting events, and he was offering huge sums of money for those rights. In rugby, he was helped along by the former England captain, Will Carling, who pointed out the hypocrisy of the administrators, the 'old farts' as he described them, who were raking in large amounts of television money while the players, who provided the entertainment and suffered the bruises, were getting nothing at all. The inception of the professional era would change the game immeasurably, but it would take time for its impact to be fully understood at Redruth's level.

It was certainly clear that the club could no longer hope to hold on to players of international calibre, who could now take their pick of clubs and get paid good salaries. A young Phil Vickery had become the latest in the line of Redruth players to gain an international cap when he had been named in the England Under-19 Colts side to play Italy at Camborne on 4 March 1995. He was one of two Cornish props in the side, along with Liskeard-Looe's Trevor Woodman. Vickery, who had started his rugby with Bude, would not stay long at Redruth. Later in 1995, he was approached by Richard Hill, the England A coach, and persuaded to join Gloucester. He would go on to have a distinguished international career, captain his country and be part of the England side that lifted the World Cup in Australia in 2003.

Vickery tells the story in his autobiography of how he came to join Redruth while working on the family farm 60 miles away near Bude. Simon Blake, who was then manager of the Colts, and the first team coach, Terry Pryor, had driven up to Bude to persuade the 16-year-old Phil to play for Redruth. He was not old enough to drive at the time, so his mother would drive him down to Redruth for training sessions, sitting in the car to wait for him to finish. His day was spent getting up at five to do the milking, working all day on the farm, then doing evening milking before travelling to training, where he often arrived late because of his farm commitments. He once said he nearly gave up rugby to concentrate on farming. Vickery played a number of games for Redruth Colts and made such an impression that, by November 1994, when he was still only 18, he was picked for the first XV for an away match at Leeds.

In June 1995, it was announced that another famous Redruth international, Dr E.K. Scott, had died. Keith Scott had joined Redruth in 1947, the year he had won his first England cap, against Wales in the Five Nations. He had won four more England caps and captained his country three times. Later, Scott had continued to serve as a rugby official and had been president of the CRFU from 1981 to 1984.

In the first week of August 1995, a squad of 28 Redruth players, along with three officials and 17 supporters, set out for a 16-day tour of South Africa. The cost had been covered by a nine-month fundraising effort which had included a number of social events, a sponsored walk between St Ives and Redruth and the issue of a commemorative shirt.

The players were following in the footsteps of previous Redruth players who had gone to find work in the South African goldfields, some of whom had gone on to play rugby in the region. The exploits of these early players had been loyally covered in the *West Briton* and when South African sides had visited Cornwall on tour, there had always been a sense of connection. Redruth legend Richard Sharp had toured South Africa with the Lions and the stories he had told of his time there had cemented the sense of affinity between Redruth and the home of the Springboks.

The Redruth side played four matches, including games against sides from Cape Town, Durban and False Bay. Their toughest encounter was against a Natal Development XV, described by one of the players later as 'bloody awesome'. Redruth won two of the four games they played and, judging by the tour programme, spent a lot of time on the beach.

One of the highlights of away games during this period was travelling on the supporters' coach. These trips, usually organised by club member Ken Tullett, necessitated a Saturday crack-of-dawn start from the club, often in total darkness, where the last item to be loaded on the bus was a large insulated container packed with hot pasties. The smell of these usually proved an irresistible temptation and they were often consumed well before the coach had left Cornwall, washed down by whatever alcoholic beverage people had brought with them. The author has never forgotten the combination of pasty and red wine as the sun rose over Bodmin Moor.

The coaches used at the time had, to be polite, seen better days. On one rainy journey up to Hertfordshire, where Redruth were due to face Tabard, one of the windscreen wipers detached itself and flew over a hedge into a nearby field, never to be seen again. There was worse on the way back. After the coach had pulled in at Exeter at around 9pm for fish and chips, it was discovered that all the interior and exterior lights had failed. The supporters' coach travelled the 90 miles back to Redruth in close convoy behind the team bus, with no lights at all. Unbelievably, everyone arrived back without incident.

The arrival of a busload of Redruth supporters at away grounds could be something of a culture shock for the hosts, particularly at some of the posher clubs like Blackheath and Cheltenham. The rather restrained behaviour of home supporters at these games was in stark contrast to the unbridled enthusiasm of the Redruth fans. It often brought back thoughts of a complaint from an unnamed Welsh international, who is supposed to have said that it was impossible to play well at Richmond: 'All that polite bloody clapping.'

It was at one game at Blackheath that Redruth stalwart Geoff Sinclair, who often drove supporters in a minibus to away games, approached the clubhouse in search of the gents toilets. A Blackheath official, resplendent in the club's distinctive striped blazer, stopped him at the door to tell him he could not come in as it was the executive lounge. 'That's alright my 'ansum,' said Geoff. 'I'm going for an executive pee.'

While the culture clash between the rugby fraternity in Cornwall and that in the Home Counties was very real, there was also an abiding respect for the county's long tradition within the game. Nowhere was that better embodied than in the experience and gravitas of Bill Bishop, who had played for Redruth in the 1950s and later became club president. From 1987 to 1990, he had been president of the CRFU and in 1991 he had been awarded the OBE for services to Cornish rugby. Bishop had already overseen the creation of the new league system in his role as chairman of the RFU competitions committee. In 1995, he became president of England's Rugby Football Union, the third Cornishman to hold the position following Percy Holman in 1952 and John Kendall-Carpenter in 1980. Now it was up to him to get a reluctant RFU to finally accept that the days of amateurism were well and truly over.

Bishop was under no illusions about what the effect of the change would be. He warned that a businessman would be able to come into a club and bring in players from outside, perhaps even an international or two who was coming to the end of his career. Of course, that is exactly what did happen and many clubs lower down the league structure felt left behind as their best players were attracted to those clubs with more money. It did not help that the RFU, which had stuck its collective head in the sand over the issue, had made no plans for dealing with a professional game. Bishop discovered that a large part of his role as president would be to bang heads together as members of the executive committee bickered publicly about the negotiations for television rights.

It took time for the professional revolution to reach Cornwall, where the overriding concerns were the number of matches clubs were expected to play, and a growing tension between club and county rugby. Redruth coach, Peter Johnson, found himself at the centre of a row when he was criticised for putting out second teams in games against other Cornish sides. He had already come under fire for suggesting that, with clubs committed to the league system, the County Championship was no longer a priority. In terms of the club's ambitions, this was inarguable, but it was an unpopular point of view and drew some heated correspondence in the local press. One writer from Truro suggested that the money Redruth made from county games helped to pay Mr Johnson's salary. This drew a swift response from the club's former secretary, John Bishop, who pointed out that Cornwall was the only county union that did not pay clubs for the use of grounds for County Championship fixtures.

It was a natural consequence of the professional era that money coming into the game would go to those clubs who were most successful and that meant prioritising the league over county commitments. Johnson did make the valid point that the club had supplied 12 players for Cornwall, but he had to be mindful of the effect on players of too many games. He also pointed out that Redruth had lost key players while they were playing for their county, including full-back Kevin Thomas, who had sustained damaged knee ligaments in a Cornwall game against Somerset.

The following season would see a further increase in the number of games the club would have to play, in another expansion of the leagues. Johnson wanted Redruth players to be contracted to the club and he suggested that Cornwall might have to look elsewhere to make up a team. His remarks were widely criticised, but it was his responsibility to focus on the right policy for Redruth. In the end, he did give players the freedom to decide for themselves whether to turn out for Cornwall and many did, with eight of the Reds appearing for the county against the Royal Navy in March 1996.

Redruth found themselves in seventh place in Division Four at the end of the 1995/96 season, finishing their campaign with a 20-20 home draw with Clifton. Yet another major reorganisation of the league system saw the top eight clubs promoted to an expanded National League Three. This would commit them to a gruelling 30-match season in which they would again face long trips to the north of England. Injuries had been a major problem the previous season and Johnson told the club that he would need a squad of 35 players to tackle life in the new league.

On 17 August 1996, before the start of the new season, Redruth turned out against Saltash in a memorial match for Ian Balkwill, a young player who had joined Redruth from Saltash at the end of the previous season. He had been killed the previous month in a collision with a lorry on the A30 at Goss Moor on the way to Redruth for a training session. A speedy winger, he had made quite an impact on his arrival at Redruth, scoring two tries on his very first appearance for the club. He had been earmarked for the county squad at the time he was killed.

A new three-year sponsorship deal with St Austell Brewery was announced before the 1996/97 season. The players' shirts, which in the past had featured a small logo for Newquay Steam beer, would carry the name 'Trelawny's Pride' emblazoned in gold and green across the chest, advertising a now-defunct real ale that had been launched by the brewery the previous year. The new shirts did not find favour with some of the club's more traditional supporters, who felt Redruth should play in an all-red strip, but the deal gave the club a necessary financial boost and it would not be long before it was a given that jerseys would be covered in logos of all shapes and sizes.

Unfortunately, the new kit did not guarantee success on the field. Redruth started the season without a number of key players, including Simon O'Sullivan, David Moyle, Stewart Whitworth and Adrian Congo, although Tony Cook and Kevin Thomas were back from injury. They had also lost the services of Nick Yelland, who had signed with Gloucester.

The first match of the new campaign was at home to Fylde and it set the tone for the whole season. The Lancastrian side arrived with one of their most famous figures, former England captain Bill Beaumont, casually stepping off the coach with lit cigarette in hand. Fylde proved far too much for Redruth, inflicting a 28-16 home defeat on a Reds side that fought valiantly but were unable to match the speed and power of their visitors.

By March 1997, Redruth were third from bottom following a 47-15 away defeat at Wharfedale in North Yorkshire, a game for which the Reds had arranged to fly up to avoid yet another long road trip. The match also saw the debut in a red shirt of two Fijian internationals, full-back Nacanieli 'Nat' Saumi, who landed a penalty and a conversion, and front-row Alifereti Doviverata. By the end of the season, the Reds had won just eight of their games and, together with Walsall, Havant and Clifton, were relegated to a new National Two South.

One incident in the 1996/97 season highlights the farcical nature of some of the decisions taken by rugby administrators without heed to the impact they would have on clubs and players. The draw for the third round of the Pilkington Cup had divided the country into northern and southern sections, to reduce the need for teams to travel long distances. However, there were more clubs from the south of the country in the draw than in the north, so Redruth, the club furthest away from anywhere in the north of England, was moved into the northern section and drawn away to Leeds. One can only imagine that someone somewhere had confused Redruth with Redditch, which is just south of Birmingham.

What compounded this fiasco was that the game was due to take place on 2 November 1996, just a week before Redruth faced another trip to Leeds for a league fixture, with all the problems that posed for player availability. It was decided that players could not be asked to take two such long trips on subsequent weekends, so the league fixture was prioritised and Redruth fielded what was essentially a reserve side for the cup game. They were hammered 96-6, with Redruth's points all coming from Chris Sidwell. A full side returned to Yorkshire the following week and suffered an 84-24 defeat in the league game. Those who took part in this debacle have never forgotten it.

What this affair underlined was the yawning gap that was opening up between those clubs which had attracted large amounts of investment and those that were still essentially amateur sides. At the time, Redruth were one of just three clubs in National Three that were not paying their players a salary. In contrast, Leeds had the backing of a millionaire and were a fully professional outfit with a side that included two Welsh internationals and Sateki Tuipulotu, a former rugby league winger who had made 20 appearances for Tonga.

One casualty of Redruth's poor season was the director of rugby, Peter Johnson. The club announced on 6 May 1997 that it would not be renewing his contract and would be abolishing the position. Johnson had been a controversial figure, but no one could accuse him of not putting the club first, even if it meant upsetting many in Cornwall who still clung to the notion that players should put county first, club second. Johnson himself moved down the road to Penzance-Newlyn, where he became assistant to the Pirates' new coach, former Welsh international Mark Ring. Nick Brokenshire took over as coach at Redruth.

One of Johnson's more revolutionary moves had been the introduction of a ladies' side at the club. As this is written, in the third decade of the 21st century, the women's game has a high profile. Club matches are televised and the England Red Roses are one of the most successful international sides in the world. However, women faced a long, hard struggle to be accepted by the rugby hierarchy, whose attitude was often openly hostile. Taking a lead from countries such as New Zealand, Italy and Japan, the Women's Rugby Football Union had been formed in 1983 to oversee the game in England, with all of the founding teams based in colleges and universities. The first Women's Rugby World Cup was held in 1991, but it was not until 1998 that the International Rugby Board, now World Rugby, officially supported the competition.

The arrival of a ladies' team at Redruth followed an approach by a group of women who had originally come together to play soccer at Truro City. They had been challenged by the Truro ladies' rugby team to play two matches, one in each code, and, against all expectations, their scratch side of footballers had beaten the rugby players at their own game. Ladies' rugby was already established in Cornwall, with teams representing St Austell, Liskeard-Looe, Truro, Helston, Penryn and Bude all playing at the beginning of the 1993/94 season.

It was not the first time that women had played football on the Redruth pitch. In August 1921, the Redruth committee had given permission for a women's game under association rules to be played at the Recreation Ground that autumn. Just two months later, the Football Association would effectively ban women from playing the sport for another 51 years. In April 1925, a note in the club minutes records that it was agreed to allow 'the schoolgirls' to play hockey on the ground, although it is not known which schoolgirls were being referred to.

Not everyone was delighted with the prospect of women's rugby in Cornwall and women often faced attitudes that were summed up by those of John Balston, a columnist in the *West Briton:*

> 'Even when the more physical aspects of the game are toned down, rugby remains a mean, uncomfortable un-beautiful way of passing the afternoon and it surprises me that girls should wish to devote time and energy to it. I do wish they would stop calling themselves "ladies" teams. No insult intended. Quite the reverse. "Ladies" is a gentle word, conjuring up images of tea on the vicarage lawn (little fingers raised as the teacups are lifted), cucumber sandwiches and perhaps a spot of croquet. Never rugby. "Ladies" is not a word to be attached to rugby players. It makes the whole thing risible. Do me a favour, ladies. Call yourselves women.'[57]

Ladies or women? There is still no agreement on the matter. In 2024, the nine women's Premiership sides all describe themselves as women, but that is not the case across the game. In the leagues covering the 2023/24 Women's Championship, the split appears to be roughly 50/50.

Redruth Ladies were soon a force to be reckoned with. They went through the 1995/96 season losing just one league game and their wins included a 27-20 home win over Marjon, then the strongest side at their level. The following season, Redruth's captain, Sarah Thomas, was selected for the South West side in the NCP Divisional Championships, while the Redruth team entered the National Knockout Cup for the first time, defeating

Henley 23-18 in the first round. In the league, they inflicted a record 105-0 trouncing on Bude. They provided seven of the Cornwall side that played Devon and they reached the semifinals of the Southern Cup, a 10-7 defeat at Reading meaning they just missed out on a final against Harlequins.

Promotion saw Redruth Ladies start the 1997/98 season in Division Three of the Devon and Cornwall League, facing sides across a large chunk of the South West. They made a strong start and their 34-5 defeat of Exeter in early November, their third win of the season, put them top of the table. Centre Sam Buckingham was emerging as the star of a talented side. They also had a good start in the South West Cup, getting to the quarter-finals with a Sally Rogers drop goal which edged them past Truro. They finished the season as undisputed Division Three champions with a 100 per cent record.

Promotion to Division Two brought stronger opposition and more travelling in the 1998/99 season, but there was early disappointment when a match official failed to appear for a game against the league champions, Avon Ladies. It went ahead as a friendly, with Avon claiming the points. A decisive 32-7 win over Exeter provided a boost in the new year and at the end of the season they welcomed Saracens Ladies, who were on a visit to Cornwall. Sarries proved why they were the strongest women's side in the country with a 98-0 win over Redruth and a 69-0 defeat of the county side.

Regrettably, the ladies' side did not survive much longer at Redruth. Despite drawing a good level of support and providing much of their own sponsorship, the team felt they were not made to feel welcome by some sections of the club and they decamped to Redruth Albany. It is perhaps a sign of changing attitudes that, at the time of writing, the club is proposing a new complex of changing rooms specifically to cater for women players and has a thriving set of female sides in the mini-junior section.

Redruth's first XV started 1997/98 in National Two South with the hope that it would at least mean less travelling.

However, there was still an 860-mile return trip to Norfolk to face North Walsham, which was as long as any journey to the far north of England. There were also five fixtures in and around London and the South East. This was still a tough league and Redruth disappointed their supporters by racing to an early lead then letting it slip away.

It was a similar story in the first round of the Knockout Cup, where a home tie against Staines looked to be in the bag, but a series of errors gifted the result to the visitors. It cost them the chance of a lucrative money-spinning tie in the next round. The Reds finished ninth in the table with ten wins out of 26 games.

One highlight of the 1997/98 season was the visit of Tonga, who faced a Redruth Presidents XV on 26 October 1997. It was the first match of their British tour and the physicality of the giant Tongan forwards proved far too much for the Reds, who lost 64-9. All nine points came from penalties kicked by 18-year-old Rob Thirlby. Redruth's attempt to slow down the Tongans by plying them with Cornish pasties at a pre-match get-together seemed only to have had the opposite effect.

That season marked the end, for a time, of Thirlby's spell at Redruth. The run-up to the 1998/99 season brought news that he had been selected for the first XV squad at Premiership side Saracens. The winger had been spotted by England star Kyran Bracken while playing in a sevens tournament in Kenya and had impressed Saracens coach Francois Pienaar. He would make his debut for them in January 1999, when he kicked 11 points in the club's victory over Cardiff in the Anglo-Welsh Cup.

He later played for Bath, during which time he was a regular in the England Sevens side, becoming the only English player to appear in both the 2001 and 2005 Rugby World Cup Sevens tournaments. He was selected for England's 2000 tour of South Africa, playing in three tour matches, although he did not play in any of the Tests. After stints with Rotherham and Gloucester, he would return to Redruth in 2007.

Back at Redruth, the club was gearing up for a new campaign under rugby manager Graham Still and coach Nick Brokenshire. They were conscious that they needed to improve on the disappointing performance of the previous season. However, a number of key players had moved on. Along with Rob Thirlby, the club had lost Rocky Newton and the two Fijian players, Nat Saumi and Ratu Doviverata. Dave Gibson had gone to the Pirates while Ian Morgan had joined Lydney. Nick Edyvean, Chris Stephens, Andy Hicks and Danny Lock were the new faces on the pitch.

It was this new-look side that faced a daunting trip to Esher for the first game of the season, the home side buoyed up by a tie-in with London Irish and a sponsorship deal with Virgin Radio. The Surrey club, which was celebrating its 75th anniversary, outclassed the Reds in all departments, romping home with a 44-3 win. Only Chris Sidwell's late penalty prevented a whitewash.

It was a sign of what was ahead. A home win against Clifton in the second game of the season was followed by a string of defeats and, at the close of 1998, the Reds had racked up just four wins out of 14 league games. Against this background, the club's decision, at the beginning of December, to appoint the former Falmouth and Bath winger, Barry Trevaskis, as a paid coach caused a major upset. The existing coach, Nick Brokenshire, and his assistant, Matt Stearn, both resigned, complaining they had not been consulted over the appointment.

Trevaskis's appointment was immediately followed by the club doing the double over Plymouth Albion, but it did not herald an improvement in Redruth's performance in the second half of the season, despite the arrival of Plymouth Albion winger Steve Walklin – although he did play a large part in Redruth's 46-13 win over basement club Havant in January. But the club managed only another two wins before the end of the season, finishing just three points clear of the relegation zone.

Even the weather seemed to be against the Reds, with the home Boxing Day fixture against Camborne being called off after torrential rain flooded the pitch. The fixture was instead played in May 1999, with both clubs agreeing it should be treated as one of the Boxing Day matches. Redruth won 66-27, having decided to field what was virtually their full league side rather than the so-called 'Holiday XV' that would have played the Christmas fixture. The month also saw a third Cornwall victory in the County Championship, with Steve Larkins and Stewart Whitworth the Redruth players in the side. Cornwall would win the trophy four more times between 2015 and 2022, but the competition would never have the same status after the introduction of the leagues.

One bright spot was the performance of Redruth Colts, who lifted the County Cup. The star of their side was the 17-year-old hooker, Sam Harrison, whose performances over the season saw him being called up to join Club England, which had been set up to give specialist training to the country's most talented young prospects.

The build-up to the 1999/2000 season saw the retirements of former skipper Dean Hussey and hooker Adrian Rutter. Simon Blake had taken over the team manager position from Graham Still in July 1999 and a number of new players had joined the club, including New Zealander Bede Brown and Fijian sevens international Lakalaka Waqanivere. Andy Hyams, who had signed from Penryn, was partnered in a strong centre pairing with the powerful Colin Laity, who had returned from injury.

Former club captain Stewart Whitworth had also indicated his intention to stand down, but he was named at fly-half when Redruth travelled to Bridgwater for the opening game of the season. The players were sporting a new strip, produced to commemorate the 125th anniversary of the founding of the club, and they produced a solid performance, beating Bridgwater 40-21, a far better start than the previous campaign.

The home game against Norwich in mid-September was a brutal one which harked back to encounters at the beginning of the century. A full-scale brawl broke out after just two minutes of play and the uncompromising attitude of the Norfolk side saw them collect three yellow cards and Redruth a crop of injuries, with Simon O'Sullivan, Ewan Cowie and Liam Trivett all having to leave the field. All three would be out for a fortnight. Redruth won the game 22-16.

By the time Redruth visited newly promoted Penzance-Newlyn in December, they had lost just two of their opening 12 games. The Pirates were now being bankrolled by one of their former players, Dickie Evans (now Sir Richard), and had the resources to buy in players. They had enjoyed a great start to their first season at this level and had eight wins under their belt. The resulting match was as tight as it could have been, with a Stewart Whitworth drop goal snatching a 21-20 win for Redruth. One disgruntled Pirates fan told the *West Briton* that money could buy players, but it could not buy that sort of commitment.

Unfortunately, the beginning of 2000 brought a crop of injuries. In a hard-fought match at home to North Walsham, scrum-half Jamie Knight was injured and Andy Hawken broke a wrist. Former scrum-half Chris Whitworth came out of retirement to join his brother, Stewart, in a half-back combination that delivered a 24-6 away win at Cheltenham. Although the second half of the season was not as successful as the first, it did include six wins, one of them a 55-16 demolition of the Metropolitan Police, who would fail to win a single league game that season. An unexpected home defeat by Tabard was followed by one-point defeats at Weston-super-Mare and Norwich. The last two matches of the season brought a second heavy defeat at the hands of Plymouth Albion and then a 33-0 home rout by Penzance-Newlyn, now a fully professional side.

Once again, the Redruth Colts were the bright spot of the season, making good progress in their National Knockout

Competition. Having disposed of Bridgwater, Camberley and Gloucester, they faced Orrell in the semi-final. The Lancashire side proved just a bit too strong on the day, winning 21-14, despite a fine fightback by the young Reds from a half-time deficit of 11-0. There was some consolation when the Colts lifted the Cornwall Cup for the 14th time.

It had been a better season, with Redruth ending in fifth place in the league, but they had finally lost their crown as the highest-placed Cornish club in the national league system. That spot had been taken by Penzance-Newlyn, who had finished second in the table, just five points behind Esher. It was perhaps inevitable that the Reds, who ran on something of a financial shoestring, would not have the strength in depth to compete against professional teams. As the world entered a new century, this disparity between the clubs with cash and those without would continue to bring fundamental changes in the game.

Chapter Twelve
The Old Order Changes

THE NEW century brought new challenges. Having had to surrender to the introduction of competitive leagues, and then to the arrival of professionalism, the RFU now found that much of the control it had enjoyed over rugby was moving towards the clubs, predominantly those in the Premiership. Having deep pockets, and the right facilities and infrastructure, would have as much impact on a club's success as the talent of homegrown players and coaches, and the support and engagement of fans. Talented players could no longer be expected to spend their playing lives with one club through loyalty if they could earn a better living elsewhere. The gap between the haves and the have nots would continue to widen, and still threatens to split the game in two.

Clubs at the level of Redruth, which straddled the divide, found it the hardest. They were neither fully professional like the Premiership and the Championship, nor completely amateur like the majority of clubs below national league level. Having adequate resources was vital if good players and coaches were to be retained and the costs of the long away trips required by the league were to be covered. Fortunately, Redruth had a long history of sound financial management, having survived many previous periods of pressure which had driven similar clubs into insolvency. It had also continued to attract good crowds. On an average week in the 2023/24 season, attendances at Redruth home games were three times that of most other National Two sides and sometimes greater than sides in National One. The continued sponsorship from local businesses and a good income from clubhouse social events also contributed to their ongoing viability.

Launceston had won promotion from South West One and laid down a marker by coming to Redruth for the opening game of the 2000/01 season and winning 34-29. The following week, in their second Cornish derby, the Reds suffered a 35-11 defeat at Penzance-Newlyn. The atmosphere at the Mennaye Field was edgy from the start. Neil Douch led Redruth out at a slow walk and the Pirates responded by delaying their own appearance for several minutes before walking out even more slowly. In the end, the home side proved too powerful.

A home defeat by Plymouth Albion in November 2000 was enlivened when Redruth legend Bonzo Johns, watching in front of the stand, politely questioned a refereeing decision. 'Shut up old man,' shouted a particularly loud Albion fan. 'What do you know about it anyway?'

As the grandstand went silent in amazement, Bonzo, a Barbarian, England trialist, and winner of 88 Cornish caps, turned round and said quietly: 'I have played a game or two in my time.'

Redruth's form fell away in the run-up to Christmas 2000 and they won just one out of six games in November and December. There was some improvement after the break, the highlight of the second half of the season being a 23-6 win over visiting Penzance-Newlyn in mid-March, ending the Pirates' hopes of promotion. Redruth again finished fifth in the table, this time having won only 14 of their 26 games.

The following season, 2001/02, they dropped to eighth place, but could at least celebrate a 48-3 win at Camborne on Boxing Day. Both Penzance-Newlyn and Launceston won promotion to National One, removing the prospect of any local derbies the following season. Redruth's closest opponents were now Weston-super-Mare and, while they no longer faced gruelling trips to the north of England, they would still have to contend with the long haul to Norfolk to play North Walsham.

A year later, Redruth had climbed one place higher, finishing 2002/03 in seventh after a mid-season change of fortunes. By Christmas 2002, they had managed just three wins out of 15 league matches, plunging them deep into the relegation zone, but they managed to pull things around, losing only one game in the final three months of the season, a 25-22 defeat at Tabard. They also beat Launceston, then a league higher, in the final of the Cornwall Knockout Cup.

The 2003/04 season continued the gradual upward trend under player-coach James Lancaster. The opening game, a first-round Powergen Cup tie against fellow National Three side Weston-super-Mare, brought a decisive 28-13 home win. Glenn Cooper scored the opening try, one of three new signings along with Ian Hambly and Scott Martin. The following week, Martin kicked 17 points against Dings Crusaders in the first league match of the season, which Redruth won 32-20.

A long journey to Walsall for the second round of the cup saw Redruth go through 32-20 to a third-round tie against Plymouth Albion in October, but that would be the end of their run. Rugby manager David Penberthy had warned his side that Albion, who had sustained three defeats on the trot, would be like a wounded animal. He was right and their much heavier pack dismissed Redruth 64-14.

Injuries meant that Penberthy was looking for players on loan for the league game at home to Weston-super-Mare. Having lost to Redruth earlier in the season in the cup game, the Somerset side turned the tables and inflicted on Redruth their first home defeat for a year. Indiscipline on the field was causing the Reds problems, not least when they travelled to a newly relegated Launceston the week before Christmas. John Navin and Paul Thirlby both picked up yellow cards and a last-minute converted try from the home side denied Redruth their first-ever league win at Polson Bridge.

By this time, the demands of league rugby meant that the traditional Boxing Day matches between Redruth and Camborne no longer held the same status or attracted the same support as they had done in the past, and much of the needle that had been part and parcel of these derbies had gone.

However, the peace was shattered when the two sides met at Camborne in 2003. The captains had agreed beforehand that if any 'nonsense' reared its head, they would both step in. Famous last words. The game had barely begun when a Camborne player ploughed into a Redruth man and a mass brawl broke out on the pitch, with both captains enthusiastically joining in. It says much for the way these things are viewed in Cornwall that no cards were issued, no individual warnings given and play eventually resumed. Camborne won 40-17. One casualty of the game was a Camborne supporter who was banned by the club for a month for offering one of the touch judges a pair of glasses.

The second half of the 2003/04 season saw a more consistent performance. Redruth lost just one of their final ten games and that was a mistake-riddled 28-13 home defeat by Launceston. Two days later, the Reds beat Launceston 59-5 in a Cornwall Knockout Cup semi-final, but the Cornish All Blacks had only fielded four first XV regulars, resting the remainder of the side for their promotion drive.

Redruth's supporters were called on to lend some muscle in the service of their club in March ahead of a home match against Tabard. Heavy snow had fallen overnight and more than 50 fans and officials turned up to shovel 4in off the pitch before the game could start. They were rewarded for their efforts when the Reds won a hard-fought game 26-15.

Redruth finished the season in fourth place, a big improvement over the previous campaign, but close enough to the play-off zone to have some critics pointing out that a little more focus could have seen them in contention for promotion. Instead, it was Launceston, in second place, who won a play-off to go back up to National League Two. Redruth's second XV had a good season, topping the Cornwall Merit Table with a performance that included a record-breaking 118-0 win over Truro reserves.

Second-row Andy Hawken decided to call it a day at the end of the season, retiring after 350 games for Redruth. He had captained Cornwall and Redruth, and been selected by the Barbarians in 2002. He told the *West Briton* that he had been making the journey to Redruth from his home at St Dennis, in the clay country, three times a week for many years and he wanted to spend more time with his family.

Nigel Hambly stepped up to take over coaching duties for the 2004/05 season. A strong running centre who had played more than 100 games for the club, he quickly showed he could combine a good tactical knowledge with the ability to inspire his players. He had to contend with the local press tipping Redruth as favourites for promotion before a ball had been kicked and he quickly moved to damp down expectations. 'Tell them to wait and see where we are at Christmas,' was his retort.

It so happened that the club, under new skipper John Navin, got off to a good start with a 35-18 win at Westcombe Park, the first time the Reds had ever inflicted a home defeat on the Kent side. It was perhaps a measure of the high expectations that Hambly had attempted to quell that a subsequent 18-7 home win over Havant resulted in spectators voicing disappointment that Redruth had failed to pick up the bonus point.

Bonus points had been introduced in the National Leagues in 2000 to encourage more attacking rugby, adding excitement to matches by making them more competitive. Teams were awarded one bonus point if they scored four or more tries or lost by less than seven points.

That match saw the home debut of former Camborne and Penzance-Newlyn forward Richard Carroll, whose shock of long blonde hair would become a familiar sight on the field and whose exploits would generate column inches in both local and national newspapers.

Against expectations, the Reds forced an away draw against Barking, who many had tipped as the form side of the season. They then threw away a possible win at North Walsham, conceding a late penalty and being marched back 10m for what was referred to as 'a bit of pushing and shoving'. The Norfolk side then had an easy kick to snatch victory.

Former player-coach James Lancaster played his last home match for Redruth against Reading the following week. He had been forced to move to London after being unable to continue his studies in Cornwall. He left just as Redruth hit a purple patch, delivering the best run of results in many years. The arrival of stand-off Rhys Gosling, on loan from Launceston, coincided with the start of a run of 15 league wins, beginning with the home defeat of Hertfordshire side Tabard on 7 November.

Redruth had also progressed to the third round of the Powergen Cup, facing National Two side Waterloo at home, but some missed chances allowed the visitors to take home a 20-8 victory. It was Redruth's last appearance in the competition; the National Knockout Cup was subsequently replaced by the Anglo-Welsh Cup and restricted to English clubs in the Premiership.

Having lost one Kiwi in James Lancaster, Redruth lost no time in signing another in the shape of Dan Goodwin, a former All Black trialist. He joined the club in November 2004 after completing his southern hemisphere season with Bay of Plenty. His flight to the UK had been funded by the Redruth Supporters' Club. Goodwin's first game was a crucial away trip to table-toppers Lydney, where the Reds squeezed a 16-15 win.

Meanwhile, in the Middle East, the former Redruth star Rob Thirlby made the scoresheet for England when they beat the Flying Fijians to win their first-ever Dubai Sevens title.

Rhys Gosling departed in December, but he was replaced by centre Duncan Murray, on loan from the Pirates, who was named in the Redruth side to face Southend on 18 December.

Redruth's 11-0 win, an unexciting game played in miserable conditions, was their seventh on the trot. It saw them going into the Christmas break fourth in the table and level on points with third-placed Lydney.

Before the Boxing Day clash with Camborne, Nigel Hambly met his opposite number, Simon Moyle, in a bid to ensure that the fracas of 2003 would not be repeated. Both clubs fielded second-choice teams, an admission that, whatever the tradition demanded, league success must come first. Hambly was clear that he would be judged on where Redruth finished in the league, not on whether or not they beat Camborne. 'It is a nice fixture for the supporters,' he said. 'But it is not what it used to be.' A late try by Camborne's Brian Andrew forced a 10-10 draw.

The second half of the 2004/05 season saw Redruth's winning run continue. In what was described as their best performance of the season, they demolished visitors Lydney 36-14. They also set a new club record of 13 league matches without defeat when they beat visitors Dings Crusaders in February. In the end, they lost just one of their final 13 games, although crucially that was a defeat against Barking, the only home game Redruth lost all season.

On 2 April 2005, Redruth beat visitors Westcombe Park to secure a second-place finish and the chance of a play-off match against the second-placed side in National Three North. Their two final matches of the regular season, wins against Southend and Hertford, ensured they would have home advantage for the decider against Macclesfield.

More than 4,000 supporters, Redruth's biggest-ever league gate, descended on the Recreation Ground on a sunny 30 April 2005. Hearts were in mouths as Macclesfield edged 9-8 in front at the beginning of the second half, but the rest of the match belonged to Redruth, who ran in four tries to win 33-14. The verdict of the Macclesfield skipper, Richard Jones, was that the home crowd, many of whom were packed into Hellfire Corner, were worth at least one extra man.

Life in National Two, then the third tier of English rugby, saw Redruth once again making long journeys to northern England. Launceston was the only other Cornish club in the league. In that first season, Redruth finished in tenth place, with Lewis Vinnicombe featuring among the top eight try scorers in the league. The Reds also reached the final of the Cornwall Knockout Cup but were beaten 15-10 by Launceston at Camborne.

It was during the 2005/06 season that an incident occurred that saw the club involved in a landmark legal case that could have had far-reaching repercussions. In October, Redruth made the trip to Halifax, where the match soon degenerated into a bad-tempered affair. During a scuffle, the Redruth second-row Richard Carroll was seen to punch Halifax prop Andrew Garvil and, following a consultation between the match officials, was given a yellow card.

It was later found that Garvil's eye socket had been broken and he sued both Carroll and the Redruth club. A hearing in 2006 awarded damages against Carroll but held that the club was not responsible for the actions of its players. In 2008, the High Court overturned the original decision and ruled that, because Carroll had a contract with the club which stipulated a match fee and a win bonus, then he was regarded as an employee. As such the club was responsible and Redruth were ordered to pay a total of almost £40,000 in damages and costs. Had the club not been insured, the financial consequences would have been severe.

The 2006/07 league campaign saw a far better performance. The side had been boosted by the arrival of New Zealand-born number eight Mark Bright. He would go on to make 119 appearances for the Reds and score 395 points in his five seasons with the club. Redruth finished in fourth place, losing just six of their 26 games. They also won the Cornwall Cup with a 43-7 win over Mounts Bay, the club that had been spun out of Penzance-Newlyn in 1999. It was the last time National League sides would be allowed to play in the competition.

Form collapsed in the early part of the 2007/08 season. The optimism engendered by an opening away win at Nuneaton evaporated following a 28-27 home defeat by Southend. 'Rubbish, diabolical and unacceptable,' was coach Nigel Hambly's verdict on his team's performance. Morale hit rock bottom when the side travelled up to Cambridge. Trailing 30-0 at half-time, the Redruth team went back into their dressing room to find it had been ransacked and a number of valuables stolen.

The Redruth players refused to come out for the second half and, after a discussion between the match officials and representatives of the two clubs, the game was abandoned. Director of rugby David Penberthy said that feelings were running high and the team had decided that the best course of action was not to play the second half. While the match officials were sympathetic, the RFU was much less so and docked the club ten points, putting Redruth well into the relegation zone.

Team spirits were low, but there was no option other than to carry on with the season, taking one game at a time. They started well at home to Blackheath but the visitors turned on a stunning display in the second half to win 34-14. An away game at Halifax brought some hope, with the Reds winning 41-17, and later came a 44-3 home win over Henley Hawks. Redruth also went through to the fourth round of the National Knockout Cup, now backed by energy firm EDF, with a 64-7 home hammering of Stourbridge.

The handful of high-scoring games restored confidence and four wins in a row during January steadied the ship, with the Reds going on to win eight of the 12 games running up to the season's end. Even so, it was not until March that Redruth emerged from the relegation zone. They finished the season in ninth place, probably a better outcome than some had predicted, but would have been two places higher without the ten-point penalty.

Redruth's director of rugby, David Penberthy, set out on a major recruiting drive during the summer, with the result that there were 12 new faces at the club when the 2008/09 season began. These included Mark Scrivener, who moved from Launceston with his team-mate Owen Hambly. The Cornish All Blacks had been relegated from National League One, reinstating one local league derby, and the promotion of Mounts Bay meant that the Reds would be travelling west for another, for the first time since 2002. The coaching team was boosted with the arrival of Jim McKay and Adrian Edwards from the Cornish Pirates and the return of former Redruth captain and coach Terry Pryor.

Rob Thirlby, fresh from his England sevens successes, was the star turn in an opening 35-28 home win over Birmingham and Solihull Bees, one of the few fully professional sides in the league. It was Thirlby again who proved the mainstay in Redruth's first-ever league match against Mounts Bay, which the Reds won 35-16 at the Mennaye Field. The home side had Josh Matavesi, one of the famous Cornish Fijian brothers, in their line-up.

In contrast with the previous season, Redruth romped through the first three months, rattling up an 11-game unbeaten run with away wins at Wharfedale, Blackheath and Waterloo. There was also a hard-fought, wet and windy, 19-13 home victory over the Cornish All Blacks, the first time Redruth had beaten them in a league fixture.

The Redruth players had been buoyed up before the game by the visit to the dressing room of the legendary Richard Sharp, who had presented them with their match shirts and shared some of his experiences playing for the Reds. He watched the match with two other great names, the former St Ives forward Roger Corin, who was watching his son, Neil, play for Redruth, and the irrepressible Bonzo Johns.

BBC Radio Cornwall came in for some criticism, having opted to feature live commentary on a Pirates away game at Manchester. The Redruth club announcer told the crowd that it was a poor show when the county's broadcaster preferred to cover a game which was 'watched by 153 people, four dogs and a horse', rather than a pulsating Cornish derby.

Redruth's optimism was soon clouded by the news that the RFU were proposing yet another major shake-up of the league system, with a plan to mirror the football leagues by creating a fully professional Championship below the Premiership. Redruth coach Nigel Hambly, reacting to the news, described the RFU as a 'total shambles' and accused the organisation of 'trying to kill community-based clubs'.

He argued that Redruth, which was topping the table and aiming for promotion to National One, would not be able to compete financially against a league comprised entirely of professional sides. David Penberthy, the director of rugby, estimated it would cost £1.25m to put together a fully professional squad and coaching set-up, and pointed out that many of Redruth's players held down full-time jobs. The RFU dismissed all such objections and voted for the new structure to go ahead.

Redruth's winning run came to an end in late November when visitors Cambridge scraped a 19-18 win. An away win at Stourbridge and a home defeat of Mounts Bay saw Redruth reach Christmas on top of the table, seven points clear of Birmingham and Solihull. And, while the league was still the main goal, the 53-0 drubbing of Camborne on Boxing Day, then Redruth's biggest-ever margin of victory over their old rivals, brought some additional festive cheer for their supporters.

Early January is not the best time to make a 482-mile trip to Northumberland and it was a freezing cold day when Redruth arrived to play Blaydon. They fought back from a 13-3 deficit at half-time and were level pegging with a minute or so to go when, agonisingly, Mark Scrivener's drop goal attempt hit the posts, leaving the Reds to share the spoils.

It signalled a disappointing January, as this result was followed by a shock 15-14 home defeat by struggling Wharfedale and then a 19-8 defeat at Launceston, the first time that season the Reds had failed to get any points from a league match. It also meant the gap closed at the top of the table. Redruth remained in pole position but were only six points clear of Birmingham and Solihull, who had two games in hand.

A run of five wins through February and March lifted spirits as two Redruth players, Luke Collins and Darren Jacques, were selected to play for English Counties against an Irish Clubs side at Donnybrook. They were back to turn out for the 25-20 win away to Cinderford, although Redruth would regret not getting the bonus point.

A defeat at Tynedale finally ended Redruth's promotion hopes, with Birmingham and Solihull taking the top spot, one point ahead but with two games in hand. While the Reds managed a narrow home win over Stourbridge, they were defeated up at Cambridge and by the time they lost away to the league leaders on 25 April, it was all over bar the shouting.

Redruth had finished in third place in National League Two, then the third tier of English rugby, the highest position they had ever achieved, and it was hard to imagine they would ever surpass it. At the time, there were 12 clubs in the Premiership and 16 in National Division One, so only 30 clubs finished higher than Redruth at the end of the season.

It left a sense of anti-climax and the club faced losing half a dozen players during the summer, including Luke Collins, who had signed for the Pirates – although he would return to play for the Reds, first on loan and then as a full signing. Richard Carroll, so long a stalwart of the Redruth pack, had announced his retirement. Rob Thirlby was departing and even Nigel Hambly confessed he was uncertain about his future.

In the event, when Redruth drew 13-13 with Cambridge in the first match of the 2009/10 season, Nigel Hambly was still in charge and Richard Carroll was still in the pack playing as well as he ever had. Darren Jacques was now captain. It was always going to be a difficult campaign for the Reds. Their income from the RFU to subsidise travel costs had fallen but they still faced long journeys to places like Tynedale, Blaydon, Otley and Sedgley Park. Redruth were still in the third tier of league rugby, but the introduction of the Championship above meant that it had been renamed National League One and they were rubbing shoulders with sides set on gaining promotion to the prestigious new league.

Defeats at Launceston and at home to promotion favourites Esher made it an indifferent start to the season and the period running up to Christmas proved patchy. Redruth reached the halfway point with only six wins from 14 games. One of the wins was a good illustration of what happened when a club ran out of money. In October 2009, Redruth ran in 15 tries for a 91-5 home win over Manchester. The northern side had seen an exodus of players and officials after suffering financial problems and had arrived without a travelling coach, with just three replacements and with a number of colts in their team.

Redruth made the long slog to Lancashire to face Sedgley Park in December, only to have the game called off an hour before kick-off. In addition to the wasted time, the club sustained a huge loss in terms of travel and accommodation costs, as did the enthusiastic band of supporters who went with them. It was a frustrating end to a disappointing period.

It did not get better after the Christmas break. A closely contested 9-7 home defeat by Launceston started the second half of the season. Injuries were causing major problems for Nigel Hambly, who was having to select players out of position. He also had to serve a four-week ban from the touchline after being found guilty of abusing match officials during the home match against Wharfedale the previous month. This had followed a decision of the referee, Luke Pearce, to allow a Wharfedale try after Redruth claimed he had halted the game. The same game had seen Redruth fined £50 for having 16 men on the pitch following a mix-up over replacements.

The club organised a meeting to discuss ways to alleviate the financial pressures, which had been caused, largely, by the huge cut in RFU funding. David Penberthy told the *West Briton* that Twickenham had historically paid half the club's travel costs, which had been £40,000 the previous season. The RFU had announced it was removing that support altogether, leaving the club to make up the shortfall.

Redruth now faced another costly away trip for the postponed match against Sedgley Park. To mitigate the expense, the club obtained permission to play their scheduled away game against Manchester on the same weekend. The Reds lost 30-18 at Sedgley Park on Saturday, 6 February, but ran out 54-14 winners over Manchester the following day. Seven Redruth players turned out in both matches.

The Reds won just six of their 16 post-Christmas matches, leaving them in 11th place at the close. There was a further blow when Nigel Hambly announced he was standing down as coach. His achievements in the role had been significant. He had picked up the reins back in National League Three and had taken Redruth to the highest league position it had ever achieved.

'I think the players need someone different,' he said. 'If I am brutally honest, perhaps we have been a little bit stale this season. I always put the club first and in that respect it is time to freshen things up.'

Hambly's departure preceded one of the worst seasons the club had experienced, in which they won just nine games. Among their 2010/11 opposition were clubs like London Scottish, Blackheath and Coventry, sides that were fuelled by large amounts of money and carried far too many big guns for Redruth to compete.

A 34-15 defeat at London Scottish had David Penberthy questioning whether some of the more senior players were as committed as they should have been, and threatening to fill the team with younger men. One of these younger players was the future England international Jack Nowell. He played 13 games for Redruth in this season, scoring 30 points, before being snapped up by Exeter Chiefs.

The first win of the season came in October 2010 when a dramatic drop goal from Aaron Penberthy to snatch victory against Rosslyn Park finally brought a smile to his father's face. It would not be the last time that Aaron's boot would rescue the Reds and he amassed more than 200 points in the season.

The Rosslyn Park match was one of only four wins in the first half of the 2010/11 campaign and even a 26-0 win against Launceston in December brought little cheer to the Redruth faithful. The East Cornwall club had gone into liquidation the previous summer after running into financial difficulties. While they had managed to re-form and start afresh, they had been deducted 20 league points by the RFU to add to their woes.

The new year saw better performances on the field and Redruth managed to win eight of their remaining 17 games. There were a number of players who turned in good individual performances, including Mark Bright, Darren Jacques, Richard Brown and lock Damien Cook, but the side was not firing on all cylinders.

The writing was on the wall when the Reds failed to secure bonus points in some vital games. There was hope as the season end approached that relegation might be avoided, particularly when an Aaron Penberthy drop goal snatched a one-point away win at Coventry. It spurred the team on and they fought to stay up, winning their final two games, but it was not enough. Redruth finished just one point adrift of survival and were relegated along with Otley and Launceston. The end of the season saw Mark Bright leave the club to join London Scottish.

Redruth arrived in a new-look National Two, which the RFU had split into north and south in a belated attempt to reduce long journeys after they had witnessed the impact of removing the travel subsidy. It ended the 400-mile-plus journeys to the north of England, but Redruth still faced long trips to Hertfordshire, London and Sussex as they began

2011/12. There were ambitious and well-resourced clubs at this level, some of whom, like Taunton, Richmond and Old Albanian, would soon move up. The league also contained Hartpury College, an up-and-coming nursery of young rugby talent.

A 27-25 defeat at Sussex club Worthing in the second week of the season was described as a wake-up call by David Penberthy. It had the required effect and Redruth reached Christmas having won 12 of their 17 matches, including a 56-12 home drubbing of London side Barnes and a fine away win at Dings Crusaders. There were also heavy defeats at Old Albanian and Richmond.

Just before Christmas, Redruth lost speedy winger Nathan Pedley, who played his last home game for the Reds against Worthing on 10 December. It followed his decision to emigrate with his family to Australia. He was a firm favourite with the home crowd and it was an emotional moment when he walked off the pitch to a standing ovation. Pedley had joined the club as a mini-junior at the age of five and dedicated his whole playing career to Redruth.

In previous campaigns, Redruth had made a poor start but recovered in the second half of the season. This year they went off the boil after Christmas, although they did sneak a one-point home win over Dings Crusaders. It came as David Penberthy announced he would be stepping down as director of rugby at the end of the season. Penberthy's association with the club stretched back nearly 50 years from when he had joined as a boy. However, just as when his brother-in-law, Nigel Hambly, had departed two years previously, he would be saying au revoir rather than goodbye.

The Reds lost eight of their final 13 games. Their late-season record was summed up by a 47-14 away defeat at Southend, with new head coach Tony Cook bewailing the inability of the side to maintain their performance in the second half. A mass brawl close to the end, which saw Redruth's Chris Fuca and

Southend's Andrew McLintock sent to the sin bin, underlined the game's frustrations.

Redruth did manage to give David Penberthy a final home win, beating Westcombe Park 21-17 on 21 April. It was followed by a defeat by Cambridge side Shelford, leaving Redruth in sixth place at the end of their first season back at this level.

There was an improvement in the 2012/13 season, both in the number of wins and the final league position. A new head coach, Adrian Edwards, stepped up to replace David Penberthy, supported by Ashley Morcom and Steve Evans. Edwards had recruited some players from outside during the summer, but he had made a commitment to bring on members of Redruth's own development and Colts squads.

Seven members of the team that travelled to Taunton in the opening game of the season were therefore making their debut. Jake Rayment, from the Colts, became one of the youngest players ever to appear in a league game for Redruth. The previous season he had been captain of the under-17 side. Chris Fuca had taken over the chiefs captaincy and led his side to a 25-15 win, despite the disruption and delay caused by holiday traffic on the M5.

A 46-24 hammering of the Cornish All Blacks in the Redruth sunshine provided further impetus for the keen young side, who went on to rack up five wins in a row, giving Redruth a great start to the season. This included a 51-23 win over Barking in East London, now back in National Two.

The departure of Sam Parsons to Australia in October was a blow, but a one-point loss at Worthing that month and a 47-15 away drubbing in early November by Hartpury College, were the only two defeats in the first half of the season. The Reds reached Christmas in third place, with coach Adrian Edwards daring to mention the 'promotion' word. Given the lack of resources and the club's continuing financial worries, he had achieved a great deal in a short time, helped by the commitment of the players and the club's supporters.

An away trip to Bournemouth on 12 January saw the game abandoned after 63 minutes. The pitch was already a quagmire when the match started and the rain had continued to pour down. Eventually, the London-based referee, Veryan Boscawen, summoned the captains and called time. Redruth were awarded the win under a rule that says the score stands if play is abandoned after 60 minutes. It is not known whether the Bournemouth players realised that the referee's name could not have been more Cornish.

The win was one of five in a six-game run that included a 10-9 win away at Polson Bridge, making it a league double over the Cornish All Blacks. However, a fine 69-0 hammering of Lydney was the last good result for a while and the rest of March saw the season go off the rails. Hartpury College inflicted Redruth's first home defeat of the season and the Reds went on to lose the next four matches, the worst result being a 64-19 thrashing at Henley. Home wins against Southend and Taunton were the only respite in the last two months of the season. Having come so close to the top, Redruth finished fourth in the table, trailing 15 points behind third-placed Hartpury College. Head coach Adrian Edwards left the club, his place being taken by his assistant, Ashley Morcom.

Redruth's fortunes dropped again in 2013/14. Although the Reds won all their home games before Christmas, they failed to win on the road until well into the new year. Two early season performances stand out. One was against London Irish Wild Geese, the amateur side of the exiles club. Redruth were 25-10 down at half-time but stormed back to win 38-28 with the help of two tries from Sam Matavesi, who was on loan from Plymouth Albion. The second was a 32-29 defeat of league leaders Hartpury College, with skipper Chris Fuca's last-minute try, converted by Ashley Hocking, winning the game.

The Reds could only manage six wins out of the 14 games played in the second half of the season and were in danger of relegation. There were problems on and off the field, as the club's continuing financial issues coincided with a string of injuries. Former skipper Darren Jacques had left the club, as had Lewis Vinnicombe, and for the trip to Southend, Morcom found himself fielding five players who had never even trained with the first XV. The team were also without their captain, Chris Fuca, who was injured, and the match became the only one of the season in which Redruth failed to score a single point.

Redruth's first away win of the season came at Exmouth on 14 February, a valuable five points helping them to avoid the relegation zone. The rest of the season continued as it had started, with the Reds winning all but one of their home matches but failing to make an impact away from Cornwall. It was enough for them to secure their place in National Two with a ninth-place finish.

Ashley Morcom announced that he was standing down as head coach because of family commitments, but he hoped to stay on in some capacity, possibly as forwards coach. It soon became clear that he would not be part of the new coaching set-up led by former Redruth winger Steve Larkins, whose appointment had been announced at the end of March. Since leaving Redruth, Larkins had been head coach at Camborne and supporters were happy to welcome back a prodigal son.

In the late summer, Redruth said goodbye to one of the giants of their post-war period. Charles Robert 'Bonzo' Johns died in August 2014 at the age of 80. Described as a true colossus of Cornish rugby, he was a man whose natural skill and mischievous personality ensured that his popularity extended way beyond the Recreation Ground at Redruth. He had begun playing for Redruth at the age of 16 and turned out for the club for the following 21 years. His early career as a coalman gave him immense strength, which made him a ferocious scrummager and devastating in the loose and in line-outs. He had been capped 88 times for Cornwall and had held the record for Cornish caps for 15 years. He had been invited to play for the Barbarians in 1962 and turned out for combined Devon and Cornwall sides against New Zealand, Australia and South Africa. Above all, he had remained a devotee of the club with which he had spent his entire playing career and he was a familiar sight at home games well into his seventies.

It was at home, in front of their loyal fans, that Redruth continued to play their best rugby and they would win only two away games in the whole of the 2014/15 season. The first gave Steve Larkins a flying start when they travelled to Southend for the first match of the season and won 36-31. Five Redruth players were making their debut, including Tommy Phillips and Todd Prisk, who were both playing national league rugby for the first time. The result proved to be a false dawn; by Christmas, Redruth had won only six out of 16 games.

Some games, such as the home defeat by Clifton in September, were lost by the narrowest margins, but losing bonus points are no substitute for actual wins and a 6-0 win over Camborne in appalling weather on Boxing Day was no substitute for league success. The frustration was summed up when, despite outscoring the Cornish All Blacks by three tries to nil, the game ended in a 15-all draw as the Reds had not included a specialist goal kicker in the side.

The second half of the season was no better, with just eight wins out of 15 games played. The only win on the road was at Bristol side Dings Crusaders, who were having a torrid season and were eventually relegated. The Reds finished the season as they had the one before, in ninth place in the table, just ahead of the Cornish All Blacks on points difference.

The first half of 2015/16 began with a restructuring of the coaching team. Steve Larkins was joined by Rob Elloway and Adrian Rutter as forward coaches, while Marek Churcher returned to the club to coach the backs. This new approach seemed to be working, with 11 wins before Christmas, four of which were away from home.

Damien Cook, son of former coach Tony, was the new skipper and he led his side to a six-try victory over Redingensians, a club that had not lost at home for 26 games. They would later rebrand as the Rams and move up to National One. There was a second away win at Bury St Edmunds but then, in late September, Cambridge came and pricked the winning bubble. Redruth's game was disrupted by errors and ill-discipline which saw three players sent to the bin.

A 17-10 home win over the Cornish All Blacks in the run-up to Christmas was another nail in the coffin for the East Cornwall side, who would be relegated at the end of the season. Redruth would not have another Cornish league derby until Camborne's promotion in 2023.

The second half of the season was just as successful, with Redruth winning 11 of their 16 games. There was plenty of scoring to thrill the crowds, including a 46-20 win over Dorking and a 38-3 defeat of Taunton Titans. These contributed to a season's total of 718 points scored, a figure that harked back to some of the glory years of the past, and saw Redruth finish in fourth place.

The following season, 2016/17, was almost as good. Luke Collins had rejoined the club after a spell at St Ives and Marek Churcher had been promoted to head coach after Steve Larkins's departure near the beginning of the season. Churcher was working with Adrian Rutter and a new addition to the Redruth set-up, the New Zealand-born Samoan centre Pale Nonu.

The latter had previously played for Rotherham Titans and Plymouth Albion, and had joined as player-coach. The club won 12 out of 16 games before Christmas, in what was an increasingly competitive league. Their ability to hold their own against tough opponents was underlined in September when the Reds ground out a 10-8 victory over visitors Redingensians, a game which saw winger Lewis Vinnicombe marking his 250th appearance for the club.

A consistent performance in the second half of the season saw the Reds finish in fifth place having won 19 of their 30 matches. However, a disappointing 22-21 defeat at home by struggling London Irish Wild Geese took the shine off Marek Churcher's last match as head coach before he set off for a role at Exeter Chiefs.

Pale Nonu took up the role of head coach in time for the start of the 2017/18 season, while continuing to play at centre. He had an auspicious start in his new role as Redruth galloped to a 58-10 home win against Old Redcliffians, a game that marked the debut as a full signing of Cornish Fijian flanker Sam Matavesi. The club's performance on the road was again disappointing, with only two away wins, and the second half of the season was patchy, but the Reds managed to hold on to fifth place in the table.

Redruth slipped back to seventh at the end of 2018/19. The damage was done in the depths of winter, when Redruth failed to win a single league game in December, although they came agonisingly close in a 35-33 defeat at Taunton. A 17-14 loss to Camborne on Boxing Day did nothing to raise morale and it was not until mid-January that the club got back to winning ways against Guernsey, and Birmingham and Solihull. With only three victories in March and April, it was not a season to look back on with any affection.

Nigel Hambly had returned to his old position as director of rugby during the 2018/19 season in what he said at the time was a temporary appointment. However, he was still in post when the Reds kicked off 2019/20, which would prove to be one of their best for nearly a decade. An injury-time try in the first match of the season saw them snatch a 10-8 victory from visitors Esher, who had been relegated from National One, much to the obvious disappointment of the BBC presenter John Inverdale, who had made a pre-dawn start from Newcastle to watch his team in action at the other end of the country.

Redruth lost only four games in the first half of the season and made sure of a satisfying 39-6 thumping of Camborne in the Boxing Day match for the Rodda's Cup, which had been awarded to the winning club in the annual clash since 2009. The momentum continued into the new year as the club strung together a nine-game winning run and hopes began to rise that they might be in the mix for promotion.

For the first time since the outbreak of the Second World War, events outside rugby intervened. As Covid spread across Europe, concerns about contagion through close contact saw the RFU terminate the 2019/20 season just two days before Redruth were to host Essex side Westcliff. At the time, Redruth were in third place in the table and only two points behind the play-off place occupied by Tonbridge Juddians.

There was a brief interlude during Christmas 2020 when the prohibition on competitive rugby was lifted and the traditional Boxing Day match against Camborne went ahead. It was a bizarre match under temporary RFU rules which banned scrums and mauls and placed restrictions on the line-out. In a strong wind and Cornish mizzle, the Reds won 21-0. It was not a great spectacle but the crowd were generous in their applause and relieved to be able to watch any rugby at all.

Terry Pryor died in March 2020. A towering figure in Cornish rugby, he had captained Redruth in its centenary season and had played in one of the great Cornish county front rows alongside Stack Stevens and Roger Harris. He had captained England B on a tour of Romania and been invited to play for the Barbarians.

His coaching career had started with Redruth Colts and he moved on to coach the first XV in their many successes at the beginning of the league system. His greatest achievement would be the later careers of those young players he nurtured and encouraged, including Phil Vickery and the Liskeard/Looe player Trevor Woodman, both of whom would win a Rugby World Cup with England.

His memory lives on, with his name proudly displayed over Redruth's main stand, and also through the Terry Pryor Trust, a charitable organisation set up by the club in conjunction with Redruth School, where he was a teacher for four decades. The trust raises money to help young people develop themselves through sport and recreation, particularly rugby union.

Terry would have been delighted by the club's performance when rugby restarted in autumn 2021. Redruth stormed through the first half of the season, losing just two of their 13 games. Disappointingly, these were both at home, an eight-point defeat by Esher and a 24-10 loss to Worthing. An even better post-Christmas performance saw Redruth finish in second place in National Two, behind Esher.

In other seasons, this would have won them a play-off for promotion against Lancashire side Sedgley Park, who were the second-placed side in National Two North. Unluckily, Redruth were denied that chance by the RFU restructuring of National League Two. Esher were promoted to National One, but the second-place play-offs were dropped.

The result of the RFU reorganisation was that National Two, originally divided into North and South, was instead divided into North, East and West. It did mean fewer games, but it did little to reduce the amount of travelling, given that the club had to make return journeys of up to 600 miles to face clubs in Cheshire and the East Midlands. Many in Redruth had a suspicion that the England map on the wall of the RFU office was not quite the same as everyone else's. In 2022/23, the first season of the new structure, the Reds finished in seventh place.

The 2023/24 season saw the revival of league fixtures with the old enemy. Camborne, who had been enriched by a new sponsorship deal, had won promotion to National Two West. The passion on the field, and in the crowd, had not diminished, as Camborne held out against a late Redruth surge to win 36-29 in the first league encounter. Jack Simmons became the first

Redruth player to score a try against the Cherry and Whites in a league game since Marcel Gomez more than three decades before. Honours were even at the second league match in December and in the Boxing Day derby.

These games continued to bring in the same huge crowds as they had done in the past, the fierce local rivalry so much a part of the game in Cornwall, just as it had been in the days before rugby, when Camborne's William Trevarthen had been killed while hurling against Redruth men back in 1705. Rugby provided the ideal sport to harness the tough competitiveness of the miners and its attraction has rarely waned.

The game of rugby has changed dramatically since the first Redruth players posed in the Brewery Field in 1875 and one wonders what those men would make of their club a century and a half later. They would find it strange to see advertisements around the ground and logos on players' jerseys, testifying to the importance of money in maintaining a modern National League side. The facilities for players are better. No more do they spend half-time on the pitch in a freezing wind sucking on a lemon and there is no need to trudge, sodden and muddy, back up Green Lane to change at Tabbs Hotel after a match. Those who were not teetotal, like John Everett, would, no doubt, enjoy the opportunity to have a beer in the clubhouse.

Some things they would still recognise. Most of them would have run out on to the ground where their successors still play, although they might marvel at the pristine condition of the turf. Old rivalries have changed little and they would feel at home at a Boxing Day derby against Camborne. And while mass brawls among spectators tend to be things of the past, they would recognise the passion and commitment of a modern Redruth crowd and the immense pride supporters have in their club and its traditions.

Redruth has both survived and succeeded despite a disadvantage of geography and a relative lack of affluence. It has maintained an unbroken tradition thanks not only to a passion for the game, but to good governance, fiscal responsibility and a deep and abiding loyalty that goes well beyond partisanship. There are more than 1,800 rugby clubs affiliated to the RFU in 2024 and, as it celebrates its 150th season, Redruth RFC holds its place as one of the top 78 clubs in England. In doing so, it has carved out a place in the game as ineradicable as the granite beneath the Cornish mining town of which it has always been an intrinsic part. Henry Grylls and William Willimott would have been very proud.

Appendix One

The Old Rivalry

'We wish each other the compliments of the season
then get stuck in.'

Redruth's Billy Phillips ahead of the Boxing Day match
against Camborne, 1952.

REDRUTH V Camborne. More than 140 years after the two
sides first met, it remains one of the best-known and most
evocative fixtures in rugby. It still brings record crowds to the
host ground, as it has for decades. The relationship has been
punctuated by rows, which often saw one or other of them
pulling out of fixtures, whether it was following the sort of
mayhem that occurred in 1912 or just over the many accusations
of foul play or biased officials.

In the seasons prior to the Second World War, the home
games between the two clubs could bring in anything up to 40
per cent of a season's gate money. Whatever the provocation for
the initial dispute, it was always the concern about the loss of
gate money that brought them back together.

The Cornish are sometimes accused of having a profound
distrust of outsiders but reserving their real enmity for their
near neighbours. Family feuds can fester for generations without
anyone really having a clue as to how it all began. The same
applies to communities and there are examples of this across
Cornwall. Newlyn and Penzance, Falmouth and Penryn, St Ives
and Hayle and, not least, Redruth and Camborne.

It was, for many years, customary for teams from the villages of St Day and Stithians to play a match on Boxing Day morning. 'Forty minutes each way and 20 minutes of injury time,' was one veteran's description of these encounters. The merger of the Newlyn and Penzance clubs in 1945 to form Penzance-Newlyn, later the Cornish Pirates, was greeted with a mixture of astonishment and disbelief given the intense, and often bitter, rivalry between the two towns, both on and off the field.

These local rivalries existed long before rugby came along but the sport provided a new vehicle to express them. In a game that, certainly in Cornwall, was often a lot more violent than in other parts of the country, it provided an ideal opportunity to work out frustrations and settle old scores. It was not just on the pitch. Quite often when boots and fists were swung among the players, brawls would break out between the two sections of the crowd. Everyone could join in the mayhem.

Of course, this was not confined to Redruth and Camborne. Rows between clubs and violence both on the field and off it were part and parcel of the game across West Cornwall. The reports of the monthly meetings of the Cornwall Rugby Union were full of quarrels and accusations of cheating, fighting, assaults on officials and claims for compensation from opponents who had failed to fulfil a fixture. These meetings often degenerated into fierce arguments, with insults flying between the committee members, who each sided with their own particular club.

But the enmity between the towns of Redruth and Camborne was often on a different level. The two communities had glowered at each other for centuries and as both got wealthier, the levels of suspicion and jealousy of each other grew. When a fire engulfed a draper's shop in Camborne in 1906, the captain of the Camborne fire brigade, who played rugby for Camborne, refused to accept the assistance of the Redruth Fire Brigade, whose captain played for Redruth. Two women died in the blaze. In a report on the tragedy, the

Cornish Telegraph opined that: 'There was no word bad enough to condemn the rivalry which existed in connection with the brigades of the two towns.'

Quite often, men from the two towns would find themselves working together, either underground in the mines or on the factory floor of businesses such as Holman, Climax or Bickford Smith. This provided an opportunity on the Monday after a game for bragging rights if your team had won and accusations of the alleged behaviour of the opposition from those whose team had lost. By the time it got to the next match, a fine head of steam had built up.

While some of the old feelings may have mellowed over the years, they have certainly not gone away. When, in 1933, it was proposed to merge Redruth and Camborne into one urban district council, it was opposed by the majority of the population of the two towns. Even now, driving on the old road from Redruth to Camborne, there is a distinct feeling of crossing into alien territory as you breast the hill and drop down into Tuckingmill.

There are still supporters of both clubs who refuse to attend the away matches for fear of putting cash into the enemy's pocket. Those that do go along bite their lip, stay in their own section of the ground and leave immediately after the final whistle to do their post-match drinking back at their home club. Tales are still told of Camborne supporters closing their eyes when the train on which they are travelling stops at Redruth Station and others who say they refuse to eat a red apple.

Between 1991 and 2023, the only regular game between the two clubs was on Boxing Day but, even now, when league positions are so important, this fixture still looms large in the calendar. One supporter was quoted as saying that he would put up with losing any number of league fixtures as long as his side could win on Boxing Day. Even though the clubs are now back in the same league, the Christmas holiday fixture still has huge importance.

While the routine violence of early years has largely gone away, tensions mean it can still bubble beneath the surface, such is the importance of this clash to both clubs. One Redruth hooker, making his Boxing Day debut in the 2000s, was warned to expect a punch to come through from the opposing side when the scrums packed down. In 2003, a mass brawl broke out among the players and both skippers eagerly joined in. Some things do not change.

Appendix Two

Cornwall's Oldest Club?

THE EARLIEST photograph of the Redruth side, taken in 1875, has the legend 'First Club in Cornwall' written on the mount. Henry Grylls, in his account of the founding of Redruth, published in 1925, wrote that it was the first to be formed in West Cornwall and, with the single exception of Bodmin, in Cornwall. He was in error, as newspaper reports show that Truro, St Austell and Bodmin were all in being when Redruth was first formed.

Redruth is lucky in that one of its founders took the time to write an account of the formation of the club in 1875, but not every club has been so fortunate. Local newspapers are often the only source of evidence for the beginning of a club, but they would have had to rely on someone sending in a report of any activities.

If we define a club as a body set up at a formal meeting and with an administration structure, then the earliest formation of a football club, for which we have newspaper evidence, is that of Truro, reported in the *Royal Cornwall Gazette* on 9 December 1871. The names of officials and a committee appeared in the paper and playing days were arranged. It would appear that, in their first year of existence, the few matches played were between sides drawn from the club itself. This was hardly surprising, as there were few other opponents at the time.

The second report of a formal meeting was at St Austell in October 1872. A month later, the new St Austell club travelled to Truro where, on a wet and windswept cricket ground, the match was drawn. On the evidence available, this could well be the first rugby match between two formally established Cornish clubs. November 1872 also saw a report in the *West Briton and Cornwall Advertiser* of a meeting of the Bodmin club at which a captain and officers were elected. The *Royal Cornwall Gazette* reported a game at Bodmin Beacon on 4 December 1872, which suggests that this was the first outing for the new side.

Although no report of the formation of a club at Penzance seems to have appeared in the press, Truro travelled to play a Penzance side in January 1873, although this may well have been an ad hoc match. One of the Truro players was named as 'Grylls' and could well have been Henry on holiday from Clifton College. In October of the same year, a report appeared in the *Cornish Echo* to the effect that the St Ives Cricket Club had decided to form a football club so that they could continue their recreation during the winter.

There was certainly enough interest to trigger a game between sides designated as 'East Cornwall' and 'West Cornwall' at Truro on 13 January 1873. None of the players were shown as coming from any particular club, although St Austell and Bodmin seemed to have supplied many players from the East while the West mainly comprised Truro men. By the time the first report of a match involving the Redruth club appeared in February 1876, there seem to have been six other clubs active in Cornwall; namely Truro, Falmouth, Bodmin, St Austell, St Ives and Penzance.

It has to be emphasised that we are relying on newspaper accounts and football was not, in the early days, high on the agenda of local editors. It is, therefore, possible that the formation of a particular club failed to make the papers. The first report in the papers of the formation of a club at Penryn, which claims to have been founded in 1872, did not appear until 1885. That is not to suggest football was not played at Penryn in the 1870s, but it never made the local press, despite the fact that there were two newspapers published in the area at the time.

There are no reports of a Penryn side in action against the few other clubs that did exist at the time.

All the clubs reported to have formed by 1875 would fold at one time or another over the ensuing years, some more than once. There were a number of reasons. Sometimes it was a shortage of players, often due to emigration, in other cases it was a lack of money. The Hayle club folded in the early 1900s when the biggest employer in the town, Harvey's Foundry, closed down. Redruth alone, despite a financial crisis in the mid-1920s, managed to field at least one side in every one of its 150 seasons. Allowing for breaks for the two world wars, it is the club which, on the evidence, has the longest continuously documented history of any Cornish rugby club.

Acknowledgements

THIS BOOK has, like a good game of rugby, been a team effort. When I announced I was writing it, the response underlined the great love and respect so many have for the club. I received many offers of help, documents and memories from people who have been part of Redruth RFC in one way or another. Many others offered support and encouragement as the project went on, far too many to thank individually.

David Penberthy, the current Redruth club president, entrusted me with the club minutes dating back to the 1890s, which have been an invaluable source of information. Charlotte Morgan, my former BBC colleague, sent me photographs and information on her father, Andy, who coached the club in the 1970s. David Dow at Swansea RFC gave me details relating to John Smith Longdon, who made such an impact on the club in the 1890s. The Rugby Museum at Twickenham provided useful information on how the scoring of the game has changed over the years.

Gerald Curtis, a former Redruth chairman sent programmes and photographs and Trevor Harvey and Keith Martin gave me their accounts of watching their first games at Redruth as boys. Grainne Lenehan, the archivist at Marlborough College, provided details of William Willimott's time there and the principal assistant keeper of archives of Clifton College, Dr Charles Knighton, was very helpful in passing on information about Henry Grylls. Carolyn Evans in Illogan gave me a number of books of newspaper cuttings relating to Redruth and Cornwall rugby from the 1950s.

ACKNOWLEDGEMENTS

The author and mining historian Allen Buckley provided valuable information and I relied heavily on his excellent biography of Bert Solomon for information about that outstanding player. His book, *The Story of Mining in Cornwall*, was also very helpful in researching the background to the industry in Redruth. Sarah Thomas, the former captain of the Redruth Ladies, shared her impressive collection of photographs and memorabilia on that chapter of the club's history.

The staff at Kresen Kernow, the Cornish archives centre, have been their usual cheerful and helpful selves. Marcus Rogers at Kernow Photo Fix waved his magic wand over some of the old photographs to remove blemishes and make them look as good as new. My thanks also go to the current Redruth officers and committee, who had enough faith to give this project their blessing and support. Without that, it could not have been written.

Particular thanks to Francis Edwards, the Cornish historian and writer. A passionate Camborne man, he provided valuable advice, not least in his reading of the initial draft of the first chapter and making many very helpful suggestions which allowed me to see the best way forward. His research has helped me shine a light on the tense and sometimes violent relationship between Redruth and Camborne over the years. I thoroughly recommend his website as a source of the quirkier elements of Cornish history and tradition.

Last, and by no means least, I am indebted to my wife, Nerina Gill. She has put up with me hunched over books, documents and computer keyboard for the best part of two years while this book came to fruition. But, more importantly, she has, as a former BBC editor, brought her skills to bear on the final version, cross-checking facts and stitching together my sometimes rambling narrative into a coherent whole. Any errors remaining are all mine.

Notes

1. Grylls, H. *50th Anniversary Booklet. Redruth RFC* (Redruth RFC 1925)
2. Norden, J. *A Topographical and Historical Description of Cornwall.* (Frank Graham 1966)
3. Carew, Richard. *The Survey of Cornwall.* (Tor Mark 2000)
4. *ibid.*
5. For a more detailed discussion as to which is Cornwall's oldest club see Appendix 2
6. Buckley, A. *Bert Solomon – A Cornish Phenomenon* (Truran 2007)
7. Grylls, H. *50th Anniversary Booklet. Redruth RFC* (Redruth RFC 1925)
8. ibid
9. ibid
10. *Royal Cornwall Gazette* 11 March 1876. Page 6
11. *Lake's Falmouth Packet and Cornish Advertiser* 11 Mar 1876. Page 1
12. Grylls, H. *50th Anniversary Booklet. Redruth RFC* (Redruth RFC 1925)
13. *Royal Cornwall Gazette.* 13 Mar 1877. Page 4
14. *Royal Cornwall Gazette.* 12 October 1877. Page 5
15. Salmon, T. *The First Hundred Years: The Story of Rugby Football in Cornwall.* (CRFU 1983)
16. *Royal Cornwall Gazette.* 19 October 1877. Page 7
17. For more on the rivalry between Redruth and Camborne see Appendix 1
18. Grylls, H. *50th Anniversary Booklet. Redruth RFC* (Redruth RFC 1925)
19. The *Cornish Telegraph.* 14 January 1879. Page 5

20. ibid
21. Grylls, H. *50th Anniversary Booklet. (Redruth RFC 1925)*
22. *Cornubian and Redruth Times* 24 Dec 1880 Page 5
23. Salmon, T. *The First Hundred Years: The Story of Rugby Football in Cornwall.* (CRFU 1983)
24. *Cornubian and Redruth Times.* 5th Dec 1884 Page 7
25. *Cornubian and Redruth Times.* 1 Feb 1889. Page 3
26. *Cornubian and Redruth Times.* 29 Jan 1892. Page 4
27. *Cornubian and Redruth Times* 15 Apr 1892. Page 5
28. *Cornubian and Redruth Times.* 22 Apr 1892 Page 4
29. *West Briton and Cornwall Advertiser.* 24 Nov 1892. Page 4
30. *Cornubian and Redruth Times.* 27 Jan 1893. Page 5
31. *Cornish Telegraph.* 2 Nov 1893. Page 5
32. *Cornish Telegraph.* 4 Jan 1894. Page 5
33. *Cornishman.* 23 Apr 1896 Page 2.
34. *Torquay Times and South Devon Advertiser.* 22 Feb 1901 Page 3
35. *Cornish Echo and Falmouth and Penryn Times.* 18 Oct 1901. Page 8.
36. *Western Morning News* 5 Jan 1903 . Page 4
37. *Cornish Echo and Falmouth and Penryn Times* 2 September 1904 Page 8
38. *Cornishman* 15th December 1904 Page 6
39. Salmon, T. *The First Hundred Years: The Story of Rugby Football in Cornwall.* (CRFU 1983)
40. *Western Morning News.* 14 Apr 1906. Page 8
41. *Cornishman.* 6 Sep 1906. Page 3
42. *Cornish Echo and Falmouth and Penryn Times.* 24 Jan 1908. Page 5
43. *West Briton and Cornwall Advertiser* 30th March 1908 Page 4
44. *Lake's Falmouth Packet and Cornwall Advertiser* 15 January 1909 Page 6
45. *Redruth 50th Anniversary booklet* 1925. Redruth RFC
46. *Western Daily Press,* Saturday, 22 November 1930, page 4
47. *Illustrated Sporting and Dramatic News,* 1932
48. Sharp, R, *Winning Rugby,* (London, Pelham Books Ltd) 1968

49. ibid
50. ibid
51. *Daily News (London)* - Tuesday, 24 September 1957 Page 9
52. *West Briton and Cornwall Advertiser* 8 Oct 1959 Page 2
53. *The Times* 6 Mar 1962
54. Sharp, R., *Winning Rugby* (London, Pelham Books Ltd, 1968)
55. *Coventry Evening Post* 5th April 1985
56. *Sunday Telegraph*, 12 September 1993, Page 29
57. *West Briton and Cornwall Advertiser* 31 Mar 1994 Page 12

Bibliography

Bradley, A.G. et al. *The History of Marlborough College 1893.* John Murray

Bradley, P. *The Camborne and Redruth Electric Tramway.* 2005 Randigall Books.

Buckley J.A. *Bert Solomon – A Rugby Phenomenon.* Truran 2007

The Story of Mining in Cornwall Cornish Editions 2005

Butler, B. *The Official History of the Football Association.* Queen Anne Press 1993

Carew, R. *The Survey of Cornwall 1603* Andrew Melrose 1953

Casey, P. and Hale, R.I. *For College, Club and Country. The History of Clifton RFC* MX Publishing 2009

Collins, T., *Rugby's Great Split. Class, Culture and the Origins of Rugby League Football.* Routledge 1998

Collins, T. *A Social History of English Rugby Union.* Routledge 2009

Gregory, C. *Cornwall – Rugby Champions.* Partridge Press. 1991

Grylls, H. *Redruth RFC 50th anniversary booklet Redruth RFC* 1925

Hughes, Thomas. *Tom Brown's Schooldays.* Dent and Co 1932

Marshall, F.L. (ed) *Football: The Rugby Union Game.* Cassell and Co 1892

Norden, John. *A Topographical and Historical Description of Cornwall. 1584.* Frank Graham 1966

Owen, O.L. *The History of the Rugby Football Union.* RFU 1955

Pelmear, K. *Rugby in the Duchy. 1884-1959* CRFU 1960

Rawle, D.L. *A Prospect of Cornwall. 1986.* Robert Hale

Richards, H. *A Game for Hooligans.* Mainstream Publishing 2006

Roodt, G. *The DNA of Rugby Football.* Partridge Publishing 2015

Salmon, T. *The First Hundred Years. The Story of Rugby Football in Cornwall* CRFU 1983

Sharp, R. *Winning Rugby*. Pelham Books 1968
Summers, D.L *HMS Ganges*. HMS *Ganges*, Shotley Gate 1966
Tangye, M. *Redruth and its People*. Michael Tangye. 1988
Tangye, M. *Victorian Redruth*. Michael Tangye 2001
Vickery, P. *Raging Bull*. Harper Collins 2010

Newspapers and periodicals

Current:

Cornish Guardian
Cornishman
Daily Express
Daily Mail
Daily Telegraph
Packet Newspapers
St Ives Times and Echo
The West Briton
Western Evening Herald
Western Morning News

Defunct:

Athletic News
Cornish Echo and Falmouth and Penryn Times
Cornish Post and Mining News
The Cornish Telegraph
Cornubian and Redruth Times
Daily News
Illustrated Sporting and Dramatic News
Lake's Falmouth Packet and Cornwall Advertiser
London Evening Standard
Morning Leader
Morning Post
Royal Cornwall Gazette
Salford Weekly News
Shields Daily News
The Sportsman
Sunday Independent
Torquay Times and South Devon Advertiser
The West Briton and Cornish Advertiser
Westminster Gazette